THE
IIMA
STORY

the DNA of an institution

THE
IIMA
STORY

the DNA of an institution

Prafull Anubhai

RANDOM HOUSE INDIA

Published by Random House India in 2011

1

Copyright © Prafull Anubhai 2011

Random House Publishers India Private Limited
Windsor IT Park, 7th Floor, Tower-B,
A-1, Sector-125, Noida-201301, UP

Random House Group Limited
20 Vauxhall Bridge Road
London SW1V 2SA
United Kingdom

978 81 8400 192 1

Typeset in Cronos Pro by Niti Mittal, Delhi

Printed and bound in India by Replika Press

Contents

To Ravi, from whom I learned through observation
To Mote, from whom I learned through intellectual engagement
To SK, from whom I learned through emotional bonding
To the IIMA Parivar, from whom I learned through shared experiences

Foreword

I have known Prafull since he joined the Indian Institute of Management, Ahmedabad (IIMA) Board of Governors during my tenure as its Chairman in 1973, but he has been deeply involved in the affairs of the Institute from the very early days. Nobody perhaps could have been better equipped to undertake the task than him.

It is a monumental task to write an account of an institution spanning over half a century, and that too with limited documentation. However, Prafull Anubhai has managed this brilliantly in his 'analytical biography' of IIMA.

In 1955 when T. T. Krishnamachari, Union Minister of Commerce, announced that the Government wanted to establish an institute of Management on the lines of the five Institutes of Technology (IITs), it inspired three outstanding visionaries deeply. Dr Jivraj Mehta, Chief Minister of Gujarat, Dr Vikram Sarabhai, scientist and businessman, and Kasturbhai Lalbhai, businessman and philanthropist, were convinced that management and technology were the keys to economic progress. They also saw it as an opportunity to locate this new school of learning at Ahmedabad and they pursued this goal with great diligence. I had the privilege of knowing each one of them. They were men of great talent and each had a dream to usher the country in the golden era of prosperity. The birth of IIMA was the result of their tireless efforts.

The Central Government provided the initial funding for covering the recurring expenses. The Gujarat government made the land available for the institute while Dr Sarabhai tied up with Harvard university with the help of the Ford Foundation (FF). Kasturbhai Lalbhai obtained the full support of the business community and committed to fund the infrastructure required. This is diligently recorded by the author in detail. As we celebrate the fiftieth year of the Institute, it is only apt that he pays his tribute to these great men.

Throughout the book, the author examines the fundamental question—what has made this Institute the premier school of management education? He discusses with deep insights the challenges faced, the means adopted, and the values stressed in the process of carrying out the mission of the Institute. He does not overwhelm the reader with empirical data but at every step reminds us the need to keep our focus on the social aspects. Circumstances change and with that so must our schools. What was needed in the mid-fifties is very different from the needs of today.

After the establishment, the task of writing the Constitution of the proposed Institute was a gigantic one. The Government of India being the main promoter demanded many veto powers, and it is to the credit of all involved that a fair compromise was finally arrived at. The Government emerged as a dominant shareholder with special rights, and the significant issue to protect the sanctity of faculty independence was achieved by and large. With the help of the FF, an academic collaboration was signed with Harvard Business School.

It should be recognized that IIMA came into being in an era of strangulation of enterprise and innovation. There was not much opportunity to practice what one was taught at the Institute and yet there was a scramble for admission. This speaks volumes of the perceived quality of education. Over a period of time, the Institute has introduced many innovative short term courses, developed case studies of Indian companies, and encouraged research by members of the faculty. In 1991, we entered the era of reforms and liberalization of the Indian economy. Free competition and globalization began to appear in our vocabulary, and the Indian industry was no longer insulated and isolated from the world economy and sheltered from world competition. With this change came the need to educate ourselves with the best tools of governance. The record of the Indian industry, its resilience, its ability to change and rise to new challenges has been remarkable.

I understand that the Indian Management Schools have made appropriate adjustments in their programmes, keeping in view the changes in the environment. And yet one can cynically ask why in spite of best practices, buttressed by high quality business education, the US business has faced a financial disaster that has brought misery to the whole world? It is agreed that the present crisis has nothing to do with management governance; it is due to a failure of human values, spurred by human greed. Management schools must take note of this in their educational planning.

Looking to the challenges of tomorrow, the Institute must stress the need to understand human society for whose purpose, economic activity is undertaken. It is important to first understand the human environment and learn to relate to them, and help the people manage their lives for better living. Disparities and inequalities that exist cannot be allowed to continue. Poverty, lack of shelter, and illiteracy have dogged us through generations and yet we have not found any concrete remedies. The deprived sections of society will not continue to be silent for too long. TV and internet educate them as to what they do not possess. Institutes like IIMA must have a social obligation embedded in their teaching and must inculcate human values and ethics to their students.

Management education imparts skills as to how best to use resources—the most precious resource being human capital. One is taught to follow a code of ethics, determine values, help in lessening social distortions, and be a useful member of society. Business has now reached a stage of maturity, and it must not depend on the Government alone to rectify the injustices of the past. The managers of tomorrow will have to deal with a host of social issues in addition to their corporate duties expected of them from their leadership qualities.

I hope that Prafull's book, along with educating his readers about the development of IIMA, generates vigorous debate on such issues. He has aroused a pocketful of dreams through the work of the founding visionaries; with faith and conviction, they made the impossible happen. *The IIMA Story* is an extraordinary book in which the author has remained silent about his own part. But one should take note of his long involvement with the Institute and the care he lavishes on it. The book bears an unmistakable imprint of it. I am sure that the readers would derive as much benefit from it as I have done, perhaps even more.

Keshub Mahindra
November, 2011

Preface

Finally this book is off my back. I have mixed feelings—a moment of deliverance, a moment of release and relief, a moment of exhilaration, a moment of gnawing feeling to do better, a moment of redemption, a moment of the joy of sharing, and a moment of resolve to revisit.

Describing events and episodes is always fraught with the problem of the blind men and the elephant. Each one perceives the 'animal' differently. The only way one can get somewhere near the actual reality is by relating the episode or the anecdote to its context and conveying the overall personality of the actors concerned. Corroborating with perceptions of others is another filter. That has been my attempt. I have tried to stand outside of myself and revisited the episodes in my mind as a spectator would. But I guess it would be impossible to escape the 'Rashomon' effect.

WHY THIS BOOK?

After the Bachelor's in Economics from the London School of Economics and with about three years of working experience, I attended the Programme for Young Executives (PYE) organized by IIMA in 1964. This launched me on a journey of management education. In those days of acute foreign exchange shortage, extensive microscopic control was exercised by the Government of India (GoI) through Reserve Bank of India (RBI). I was selected to attend the Programme for Management Development (PMD) at Harvard for the spring batch of 1965. This would not have been possible but for the funding support provided to IIMA by Ford Foundation (FF) to sponsor two executives from among the participants of its Executive Development Programmes (EDPs) every year.

Then came a turning point. Dr V.L. Mote under whom I had worked for about a year in Calico Mills joined IIMA in 1964. He became the Chairman of the Post Graduate Programme (PGP) in 1965. Professor K.V. Ramnathan had taught Management Accounting II to the first batch of 1964-66. For the 1965-67 batch he was unavailable as he planned to pursue further education in the US. Dr Mote asked me if I could take that course at short notice. I had a latent ambition to teach. This invitation was the perfect opportunity. Without quite realizing what I was taking on I grabbed it; a case of 'inner voice' overtaking reason. I managed to teach that batch, was luckily well received and not hooted out. The students provided very positive feedback. This acted as a great tonic for me. Mind you, they observed me with great curiosity as from amongst a group of executives designated as Faculty Associates I was the only one who had committed to teach a full course. Not just students, even the other faculty and Director Ravi Matthai were probably equally curious.

This launched a deeper association with IIMA. My engagement in teaching continued. I moved from Management Accounting II to Management Control System (MCS) and then Business Policy. My teaching was not based on scholastic or erudite learning and research. It was rooted in my conceptual understanding, clarified and reinforced by my practical experience. In an atmosphere conducive to experimentation and innovation, I came up with a revised design for the programme for small and medium industry. I got involved in EDPs and got happily sucked into IIMA academic community and their plans. I enjoyed it immensely and greatly benefitted from it. That has not stopped even today.

In 1977, Shrenik Lalbhai suggested to the IIMA Board of Governors (BoG) that I be invited to the board as an IIMA Society member. I joined and remained a member of the BoG for a continuous period of twenty-seven years, except for about two or three years in between. My worm's eye view was complemented by a bird's eye view; a teacher's view now supplemented by a policy maker's view. I grew with IIMA and IIMA grew on me.

I saw conflicts, disconnects, rivalries, and even fundamental power struggles. I was either a party or a ringside observer to many a momentous decision. I saw many changes in leadership, both at the Board as well as at the institute level. I saw a severe resource crunch and the climb out of it. I saw wonderful buildings and also an extension of them by a different architect; a promising young architect trying to match his imagination to a pioneering master. I saw yesterday's students become and emerge as global business and academic leaders. I saw the transformation of a struggling institution in a corner of the country to a national icon. I saw the early struggle to get recognized by students, academia, business, and government to a time when everyone wanted an association with it in some way and considered it to be a privilege. Everyone thrived.

This was a great story of institutional evolution. I was a close witness and an enthusiastic participant. The idea of this book germinated.

The story had to be told. It needed to be widely understood. It could provide valuable learning. It was unique and exciting. Due to my long association with the Institute, almost from the beginning, I had multiple perspectives. I was an inside-outsider. I happened to personally know all the key players—Kasturbhai Lalbhai, Vikram Sarabhai, Prakash Tandon, Ravi Matthai and so on. I was privy to many discussions and decisions and also familiar with their context. To tell this story it was not easy for me to bypass me. I selected myself.

Fortunately, I was encouraged by people at different levels. They pledged full support and encouraged me, not that I was reluctant and required to be egged on. So, like my first decision to plunge into teaching at IIMA in 1965, my inner voice again overcame reason. I committed myself to writing about this journey, interpreting and deriving insights in my own way, blithely unaware of the enormous amount of work and commitment of time it would involve.

This was my first attempt to write a book. I had not even a ghost of an idea what it would involve. I am neither a scholar nor an institution theorist. I have not formally studied institution building though my entire focus is on the same.

My perspective is that of an observer and practitioner and not of a scholar. I have had the opportunity to be associated with many diverse institutions in education, arts, healthcare, and social work. I have been a party to examining issues, debating them, deciding on them, and in many cases implementing and finally monitoring and reviewing them. I have therefore had opportunities to observe what works and what does not, the why and how of it as well. This is not formal knowledge or a theoretical construct. Here, I am looking at IIMA from this very perspective.

Initially my reason for writing this book was somewhat vague. Most people encouraged me as they felt that some of the facts about IIMA's beginning and initial years and many others relating to governance would not be known to people unless I share them. Soon I was clear that what I wanted to share was my understanding of how institutions are built. What it takes to make them what they are. IIMA was an apt case as I had a ringside seat for nearly forty-five years.

As I was engaged in building the Ahmedabad University established in 2009, I faced enormous pressure and responsibility. At the same time I must confess that it helped develop a much sharper focus and deeper insight in the structure, values, policies, and processes of IIMA and vice versa. There is no better teacher than practice. Responsibility for results hones the decision making process, induces reflection, and lends balance to proclivities for heroics. There is no overstretch in what one can pursue, there is always room, often unbeknown to us.

I would like to caution the reader that this is not a history of IIMA although there is a historical perspective. It is not a chronicle of events relating to IIMA although there is narration of many important episodes. The best way to describe it is, I believe, as an 'analytical biography' of IIMA.

Many of the values and processes described here, as illustrations of the unique culture at IIMA, may be taken for granted at universities in developed countries. For example, faculty autonomy in academic matters or the sanctity of schedules are taken for granted in most leading Schools in the US and UK. However these had not taken root in India. Therefore, to a reader abroad such observations and examples may appear to be a little trite. I would urge readers to view them in Indian context.

My most helpful assets in meeting this self-invited challenge were a curious mind, a watchful eye, and perceptive friends. They refreshed my memory, provided different viewpoints, corrected factual errors, and spared a lot of their time. I also got access not just to IIMA papers which unfortunately have significant gaps, but some invaluable documents from Vikram Sarabhai's papers, Kasturbhai Lalbhai's papers, Harvard Business School (HBS) Archives, and FF Archives. Without the benefit of this access, my story would not have captured the nuances of various relationships and the supporting documents for my interpretation. I am grateful to Mr N.V. Pillai, Chief Administartive Officer (CAO) of IIMA; Padmanabh Joshi, Vikram Sarabhai's biographer; National Archives of India, New Delhi; Raschel Wise of HBS; and Idelle Nissila of FF, New York. Balkrishna Doshi, the renowned architect, provided insight into the mind of legendary Louis Kahn. I am ever so grateful to him.

Keshav Mahindra illuminated the nuances of some of the defining moments. Narayana Murthy's handling of *l'affaire* fee reduction was a practical demonstration of values and leadership. Shrenik Lalbhai helped understand Kasturbhai better. All former directors from Samuel Paul, Vijay Vyas, Narayan Sheth, Pradip Khandwala, Jahar Saha to Bakul Dholakia and the present incumbent Samir K. Barua gave their valuable time, provided relevant information, and clarified issues.

Many former and current faculty members filled in the details of various critical events and presented a kaleidoscope of viewpoints. I would like to make special mention of Prof. V.L. Mote, the late Prof. Udai Pareek, Prof. T.V. Rao, Prof. A. H. Kalro, Prof. K. Balakrishnan, and Prof. B.H. Jajoo. H. Anil Kumar, the IIMA Librarian, was a great help in identifying and providing relevant sources promptly. My thanks are due to him also.

The biggest contribution came from Prof. Dwijendra Tripathi. Encouraged by his generosity, I kept on encroaching on his precious retirement time and drew upon his sharp memory and incisive insights. He meticulously read and re-read each draft of the various chapters, provided valuable tips and guidance, and pointed out lapses in my perspective. He did this with clinical precision and professional detachment, not letting his own views colour his comments. As I mentioned earlier, I am a novice at writing books. But for him, I would probably have been exhausted and might just have abandoned the project.

U Harindran, my assistant at IIMA, has been a great help. He checked facts, researched data, read my illegible handwriting, and did some initial editing to improve readability. His association with IIMA has been as long as mine or may be even slightly longer. That gave me a great sense of comfort and a rare sounding board; that his emotional investment was like mine provided a most fortuitous coincidence.

Mr B.G. Varghese, my secretary at Ahmedabad University pitched in with some valuable support. During all my professional life I have used various forms to express myself. I write, more often dictate, and sometimes converse. He patiently typed out my recorded dictation and also garbled writing. That expedited the process and often helped capture my ideas which would have escaped me, had I restricted myself only to writing. My thanks are due to him. Mr Laxmandev Gohil and Ms Nina Badlani of the Accounts Department of IIMA helped in compiling financial data in different ways for all these years as per my request. My thanks are due to them.

I am ending the book now. *The project, however, has not ended.* Many ideas, questions, and issues still swirl in my mind. Often I get the feeling that some words need to be changed to capture the exact meaning I want to convey, to develop a different perspective or to add or omit a detail. It is endless, it is tiring and beyond a point it is even pointless! The most that I expect from this endeavour is to trigger some thoughts, inform some ideas, and refine some actions. That is the hope, may be the purpose, and perhaps the hidden driver.

Introduction

Way back on February 5, 1955, T.T. Krishnamachari (T.T.K.), India's Minister of Commerce, gave the keynote address at Ahmedabad Textile Industry Research Association (ATIRA)'s first management conference. At the time, Vikram Sarabhai was the director of ATIRA and Kasturbhai Lalbhai was the chairman. In the course of his address, T.T.K. (as he was popularly known) stated:

'Sometime back my colleague, the Minister of Education, appointed a committee.

The purpose of that committee was:

1. To establish a sort of Institute of Management,
2. To establish an Administrative Staff College.

I do not know what impelled him amongst the fifteen Ministers and forty odd Deputy Ministers and Ministers of State to choose me to be the Chairman of the Committee. Anyway, we are now supposed to be formulating plans for establishing a Central Institute of Management and also for the starting of an Administrative Staff College.'[1]

T.T.K.'s comments alerted Vikram Sarabhai. The idea of IIMA began to take shape in his mind. He wanted Ahmedabad to be the location for this institute.

At the time, Mumbai was India's undisputed commercial and financial capital. Ahmedabad by contrast, was a small, single industry city in the western corner of India. It was barely one-sixth the size of Mumbai, and unlike its cosmopolitan rival, Ahmedabad was essentially a Gujarati city. Most of the country's leading professional managers were based in Mumbai, Calcutta, and Madras, as were the country's oldest universities. Ahmedabad was little more than an appendix to Mumbai. How the city came to be chosen as the venue for the IIMA is an absorbing tale of leadership, politics, and of how a small yet focused group can overcome a greater yet diffused contender.

The late 1950s were a fascinating period in India's history; ten years of freedom, ten years of building a new nation, faced with the stark reality of a poor and backward society. Faith and aspiration battled against three hundred years of darkness and oppression. A small, progressive minority was trying desperately to wake the majority from centuries of stupor. The whole effort was palpable.

Rabindranath Tagore's words gave expression to the faith of this minority.

With the launch of Sputnik, the Soviets were winning the space race. Colonialism was in its last throes, although the memories still rankled. Suez could not be held forcibly by the colonial powers. While Pakistan chose to ally itself to the USA, India asserted its non-alignment. This policy of non-alignment irritated the western powers, bringing India politically closer to the USSR. The ravages and shortages brought about by the Second World War had come to an end. The Western economies were quickly rebuilt. Demand for Indian textiles—the only manufactured commodity exported—tapered off. Indian commodities were faced with global competition. The country needed capital, technology, and skills. The wartime foreign exchange reserves were fast depleting. Given the political stance, inward looking economic policies became inevitable. The country was faced with crippling regulations in all spheres of economic activity. Entrepreneurship was throttled. Economic initiatives could

---

[1] From ATIRA archive papers: 'Inaugural address by Shri T.T. Krishnamachari, Union Minister of Commerce and Industry', ATIRA Archives, Ahmedabad, p.11.

only be pursued with government blessings. An unhealthy relationship between industry, commerce, and government began to take root. Bureaucracy flourished, rules and red tapism crippled industry as private enterprise was marginalized. The whole country was being managed as one gigantic government enterprise.

It was in this climate that an institute of management was first conceived and then came into being.

On December 11, 1961, the Memorandum of Agreement (MoA) was signed by Dr Jivraj Mehta, Chief Minister of Gujarat; Kasturbhai Lalbhai; and Vikram Sarabhai among others. The first meeting of the BoG was held on February 28, 1962. The Institute was born, functioning from loaned premises, with a scientist as the part time Honorary Director and a Chief Minister of a State as Chairman.

Over the course of the next few years, the faculty was recruited and a relationship with HBS was forged. Work on the campus buildings began, funding trickled in and by July, 1964, the first batch of 48 students arrived.

In the early to mid 1960s, management as a profession was still in its infancy, it was neither fully understood nor appreciated. People failed to realize that not only was there a need for a good supply of trained manpower but that demand also had to be assiduously created. The promotion, sustenance, and growth of managerial talent was a key task. How things have changed over the years; from a time when industry had to be wooed, cajoled, and entreated to take notice of the talent IIMA had to offer, to a scenario where industry leaders were vying with each other to attract its finest alumni. This in itself shows how a small but committed initiative can develop into an iconic mass movement. Remarkably, all of this was achieved in the relatively short period of ten to fifteen years. Since then the reputation of IIMA has grown consistently. It has become the 'confidence' of the nation.

The IIMA began with the faculty strength of just thirteen in 1963 and by 1990 it had grown to eighty three. Since then its full faculty strength has remained between seventy- five and ninety over the last two decades. (For full details, see Appendix 5).

The first tiny batch of 48 PGP (MBA) students has now grown to 353 students in 2011. On a cumulative basis 8902 students graduated from long duration programmes including 8153 PGP students. In short duration programmes it has grown from 120 in 1963–04 to 47437 (cumulative) in 2011.

IIMA's leadership has been provided by a total of ten chairmen and ten directors over the last fifty years (See Appendix 2 and 3). All the chairmen were leading industrialists except for one who was a renowned economist and bureaucrat, and one educationist. All the directors except Dr I.G. Patel came from within the Institute itself.

In 1966, placing that first batch of forty-eight students proved to be a real struggle. The average salary offered to students was about Rs 825 per month, a princely sum in those days, and they were placed at middle management levels mainly in the manufacturing industry. Today, all students receive multiple offers and many foreign placements. The average salary has climbed to Rs18 lakh per year and most students enter the financial and consultancy sectors at a fairly senior level.

Currently many large Indian businesses and several multinational corporations can boast of CEOs from IIMA.

Over the last thirty years, newspapers and magazines have been ranking business schools from around the globe. To begin with Indian institutions weren't even a blip on the radar. IIMA was the first Indian business school to achieve international recognition. In 2002, IIMA figured in the top 60 in the Economist Intelligence Unit's list. The same survey ranked the IIMA as the most selective management school in the world. Within other parameters, such as teaching, it was ranked amongst the top 10. And in 2011, IIMA was ranked number 7 in *Financial Times* (FT)'s global ranking of Masters in Management Programme.

However, on research and the entry level salary of graduates, IIMA consistently ranked far lower. In regional rankings, such as Asia Pacific, it was in the top five and for a couple of years stood as the top institution. Within India, IIMA always topped the charts by a wide margin.

The faculty of IIMA come from a diverse range of backgrounds. Initially, some came from industry, some from government, some from universities, a few from the NGO sector and, lately, many from the Fellow (Doctoral) Programme in Management. During the first five years, nearly every faculty member was trained at the HBS. They all shared the common case method pedagogy and General Management bias of HBS. Right from the word go, emphasis was placed on practice orientation and the problem solving approach. The general ethos of HBS greatly influenced the Indian faculty's orientation, teaching, and research skills. This was transmitted by the HBS faculty who came to IIMA. About fifteen of them came for periods ranging from three months to two years.

Rather than choosing to focus only on the business and corporate sector, the IIMA positioned itself towards management problems of all sectors of the economy. One reason for this was due to its partnership with the government; the large public sector was another, but the major factor was due to the social commitment of its early leaders and the progressive outlook of ministers such as C. Subramaniam.

Because of this background, IIMA became the first port of call for not only the corporate sector but the social and public sectors as well. IIMA's partner HBS insisted that faculty members should be permitted to engage in consultancy for up to 53 days a year, just as they did at HBS itself. This opened up an important avenue to the faculty, allowing them to understand and experience contemporary management concerns. Organizations such as Air India, Larsen and Toubro (L&T), State Bank of India (SBI), and the Ministry of Agriculture all came to IIMA, giving the faculty insights into real life problems and helping to develop a multi-disciplinary approach. It also honed their problem solving skills, and allowed them to appreciate the complexity of reality, its ambiguity, and the limitations of 'academic' solutions to managerial problems.

One of the most valuable aspects of IIMA's association with HBS was that of research in practice. From day one, the Indian faculty became engaged in research into the practice of Indian business. Vikram Sarabhai had emphasized that every faculty would undertake all the four 'academic' activities of teaching, research, consulting, and case writing. Each activity helped to reinforce the other. It is also a reflection of Vikram's own varied background. He did research in physics, while simultaneously running his business. In the first ten years, 587 papers were published and 1,361 cases and technical notes written by the IIMA faculty. As of 2010–11 the tally was 4,015 papers and 4,836 cases and technical notes. IIMA was unique in the roles played by its faculty. Although it drew upon HBS for its experience and structure for faculty organization and mix of activities, it also found its own solutions in the Indian context. Unlike anywhere else in India at the time, the IIMA faculty played crucial administrative roles. PGP administration, admissions, evaluation, placement, and executive education were all handled by the faculty. Whether this was a good thing or not, has been hotly debated by the faculty over the years, but it did have its rewards. The IIMA faculty has emerged as a huge talent pool for the position of directors and CEOs of numerous educational institutions. Over the last forty-five years, the IIMA faculty has provided sixteen Directors for IIMs and other institutions.

In the late 1950s and early 60s, Architecture as a profession was relatively unknown and certainly under-appreciated. Vikram Sarabhai's sensitivity and Kasturbhai Lalbhai's experience ensured that the IIMA buildings were not boxed spaces like other similar institutions. The best architects of the time were engaged and renowned foreign experts such as Louis Kahn were invited. The results are there for everyone to see. Today, the IIMA buildings have become the iconic image for our business and management education institutions.

Kasturbhai headed the building committee for 17 years, keeping a sensitive and watchful eye on the aesthetics, functionality, and costs. The Institute itself began in a bungalow in Shahibag. The Gujarat Housing Board provided temporary accommodation for both faculty and staff from July, 1964 to March, 1966. Because the buildings weren't scheduled to open before July, 1965, classes started in ATIRA. One seminar room and two small classrooms were made available at an annual rent of Rs 5000 plus electric bills and other incidentals. The Gujarat Housing Board provided 18 of their 34 flats for student housing close to Ambawadi about couple of kilometers from the campus. In 1970, IIMA had just a few buildings, measuring a total of 1,15,000 sq. ft. By 2011, the campus had grown to a massive 16,53,000 sq. ft. Thanks to its continuous growth and development, the IIMA campus has always worn the look of a masterful work-in-progress.

Few people realize that the Public Private Partnership (PPP) model, which is currently very much in vogue as an organizational form for large public projects was actually adopted by IIMA way back in 1961. To begin with, IIMA was funded by four promoters: the GoI, the Government of Gujarat (GoG), local industry, and the FF. GoI gave annual grants to meet the operational deficit. GoG provided part of the equipment costs and about 65 acres of land; local industry pledged to meet the cost of the buildings and equipment; and the FF met the entire foreign exchange costs, which included the cost of the HBS collaboration, faculty, training abroad, and funding for the library.

In 1966, its first full year of operation, IIMA's receipts from the Post Graduate Programmes (PGP) were Rs 3.13 lakh and Rs 2.89 lakh from short duration programmes. Its consultancy income was Rs 14,000 and the grant from GoI was Rs 11.81 lakh. The respective figures for 2011 were a total of Rs 6159.11 lakh from PGP and other long duration programmes, Rs 2055 lakh from its short courses, a total of Rs 2664 lakh in consultancy income, and zero grant from GoI.

On the expenses side, in 1966, expenditure on the Post Graduate Programme was Rs 2.8 lakh, Short Duration Programmes (SDPs) Rs 2.4 lakh, and establishment expenses Rs 11.82 lakh. In 2011, these were Rs 1879 lakh for PGP and other Long Duration Programmes (LDPs), Rs 1018 lakh for SDPs, and Rs 4707 lakh for establishment expenses.

In 1966, immovable property was worth Rs 48 lakh and investment nil, but in 2011, immovable property grew to Rs 10477 lakh and investments to Rs 29401 lakh.

No grant has been sought or received from the GoI since 2003. Of the total assets created by March 31, 2011, of Rs 14891 lakh, Rs 3158 lakh came from GoI and Rs 11733 lakh from internal generation and other sources. IIMA belongs to a handful of institutions which have fully provided for pension liability of its staff.[2]

Few successful institutions began under such unique conditions. None have seen such a long and consistent history of growth and excellence. Unlike other institutions, the IIMA has the courage and drive to constantly question itself and strive to surpass its own records. The passion and commitment of the faculty, students, staff, and the BoG cannot be found elsewhere. Its monumental physical and intellectual presence is unrivalled. But why? How did this happen? In a country with a myriad of institutions all struggling to achieve excellence, let alone maintain it, we ask 'Why IIMA is what IIMA is?' This is the central question I am attempting to answer. In my view, five elements have contributed to it—the circumstances of its birth and initial resource mix, the collaboration with HBS, governance structure, its early leadership, and values and processes. All of these factors formed the DNA of the Institute. We will discuss these elements throughout the course of this book

---

[2] Many of the financial data mentioned in this and Chapter 9 – Finances, have been regrouped according to the purpose of analysis.

1

Why IIM?
If IIM, Why Ahmedabad?

THE BIRTH PANGS AND THE DNA OF AN INSTITUTION

> 'Jab Kutte pe sassa aya tab badshah ne shaher basaya': Where a rabbit overpowered a dog and King Ahmedshah founded the city.
>
> According to legend, King Ahmedshah was once looking for a site to found a great city. He came to the banks of the Sabarmati where he saw a rabbit overpowering a dog. Greatly impressed by this spectacle he chose the site to build a city in his name. That is how the city of Ahmedabad was founded and named.

The year was 1955, and the people were still basking in the glow of political independence. Although the urge to participate in the building of a nation stirred many young hearts, the country was one of huge contrasts. There was ignorance and there was a thirst for knowledge. There was superstition and there was scientific spirit. There was deprivation and there was pride. There was exploitation and there was altruism. There was indolence and there was momentum. There was fatalism and there was self belief. There was an air of resignation and there was a feeling of being in charge. There was simplicity and there was creeping materialism. There were islands of opulence and there was a vast sea of poverty. There were secular ideals and there was caste consciousness. There was degrading dependence and there was fiery independence. There were privileges and there were supplicants. There was much to be depressed about and much to cheer. A sense of nostalgia was giving way to hard reality. The focus was shifting from the heroics of liberation to the challenges of construction. A generation was moving out, another taking charge.

It is in this national milieu, that the Nehru government thought of establishing a national institute of management. Beginning in Kharagpur, in 1950, the government had already established five Indian Institutes of Technology (IIT). It is interesting to note that both technical and management education were given priority over the development of universities. Nehru believed that these along with projects such as Bhakra Nangal were the true temples of modern India.

We are going to examine two important questions, the first being how was the institute for management education conceived, and the second, how did it come to be established in Ahmedabad?

THE DECISION TO ESTABLISH

The decision to establish an institute of management was taken in 1955 when the Government formed a committee to look into all the options available before making its recommendations. Up until that time, management education was almost non existent in India. The universities of India had modelled themselves on their British counterparts and had remained oblivious to the development of business education in the USA. At the time, Harvard had been teaching business for almost half a century and the Wharton and Tuck Schools a few decades more.

It is true that India did have its own colleges of commerce, but these had grown up as part of the universities. Commerce fell between a proper discipline in higher education and vocational training. The main emphasis was on finance, banking, accounting, and secretarial practice. There was very little practical work, and research in the field was completely unheard of. In short, Commerce was not considered worthy of scholarly pursuit. Most high level policy makers had a background in the liberal arts or law, and students of commerce were condescendingly viewed as little more than prospective low level functionaries. It is true that Local Management Associations (LMAs), were being established, but Commerce colleges and universities never cared to establish links with any of them.

These Commerce colleges were unable to produce the high level personnel that India so desperately needed to execute its progressive programme of economic development based upon the central planning model. The nation needed something different. The public sector was rapidly expanding and this helped to bring about an awareness of the urgent need for management training.

The United Kingdom had established the Administrative Staff College in Henley-on-Thames in 1945. Progressive private businesses had also begun taking steps towards management training. They recruited graduates from the Arts and Commerce faculty and organized on-the-job training within their companies. Some high level businessmen even sent members of their families over to the USA for MBA studies.

Not surprisingly '... in 1953, the All India Council for Technical Education, in advising the Government of India (GoI) on the expansion of educational facilities to implement planned industrialization, heavily discounted the resource potential of the commerce colleges and recommended the establishment of an entirely new set of "management studies" programme.'
(Hill Thomas & others, *Institution Building in India*, p.11)

As an outcome of this, programmes for management studies were established at several universities. However, by 1960, it had become apparent that these programmes catered only to the needs of the lower levels of management. This was mainly due to the fact that, until this point, no Indian University had ever connected with industry or commerce for research or study. Many of them began running evening and part-time programmes. All India Management Association (AIMA) and Local Management Association (LMA) followed suit and Administrative Staff College of India (ASCI) also ran short term programmes. Still, this was not enough. The programmes lacked both depth and rigour. To quote a competent contemporary study '... most of the existing institutions and associations are meant for people already employed in business and other organizations. There is, however, a real lacuna of educational facilities preparing young men and women for professional careers in management.'
(Hill Thomas & others, *Institution Building in India*.)

All these developments led to the initial idea of a specialized national institution of management. It is much to the credit of the government of the time that they foresaw the need for a formal education in this field, so early in the history of the fledgling republic. They fully recognized the value of education as an instrument of economic development.

In 1955, Dr Humayun Kabir, the Minister of Scientific Research and Cultural Affairs, established a committee under the chairmanship of T.T. Krishnamachari, probably the only Cabinet Minister who came from an industrialist family. Based upon the recommendations of that committee, the Indian Management Education Study Team visited the USA and submitted their own report. In the meantime, the Ford Foundation (FF) had become increasingly active in its support of the development of both technical and management education in India. The FF had established an office in Delhi, led by such senior personnel as Dr Douglas Ensminger. By 1958, they were playing a large role in establishing educational institution like IIT Kanpur.

In March, 1955, Dr Douglas Ensminger held discussions with both the Indian and the US governments regarding prospective aid for the establishment of institutions of higher learning in the fields of technology and management. The initial dialogue took place between representatives of both governments and the University of Mumbai. Dr John Matthai was the Vice Chancellor and Dr C.N. Vakil was Head of the Department of Economics at that time. In April, 1956, the Foundation approached Harvard Business School (HBS), asking for their assistance by sending a team to study and prepare a report on the establishment of such an institution. In 1957, Professor Richard Merriam and Professor Harold Thurlby of HBS arrived in India. They prepared a report of their findings and recommended the formation of a business school, based primarily upon the American model. Their most important point was that such a school be completely independent of the university system. Understandably, perhaps, Mumbai University reacted adversely and from that point on showed no further enthusiasm for the project. The FF continued to push but without any positive response. In late 1957, Dr Matthai left his post as Vice Chancellor of the university, but his successor was also unwilling to progress further with the proposal. The FF considered the Business School of the University of California at Los Angeles (UCLA) as a possible partner. Associate Dean George W. Robbins of UCLA submitted a report, dated December 20, 1959, which was more or less along the same lines as the earlier HBS report. Robbins observed that after establishing one institution and learning from its experience, India should go ahead with establishing more. This report was accepted by the Planning Commission of the GoI on December 28, 1959. The FF still hoped that Mumbai University would come around and that the institution would be established there. However, the basic sticking point regarding the autonomous status of such a school could not be overcome.

The Robbins Report was accepted by the Government, with one small but fundamental change. While the exercise was initiated to explore the establishment of a national institute of management, the Government had, by now, decided to establish not one, but two institutions. To begin with, the institutions were to be established in Calcutta and in Mumbai, one in the far eastern corner and the other in the far west. Both Calcutta and Mumbai were considered the industrial hubs of the entire nation, the Multi National Companies (MNCs) and other large Indian enterprises all had headquarters there. The entire process can be summarized thus:

'In both business and education, Indian practices have long been largely indistinguishable from British. Consequently, although all of the institutions heretofore described were patterned on foreign (i.e., British) prototypes, none was in any important respect alien to its new environment. In contrast, at the time of independence, relatively few Indians were familiar with corresponding American practices, which differed quite sharply in many ways from those prevalent in India. That the American management education model was adopted as early as 1960 testifies not only to the receptivity of Indian leadership to innovation, but also to the promotional effectiveness of the FF, which lent active support to Indian management development efforts almost from their beginning.'[1]

'Interestingly, although the proposal was specifically for a single such institution, and although all prior discussion had focused on Mumbai, the Foundation was soon committed to assisting with two institutes neither of which was ultimately located in that city.'

(Hill Thomas & others, *Institution Building in India* p.16)

Thus there were three distinct cycles of development of management education. 'The first, commencing in 1913, produced the colleges of commerce; the second, beginning in 1953, yielded several management studies programmes and the administrative staff college; and the third, which started in 1961, resulted in the management institutes.'

(Hill Thomas & others, *Institution Building in India* p.19)

---

[1] In addition to meeting the foreign exchange requirements for building the management institutes at Ahmedabad and Calcutta, the Foundation has supported a number of other activities pertinent to management technology transfer from the United States to India. These include: (i) selective augmentation of TCM/USAID programmes for observational visits by Indian leaders to the States; (ii) provision of American consultants on various aspects of management development to both the Government of India and such institutions as ASCI; (iii) establishment of an All-India Management Association (AIMA) to integrate and strengthen development activities of the pre-existing other, international teacher training programmes at both Harvard University and Stanford University. (The International Teachers Programme at the Harvard Graduate School of Business Administration was started in 1958; the International Centre for the Advancement of Management Education at Stanford dates from 1962. The Ford Foundation has provided some financial assistance to ITP and has been the sole source of grant support for ICAME.); (iv) sponsorship by AIMA of an annual Advanced Management Seminar staffed (at first wholly and later in part) by American professors; and (v) not specific to India but utilized as heavily by that country as any other. Hill Thomas & others, *Institution Building in India* p.15

Why an independent institution was mooted in the first place? Business schools were run as part of established universities all over the world, with only a handful of exceptions. It would seem that both the Professors from HBS and Dean Robbins believed that the Indian universities were not suited to establish a programme of management that was practice oriented. The universities regarded themselves as great purveyors of liberal education in the British tradition. They had no connection to the real world of business practice.

Another key factor in the decision was the establishment of independent institutions of science and technology. The government realized that technology and management were key to the development of industry irrespective of ownership. It was an investment in the future, which also fitted in with their overall objective of economic self reliance right across the board from the manufacture of textiles to the development of nuclear power.

WHY AHMEDABAD?

The whole process from the initial idea to the final decision to actually establishing an institution of management education took a total of five years, but after the Robbins report, the pace quickened and things began moving much more rapidly. The government accepted the report immediately, deciding to establish two institutes instead of one. This decision was surprising, because the launching of a management school was considered by many like Professor Herbert Simon to be a high risk venture. It is unclear to this date whether the decision was made as a response to political pressures or with the specific idea of developing a healthy spirit of competition between the two institutes. From the very beginning there was no question over Calcutta as the location for one of the proposed institutes. Ahmedabad however, was entirely another matter for the city had little to commend itself as the location for the other.

Ahmedabad was a single industry city, provincial and regional in character and a fraction of the size of Calcutta. Mumbai, the clear favourite, was much bigger, cosmopolitan in character with a diversified industrial base, and it had already established itself as the hub of professional managers. Some quarters believe that Calcutta and Ahmedabad were chosen because of the regional connections of both Dr Humayun Kabir, the Minister in charge of the project, who was a Bengali, and the Secretary, Professor M.S. Thacker, a Gujarati.

In March, 1961, Professor Hill hinted in a report, the pressure from the business community as a possible reason for the decision.

'Although Robbins proposes a single national institution, the Indian government has decided to establish two, one in Calcutta in the east and one in Ahmedabad in the west. Since it is apparently accepted that both institutes will emphasize residential courses on an All-India basis, and since it is generally conceded that staffing presents a major problem, this decision is easily attacked on logical grounds. The Indian business community is, however, rather sharply divided into eastern and western sectors, and it may be assumed that the decision does have political merit. While I am certain that the simultaneous establishment of two schools will considerably extend the period required for either to reach maturity, I do not consider this an insurmountable handicap. I am somewhat more concerned by the possibility that, if political considerations dominate in this instance, they may in others.'

There may very well be some merit in these speculations but many other events were taking place behind the scene. Vikram Sarabhai, taking his cue from T.T. Krishnamachari's keynote address at Ahmedabad Textile Industry Research Association (ATIRA) in 1955, had been paying close attention to these developments. Following the Indian government's acceptance of the Robbins Report of December, 1959, he became increasingly active.

Gujarat State was formed in 1960 and Dr Jivraj Mehta was named Chief Minister. He was a very enlightened, progressive politician. Vikram Sarabhai decided it was time to swing into action. Vikram wanted the proposed institute to be located in Ahmedabad, and together with Kasturbhai Lalbhai, he decided to enlist the support of Dr Mehta.

Thanks to the personal pull of Kasturbhai and Vikram, the solid support and lobbying of the Government of Gujarat (GoG), and Ahmedabad's reputation in the field of education—the Indian government agreed to shift the location of the institute to Ahmedabad. Kasturbhai was the Chairman of the Ahmedabad Education Society, which had established several leading educational institutions in Gujarat and also promoted Physical Research Laboratory (PRL), National Institute of Design (NID), and ATIRA. He had also provided half the initial costs of establishing the LD Engineering College in Ahmedabad. Kasturbhai's support gave the project a strong sense of credibility. Mumbai may have been bigger but it lacked any single champion with the passion and commitment of either Kasturbhai, Vikram, or Dr Jivraj Mehta.

The triumvirate of Jivraj Mehta, the Chief Minister of Gujarat; Kasturbhai Lalbhai, the undisputed business leader of the new State; and Vikram Sarabhai, the visionary scientist-businessman, was a powerful combination, rarely seen in public life. While Jivraj Mehta and Kasturbhai Lalbhai were of the same generation, Vikram was a generation apart. Jivraj Mehta was a physician educated in India, Kasturbhai was not even a college graduate, and Vikram was a research scientist trained at the Indian Institute of Science (IISc) and Cambridge. These three men were very different, but they all shared one passion and that was the establishment of a new institution in the field of management. At the time it was believed that, at the very best, this institution would train perhaps a few hundred students and industry managers. The staff and faculty would be relatively small and local Gujarat students and workers would not be given preferential treatment. It is common for politicians and industrialists to think 'what's in it for me?' The answer as far as these three men were concerned, was 'very little'. There was no reason for them to stake their reputations or commit their funds to this seemingly insignificant project. But together they shared a great vision and extraordinary qualities. And, they were determined to make that vision a reality.

Dean Robbins had observed, 'The Institute should be located geographically (1) where there exists varied types and sizes of business to serve as a laboratory for the faculty and students, (2) where adequate resources are available, and (3) where the environment is favourable to vigorous growth and experimentation.' He had underlined the need for collaboration between business, government, and education. The trio sensed the opportunity in this observation and made it the basis of their actions. Jivraj Mehta immediately committed 65 acres of prime land, Kasturbhai offered to underwrite the cost of buildings on behalf of the local business community, and Vikram mobilized support from the Ahmedabad business and professional community.

Jivraj Mehta toured the country, canvassing support at the political level. Kasturbhai also used his contacts in government to promote the cause. Vikram wrote to V.T. Krishnamachari, the Vice Chairman of the Planning Commission, in May, 1960 (see Appendix 1). He also orchestrated the support of the Ahmedabad Management Association (AMA), Ahmedabad Millowners' Association, and the Gujarat Chamber of Commerce. Vikram's relationship with Professor M.S. Thacker, a fellow scientist, who was also the Secretary of the Ministry of Scientific Research and Cultural Affairs helped matters. G.L. Mehta, a former Indian Ambassador to the United States and Chairman of ICICI, also weighed in with his support. He had great regard for both Kasturbhai and Vikram.

Vikram made a powerful case for Ahmedabad. The main thrust of his argument was the city's track record of establishing such pioneering institutions as ATIRA through private initiatives. Vikram pointed out to V.T. Krishnamachari, the Vice Chairman of the Planning Commission, the climate for management and research in Ahmedabad and the initiatives already taken in that area. He argued that at ATIRA research was already being used as an important tool in improving business and management practice. A relationship with both Massachusetts Institute of Technology (MIT) and HBS had already been forged. Indeed, the fact that a three-month residential programme for senior managers was organized within just two years of its establishment demonstrated three things: a strategic understanding of the market, the availability of programme design skills, and the confidence to deliver it. Vikram underlined that while ATIRA had begun with contributions from local industry, it now attracted an all-India membership. Indeed, the establishment and success of ATIRA as the first private co-operative research establishment in the country proved a powerful pull towards locating IIM at Ahmedabad.

So many heavyweights came together to swing a decision to establish a 'miniscule' institution in Ahmedabad in a field which hardly had any public awareness. It was an amazing spectacle! The decision was clinched. Indian Institute of Management Ahmedabad Society (IIMA Society) was formed to implement the project.

The GoG displayed a monumental commitment to the initiative, which is captured in the following episode. During the first meeting of the Board of Governors (BoG) on February 28, 1962, the Chairman raised the issue of the proposed acquisition of land. The total area of land to be acquired was about 65 acres and the cost to acquire it was Rs 27 lakh. The GoG undertook to facilitate the acquisition process and to donate the funds as its contribution to the Institute, while the Institute itself was to make the payment for the land. The GoG gave the following schedule for payment:
1. 40 percent of the amount to be paid in March, 1962
2. 30 percent of the amount to be paid in April, 1962, and balance
3. 30 percent of the amount to be paid in April, 1963

(It appears that there must have been a budget allocation constraint because the total payment to be disbursed in 13 months was cleverly spread over three financial years—FY 62, FY 63, and FY 64).

In the same meeting, while discussing the issue, the Chairman reported that the Bank of India had agreed to grant a loan of Rs 16.60 lakh (60 percent of the total amount) at the request of the Society (IIMA Society). This loan along with the initial 40 percent contribution would enable the Society to make the full payment to acquire the land. The Bank of India sanctioned this loan under the condition that 50 percent of the amount borrowed would be repaid in April, 1962 and the balance in April, 1963. The loan was to come in the form of a cash credit facility and interest was to be 1.5 percent above the bank rate, minimum 5.25 percent. It would be a clean advance until the Society obtained the title and created an equitable mortgage by depositing the title deeds. It was therefore stipulated that the GoG would give a guarantee for it. Jivraj Mehta, the Chairman, and V. Isvaran, the Chief Secretary, were authorized and empowered to *attend at the Bank of India* and deposit the title deeds of the Society's immovable properties. Furthermore, as this was done in order to accommodate the State Government, it was agreed that the interest on the same would be borne by the GoG. In the end, at the next board meeting on June, 30, 1962, it was revealed that the GoG had paid the full amount and the possession of the land was handed over to the Institute without having to take the loan from Bank of India.

For a Chief Minister of a State to offer to attend a bank to sign the papers for a loan for an institute which hadn't even opened its doors was unthinkable in any context. The passion and commitment shown by the Chief Minister must surely have had a positive effect on the minds of both the FF and HBS. As we will see, later on when it came to such issues as the selection of a Director, or basing a research centre in Mumbai, the voice of Jivraj Mehta would always have a great impact.

People are often perplexed by the selfless commitment of these captains of industry and by the 'pull' they managed to exercise. Few people realize that Vikram's father, Ambalal Sarabhai had previously helped to fund Gandhiji's movement. Kasturbhai had also been a contributor. The Nehru family were also linked to both Vikram and Kasturbhai's families.

It is worth reflecting how these two stalwarts from the leading industrial families of Gujarat were so deeply committed to the public cause of education and strove so hard to ensure that the IIM was finally established in Ahmedabad.

The idea of Indian Institute of Management, Ahmedabad (IIMA) came up during a burst of institutional activity in Ahmedabad. These institutes were modern, larger in scale, innovative in governance structure, and international in character. PRL, ATIRA, NID, IIMA, and the School of Architecture were a far cry from the traditional commerce, science and arts colleges. A spirit of adventure, combined with confidence, drive, and a burning desire to build a modern India prevailed. Certainly, the inspiration and the models came from the West, but the concern and relevance were all acutely Indian.

Strangely enough, these initiatives came not from educationists, politicians, social workers, or landlords but rather, they were the creation of two remarkable industrialists. Two men who were used to dealing with global competition, who were no strangers to the concept of investments and return, costs, and viability. Vikram Sarabhai and Kasturbhai Lalbhai were disturbed by the consequences of the nation's long political subjugation, economic backwardness, poverty, and social divisions; they wanted to build a new liberated India. Their motives and values were fundamentally different from those who were interested in building and founding ordinary educational institutions.

Vikram and Kasturbhai had no interest in starting medical or law schools. To them, the key priorities for the budding republic had to be economic enterprise, science, technology, management, design, and architecture. These disciplines were all new and innovative. All programmes all placed a strong emphasis on research, scientific methods, and problem solving orientation. According to Vikram and Kasturbhai, these were to be the building blocks for their shared dream of a new India.

Of course, Mumbai had more than its fair share of industrial giants but none of them worked together as a close-knit group, nor did they align themselves with the state government for a common cause. It is quite likely that the Maharashtra political leadership had little understanding of business or a close working relationship with local business leaders. On top of this, the Mumbai University remained adamant that any proposed institution should function within the existing university structure.

And so it was that a mighty coordinated push at Ahmedabad, combined with a lacklustre campaign at Mumbai, clinched the issue against all odds. Mumbai may well have had the support of the FF but at the end of the day it was an alliance between local industry and local government, based on a shared vision, mutual trust, and integrity that won the deal. The 'rabbit' had overpowered the 'dog' once again! IIMA was born.

THE OUTCOME OF THE CHOICE OF LOCATION

Owing to the great debate over location, the final decision on IIMA came somewhat later than that of IIM Calcutta. IIMC held its first planning meeting on February 18, 1960. IIMA was not to hold its first meeting until five months later on July 20, 1960. Dean Robbins as the representative of the partner institution UCLA, could not be present for the meeting. Soon, the partner was to change, which provides yet another twist in the story.

HBS Project Director Harry Hansen's balanced observation on the location of the Institute is worth noting:

'Although the question of location of the Institute in Ahmedabad was not a question involved in this survey, a few observations should be made. The choice of Ahmedabad as a site has many advantages. There is interest and support for the Institute among prominent industrial leaders in Ahmedabad who have for a long time demonstrated an interest in education. With regard to the business community generally, either group or individual discussions were held with approximately seventy-five executives. As might indeed be expected no negative views concerning the proposed Institute were expressed, but beyond this there was lively interest and discussion concerning its objectives and plans. Indeed it can be argued that because Ahmedabad is not a very large international or cosmopolitan city that its leading citizens will readily rally to the support of the Institute. To illustrate, there does not appear to be any doubt among Ahmedabad's leaders that the business community will deliver its expected rupee support. As for the State Government, officials manifest keen interest in the Institute and show every indication of continuing support in this early planning stage. As one illustration, the State Government has made available an excellent and ideally situated tract of sixty-four acres of land. As an over all observation, the long association of Mahatma Gandhi with Ahmedabad provides a unique climate that may prove most conducive to the support of the Institute by the community.'

'On the negative side Ahmedabad, and for that matter Gujarat State itself, does not have the diversified industry and trade of a large metropolitan centre. This means that a great deal of research will have to be done in the other parts of India with the nearest and richest source being Mumbai. Thus, it will be necessary for the Institute's staff to establish cordial and effective relationships in the latter area. This may become complicated if Mumbai itself develops its own Institute along similar lines in the future. One would hazard the guess that should this happen the Ahmedabad Institute would diminish in importance despite the expected growth and diversification of industry in Ahmedabad and Gujarat State. A point also of some importance is that a Mumbai location would enable the Institute to draw upon as occasional lecturers and visitors some of the many business and governmental leaders, Indian and foreign who visit Mumbai.'

'A second negative point is that Ahmedabad, when compared to Mumbai, is not as attractive an assignment for people of the professional calibre wanted from abroad. Schooling opportunities for children are limited (although the interesting development of Shreyas is an exception for younger children). Opportunities for adult recreation and cultural and intellectual development are also limited except for the unusual person. The Indian faculty group itself would probably prefer the wider business contacts of Mumbai. Thus, one may expect some difficulties that are related to the location in recruiting staff.'

'No location can be ideal. There is no doubt that the Ahmedabad location promises a healthy soil in which the Institute can grow. One point of great importance, however, should be made. The Institute of course is an All India Institution, but it will at the outset draw largely from Western India and from the Ahmedabad-Baroda-Mumbai complex. From the very beginning the Institute should in some positive manner demonstrate its orientation towards this area rather than Ahmedabad alone. For example, the Institute should early establish a research base in Mumbai and have quarters available there for administrative and research purposes as well as some living facilities for visiting staff. The Director should direct a reasonable proportion of his time to working with Mumbai's businessmen.'

The following observation by Professors Hill, Haynes, and Baumgartel provides a succinct summary of the outcome.

'While the precise nature of the events leading to the change of location from Mumbai to Ahmedabad have been obscured by time, the major determinants are generally assumed to have been (i) opposition by the University of Mumbai to IIM autonomy and (ii) the promise of strong private sector support in the Ahmedabad area. In any event, such support did materialize in the form of an excellent physical plant, including a sufficiency of on-campus faculty housing. In contrast, IIMC still remains in what are now grossly inadequate 'temporary' quarters.'

(Hill Book p. 16)

To recapitulate:
1. Both the local industry and its leaders played a huge, unprecedented role in this period in the following respects:
   (a) Changing the location from Mumbai to Ahmedabad.
   (b) Providing funds for the initial infrastructure.
2. Vikram Sarabhai agreed to be the first Hon. Director.
3. Kasturbhai Lalbhai served as Chairman of the Building Committee for seventeen years.

4. AMA, PRL, and ATIRA brought network links for programmes, visiting faculty, and research.
5. An active role was played by Madanmohan Mangaldas and Navnitbhai Shodhan as members of the BoG.
6. Ahmedabad Millowners' Association and Gujarat Chamber of Commerce provided much needed support.

We seldom realize how great an impact the leadership qualities and values of pioneers have on the conduct and development of an institution. Just as it does in human beings, DNA plays a huge role in defining the personality and culture of an institution. The distinction between 'nature' and 'artifact' gets blurred. As we trace the later development of IIMA we will have an opportunity to study the true impact these leaders and pioneers had upon the institution.

THE LAUNCH

Momentum for the IIMA project really picked up with a letter from Professor M.S. Thacker, Secretary of the Union Ministry of Scientific Research & Cultural Affairs to Jivraj Mehta, Chief Minister of Gujarat, dated November 15, 1960. This letter set out the conditions for establishing the institution in Ahmedabad. The Robbins Report was also enclosed as an attachment to the letter (See Appendix 2).

Mr V. Isvaran, Chief Secretary, GoG accepted the letter and report on behalf of the Chief Minister by a letter dated December 3, 1960 (See Appendix 3).

Vikram, Kasturbhai, and Isvaran then set to work, laying the foundations of the project. A number of formalities still had to be completed, initial funds had to be raised, a constitution had to be prepared and negotiated, and perhaps most importantly, an academic structure needed to be created. Isvaran took care of all the government procedural formalities, while Kasturbhai enlisted the support of his fellow industrialists and formed the Society. Vikram handled the academic side, enlisting the collaboration of HBS and consolidating support from the FF. While HBS agreed to provide academic support, the FF committed themselves to funding the cost of HBS support and library. The first genuine and highly effective PPP was successfully formed in India in 1961 between the GoI, the GoG, and industry, with the FF acting as a US facilitator. This feat was unique and remarkable in many ways.

To begin with, two Governments were involved—the Indian government and the GoG. Professor M.S. Thacker represented the Indian government. He was a Gujarati, who became attracted to the project and to Vikram due to the latter's commitment, sincerity, and personal magnetism. Isvaran handled matters in the GoG with the Chief Minister's blessings and support. Kasturbhai's reputation and credibility proved crucial in gathering support at high levels. People had faith and confidence in the project, knowing that once Kasturbhai and Vikram set their minds to it, then things would surely happen. The project was not one to be initiated for private gain but for public good and no matter what problems arose, they were sure to see it through to the end.

In developing the academic structure, Vikram was assisted by Kamla Chaudhary, a close friend who had worked with him previously at ATIRA. An innovative thinker, who liked to question conventions, Kamla approached the new institute with enthusiasm, suggesting that before launching the flagship two-year MBA course, they begin with a 3-Tier Programme.

This proved to be not only a great and successful innovation, but it also founded a strong academic value whose imprint is visible to this day. The reasoning was as follows: Management in Indian industry needed professionalizing. Indian businesses were all founded by entrepreneurs and most were family managed. In order to effectively change and modernize business practices, work needed to be done right across the board from the top to the senior and down to middle management. This is how the 3-TP concept was formed. Furthermore, if the institute were to enlist the support of Indian businesses for case studies, research and placement, it was necessary that they become informed about modern management practices as well as the institution. Live contact with industry was established. Even today, most other institutions of higher education have failed to bridge the gap between 'town and gown'. It is a basic shortcoming in the education system that the IIMA overcame and embodied as a core principle right from the beginning.

At the time, the only institutional model was the Hyderabad based Administrative Staff College of India (ASCI). ASCI was itself based on a similar institution founded by the British Government at Henley-on-Thames. The main principle of academic policy at ASCI was that there would be two sets of faculty, one dealt with teaching and the other with consulting. The two were distinctly separate and specialized. Vikram disagreed with this approach and decided to establish a more integrative system. He felt that at IIMA, all the faculty should be engaged in all four academic activities—teaching, research including case writing, consulting, and academic administration. This was the policy at HBS and Vikram endorsed it for IIMA. HBS had pioneered the case method which would establish live contact with 'reality' and the business world. The pros and cons of this pedagogy are open to debate, yet the prime contextual gain was that it promoted and developed contact with Indian Industry. This ground breaking initiative contributed greatly to the unique methods and development of IIMA.

THE CHRONOLOGY OF EVENTS

1953	AICTE formed
1955	Cabinet Committee chaired by Minister of Commerce, Shri T.T. Krishnamachari
1957	'Report of a visit to the United States' prepared by the Indian Management Studies Team published in 1959 by the Ministry of Scientific Research and Cultural Affairs
1956	'Merriam–Thurlby' of HBS Report prepared for FF
December 1959	Dean Robbins Report
November 15, 1960	Letter from GoI announcing the decision of Ahmedabad location
December 3, 1960	Acceptance by Isvaran, Chief Secretary of Government of Gujarat

I. THE CLIMATE FOR AN ALL-INDIA INSTITUTE OF MANAGEMENT IN AHMEDABAD

The unique labour management relations in Ahmedabad are well known. They constitute an important basis for the prosperity of the industry and for a climate in which progressive endeavour is possible. They make it impossible for management to concern itself with major problems of development in other areas.

As early as 1947, when the textile industry of Ahmedabad decided to establish the first large scale cooperative research association in this country on the model of the British Research Associations, it was also decided that ATIRA should deal not only with technological problems, but with questions related to management and the human factor in Industry. The organizers of ATIRA were indeed conscious of the fact that technological innovations and improvement of productivity are closely related to social factors within the industry and that unless the multi-dimensional character of our problems is recognized and studied simultaneously in its various facets, progress would be slow and difficult.

Over the previous twelve years, ATIRA had endeavoured to promote the application of the scientific method to various aspects of industry including management. It had organized programmes for training in Human Relations for top and middle management, for supervisory training, and for the introduction for Statistical Quality Control and Work Studies in industry. Apart from annual management conferences, ATIRA had in the past organized residential courses for top management. In 1956, a three-month Executive Development Programme (EDP) was held there with the assistance of Dr Sutherland, Director of the Tavistock Clinic, London. The training programmes were backed by active research undertaken on real problems of industry, and therefore the training was oriented towards current needs and reflects forward thinking in the field of management. I enclose, for your kind information, some literature related to ATIRA's activities in the field.

The Calico Mills over the past five years has conducted an extremely interesting series of studies dealing with Technical Innovation, Work Organization, and Management. The study was made by Mr A.K. Rice of the Tavistock Institute of Human Relations and other social scientists, and the results of the study have now been published in a book entitled *Productivity and Social Organization – The Ahmedabad Experiment* by A.K. Rice. The new concepts of organization and management arising from the study have found widespread acceptance and have been successfully implemented in the Calico Mills. This has led to rethinking of organization and administrative practices in other units of the industry as well.

In Ahmedabad, there is today a great interest and a consciousness of the problems of management and of the need for professional management to replace the traditional owner entrepreneur manager in the large and growing industrial and commercial establishments of the city.

(See Appendix 1 for Vikram's letter to V.T. Krishnamachari on p. 240)

II. EXISTING ORGANIZATIONS IN AHMEDABAD WHICH WOULD BE SUPPORTIVE TO THE PROPOSED ALL-INDIA INSTITUTE OF MANAGEMENT

1. Professional and Research Bodies

Mention has already been made of the work of ATIRA. About three years previously, a new Centre for Group Dynamics was established at ATIRA to widen the field of research in the operation of small groups from the industrial setting to the area of public administration and cooperative. Dr Kamla Chaudhary, Head of the Human Relations Division of ATIRA, was the Director of the Centre which collaborated with the Centre for Group Dynamics of the University of Michigan. The Human Relations Division at ATIRA also had active research relationships with the MIT and the School of Business Administration at Harvard.

The BM Institute at Ahmedabad had trained staff of senior social scientists including psychologists, psychiatrists, and psychoanalysts. It was deeply interested in training and in the social problems in industrialization. It was then collaborating with ATIRA in organizing management courses in the field of Human Relations.

The AMA was a young but active body which offered a forum for individual managers to organize programmes and partake in management studies. This association actively collaborated with bodies like ATIRA in a number of programmes.

The Textile Association had a membership of more than 2,000 active supervisors and members of top and middle management of the textile industry in Ahmedabad. Like the Ahmedabad Management Association, it also collaborated with ATIRA and organized study programmes of its own.

2. Educational Institutions

The Gujarat University has a postgraduate department of Social Sciences and a postgraduate department of Psychology and Education. For the Second Five-Year Plan, the University had proposed a School of Business Administration which was approved by the State Government. However, on the recommendation of the Godchild Committee, the scope of the proposal was later altered and the University had then instituted postgraduate diplomas in Business Management and in Industrial Management. The University also ran courses leading to a diploma in labour welfare.

(See Appendix 1 for Vikram's letter to V.T. Krishnamachari on p. 240)

III. LOCAL SUPPORT FOR THE PROPOSED ALL-INDIA INSTITUTE OF MANAGEMENT

Apart from the professional support of the various institutions indicated above, it is clear that local financial support and initiative to carry forward a training institute for management would be forthcoming in an ample measure if it were decided to locate the Institute in Ahmedabad. The Ahmedabad Millowners' Association, ATIRA, the Gujarat Chamber of Commerce, the Ahmedabad Management Association, and individual units of industry and commercial houses would, I am sure, wholeheartedly support the present move. Even though the initial support from private industry may originate in Ahmedabad, this would not in any way prevent the functioning of the proposed Institute of Management on a truly All-India basis. We have the example of ATIRA where even though the main funds for the creation of ATIRA were found from Ahmedabad, membership was thrown open to the textile industry throughout the country. Today, a third of the members is from outside this area.

2

The IIMA Constitution

THE BACKGROUND

In 1961, IIMA was founded as a public private partnership between the following four constituents—the GoI, the GoG, local industry, and the FF.

This partnership followed the advice of Dean Robbins, whose report of December, 1959, underlined the need for close collaboration and involvement of local industry in management education. The report proposed the formation of a Society wherein the rights and responsibilities of all the partners could be defined. The report went on to say:

> 'The Institute may be organized in one of three ways: (1) as a department in a university, (2) as an autonomous society of the State, or (3) as an autonomous society organized under the Societies' Registration Act (XXI of 1860). The third method is recommended.
>
> The third method has ample precedent in India and permits rapid, independent action based upon appropriate collaboration of business, government, and education. While it may restrict the type of degrees to be awarded, this method provides ample compensating factors in freedom and flexibility.'

Based upon this recommendation, the GoI proceeded to select the partners. The FF had been an important agent in the formation and development of the project; however, being a non-Indian entity it was not accorded a permanent stake. The GoI was the chief promoter and all the partners contributed resources. The contribution each party was expected to make was specified in the Planning Committee meeting of July 29, 1961:

1. 'The GoI was to provide 12 lakh of rupees annually for recurring expenses of the Institute;

2. The State Government of Gujarat was to provide the land amounting to approximately 64 acres examined [sic] at Ahmedabad;
3. The local business community was to provide up to Rs.30 lakh as the need arises for buildings and locally procurable equipment;
4. The FF was to provide dollar support for a programme which in its judgment will be adequate for the job to be done.

(Note: 1. Later in the first BoG meeting on February 28, 1962, it was observed that the term 'local' is not appropriate, as the Institute is of an All India character and members of business and industry in the country as a whole are showing interest in promoting the Institute.
2. Locally procurable equipment will be the responsibility of State Government and Industry in the ratio of 50:50').
Source: IIMA records.

The essence of partnership is that partners with independent objectives and different agendas come together on the basis of common goals. They contribute by way of either funding or participating in governance, in order to achieve these goals. A constitution captures this arrangement, defining the goals and the respective rights and obligations of the partners. While designing this constitution, future needs and contingencies must always be kept in mind. This may involve a variation in the rights of existing partners and even the induction of new partners. Processes enabling these changes to take place smoothly have to be provided for within the constitution and future problems need to be anticipated before they arise.

THE CONSTITUTION–MEMORANDUM OF ASSOCIATION (MOA)

As we have already seen, the decision to establish IIM at Ahmedabad was taken around November 1960, after protracted and strong lobbying led by Vikram Sarabhai. It was unique that 'local industry' pledged to fund the estimated cost of building the infrastructure. Local initiative spearheaded by Vikram was very strong and the other partners involved in the project had all expressed tacit faith in him. Now that they had achieved that first step, it was time for the Memorandum of Association (MoA) to be drafted.

An MoA is the constitution of an institution. It sets out the objectives, values, governance structure, checks and balances, and accountability mechanism. All of these factors reflect the motives and aspirations of the original partners or resource providers.

After consulting Kasturbhai Lalbhai, Vikram assigned the task of drafting the MoA and incorporating the governance structure for the Institute to Chandraprasad Desai, General Manager of Arvind Mills and a confidante of Kasturbhai. After looking over the initial draft, Vikram annotated his own comments and together they produced a draft MoA for IIMA in March 1961. However, this draft underwent several substantial changes over the next four months by the time the Planning Committee meeting was held in July 1961. The GoI bureaucrats worked on it extensively. While the original draft that Vikram had provided attempted to reflect the true nature of PPP with a healthy balance of rights for all the partners, the final draft asserted the primacy of the GoI. The Government was accorded the status of a 'dominant shareholder' with far-reaching special rights. The Institute was almost reduced to becoming an entity of the GoI itself. A comparison between what was originally designed and what was eventually delivered is revealing:

TABLE 3.1 IIMA MEMORANDUM OF ASSOCIATION

Provisions as Proposed	Provisions as in the Final Document
The Council (Board) shall appoint the Director of the Institute.	The appointment to the post of Director shall be made with the approval of the Central Government on such terms and conditions as may be decided by the Central Government.
The Council may elect a Chairman of their meetings, and determine the period for which he is to hold office, and unless otherwise determined, the Chairman shall be elected annually.	Chairman to be appointed by the Central Government in consultation with the State Government.
The Council shall have the powers to frame bye-laws which may provide for the classification and method of appointments and the determination of the terms and conditions of teachers and other staff of the Institute.	The Board shall have the powers to create teaching, administrative, technical, ministerial and other posts under the Institute other than the post of Director and to make appointments thereto provided that the posts so created are in the cadres and scales of pay as approved by the Central Government in consultation with the State Government from time to time.

The Council shall have the powers to purchase or otherwise acquire for the Society any property, rights, or privileges which the Society is authorized to acquire at such price, and generally on such terms and conditions as they think fit.	The objects for which the Society is established are… to acquire and hold property provided that the prior approval of the Central and the State Government is obtained for the acquisition of immovable property.
Once at least in every year accounts of the Society shall be examined and the correctness of the Income and Expenditure Account and Balance Sheet ascertained by one or more properly qualified auditor or auditors. Auditors shall be appointed and their remuneration fixed by the General Meeting of the Society.	The annual accounts of the Board shall be audited by the Auditor General of India or any other authority as may be decided by the Central Government in consultation with the State Government and any expenses incurred in connection therewith shall be payable by the Board.
	In case the Central Government is satisfied that the Society or the Institute is not functioning properly, the Central Government shall have the power to take over the administration and assets of the Institute in consultation with the State Government.
If upon winding up or dissolution of the Society, there remains, after satisfaction of all its debts and liabilities any property whatsoever, the same shall be given or transferred to some other institution or institutions having objects similar to the objects of the Society.	If on winding up or dissolution of the Society, there shall remain after satisfaction of all its debits and liabilities any assets and property whatsoever the same shall not be paid to or distributed among the members of the Society or any of them but shall be dealt with in such manner as the Central Government in consultation with the State Government may determine.

The impact of this design of the constitution on the governance of the IIMA will be dealt with later in Chapter 7 on Governance.

IIMA'S MISSION AND OBJECTIVES

Based on the MoA, IIMA adopted the following mission and objectives initially.

Mission

1. To play a pace-setting and innovative role in management education and research.
2. To influence management practice and thought at the enterprise level.
3. To influence public policy in domains that interface strongly with business and industry.
4. To acquire an international focus, develop expertise, and become a centre of excellence, in international management, and to internationalize IIMA's operations and linkages.
5. To contribute to the improvement of quality of management education in the country by building the capabilities of other management institutions through institution building and faculty development programmes.

Objectives

1. To provide educational facilities for training young men and women for careers in management and related fields in any form of organization.
2. To improve the decision-making skills and administrative competence of practicing managers.
3. To develop teachers and researchers in different management fields.
4. To create knowledge through original research, both applied and conceptual, relevant to management and its underlying disciplines, and to disseminate such knowledge through publications and programmes.

THE ORIGINAL RESOURCE MIX

The policy on resource mix casts a long shadow on the development of any institution. Indeed, it determines the very character of the institution itself. The constitution reflects this by way of highlighting the respective rights of the resource providers. Very often it boils down to the syndrome 'beggars can't be choosers'. Needs change over time and new sources have to be tapped. New stakeholders often emerge and questions over the reallocation of rights are certain to crop up. The constitution should have the flexibility to accommodate the future need to raise resources. In a dynamic environment it isn't easy to look into the distant future and anticipate new scenarios. However, shrewd judgement, careful thinking, and a little bit of prescience can provide a good balance between security, resource head-room, and certain degrees of freedom. It is a design challenge. In the final analysis, it requires wisdom to reassess the mission and goals of the institution and constructively examine its alignment with the goals and agenda of each partner.

The initial resource mix was primarily based on the budget estimates prepared by Dean Robbins. It also contained his views on the resource mix. His estimate was as follows.

'Estimates of costs of capital equipment and operation must necessarily be very rough. There has not been sufficient time for a detailed study of cost data in India as a basis for computation. Hence the figures here should be taken as indicative only of a general order of magnitude.'

TABLE 3.2: CAPITAL EXPENDITURE NEEDS

Capital Expenditure Needs	By 3rd Year (Rs)	By 10th Year (Rs)
Land	No estimate	No estimate
Building	10,00,000	30,00,000
Equipment	6,00,000	8,00,000
Library	2,00,000	3,00,000
Total	18,00,000	41,00,000

TABLE 3.3: ANNUAL BUDGET FOR OPERATIONS

Annual Budget for Operations*	By 1st Year (Rs)	By 10th Year (Rs)
Academic salaries and wages	3,50,000	7,00,000
Other salaries	50,000	4,00,000
Other expenses	60,000	3,00,000
Total	4,60,000	14,00,000

*Excluding hostelry operation

'Fee income should support practically all the cost of advanced management courses and conferences. Tuition fees for the regular graduate programme should not be expected to meet more than a fractional share of costs of that programme. Other income should be sought from (1) government, (2) regular contributions from business members of the Society and others, (3) grants from foundations, (4) sale of printed material, and (5) contract research (for which no estimates of costs are included above)'.

The partners committed their contributions based on these estimates. This was frozen and recorded in the first meeting of the Planning Committee and later in the Board meeting on February 28, 1962, as mentioned previously.

CONTRIBUTION FROM THE FORD FOUNDATION

A letter, dated September 24, 1962, from Mr Joseph M. McDaniel, Jr Secretary of the FF to Dr Jivraj Mehta, addressed to IIMA, notified the Institute of a grant of USD 471,000 for a two-year period to develop the Institute's training and research programme. Of this USD 471,000, a payment of USD 5,000 was to be made to the Institute for architectural services, and the remaining USD 466,000 was to be paid to Harvard University. Following is the break up (See p. 50 for a detailed break up).

TABLE 3.4: BUDGETED FUNDS FOR PAYMENT TO HARVARD UNIVERSITY IN CONNECTION WITH THE INDIAN INSTITUTE OF MANAGEMENT, AHMEDABAD

Item	Budget (in USD)
Long term foreign advisers*	215,000
Short term consultants	60,000
Fellowships	65,000
Books and equipment	75,000
Project administration costs	29,000
Overhead	21,700
Total	465,700

Beginning with this resource mix, IIMA covered ground breaking terrain. The future changes in the pattern of the resource mix were a reflection of changes in the environment for management education, the policies of the GoI, internal policy and, of course, the growth of the institute itself. It also reflected the latent tension between GoI control and institutional policies and aspirations. New strong stakeholders like alumni and faculty emerged and the roles of the various stakeholders changed.

THE IMPACT OF GOVERNMENT INTERVENTION

In some respects the decisions on the original resource mix was reflected in the MoA. For example, the GoI undertook the responsibility of providing running grants to make up for the shortfall of revenue in meeting the current costs. Therefore, it would only be logical for the GoI to stipulate that the salaries of faculty, which would be the most important item of expenses, should require their approval. Similarly, the clause relating to budget submission, approval, and the auditing of accounts also seemed fair, although one could argue that the MoA should have stipulated that as soon as the Institute became self reliant these clauses would be open to review.

What is less clear is the clause relating to the appointment of Chairman and the Director. Here the reins were handed to GoI. There is no evidence of any debate or discussion on the issue despite the far reaching departure from the draft prepared by Vikram. It could very well have been either a simple act of faith or, perhaps, a sign of exhaustion or even an underassessment of the potential mischief this could cause. In spite of the basic conception of public private partnership (PPP), the dominance of the GoI was evident from the start. We have to ask, is this not overdue for amendment?

The BoG is the main organ through which any institution is administered. The composition of the Board of IIMA was as follows:

1.   Chairman to be appointed by the Central Government in consultation with the State Government.
2-5.   Four representatives of the Central Government nominated by the Ministry of Education, GoI.
6-7.   Two nominees of the State Government representing its concerned departments.
8.   A representative of the All India Council for Technical Education.
9-12.   Four members of the General Body of the IIMA Society to be elected for 2 years by the members of the Society from amongst themselves.
13-16. Four persons to be nominated by the Central Government in consultation with the State Government to represent Commerce, Industry, Labour, and other interests.
17.   A representative of the All India Management Association.
18.   A representative of the National Productivity Council of India.
19-20. Two Professors of the Institute to be nominated by the Chairman of the Board (for 2 years.)
21-24. Not more than 4 members co-opted by the BoG as a whole.
25.   Director of the Institute (ex-officio member).

An Officer of the Institute nominated by the Board of Governors will work as ex-officio Secretary to the Board.

Hence, it is evident that the GoI has considerable control of the composition of the BoG. This is discussed in greater detail in Chapter 5.

Another limit placed upon the BoG was relating to the expansion of the Institute through the requirement of approval for the acquisition of real estate. Again, this was possibly agreed to as an act of faith. And, in fairness, it has to be said that it is almost impossible to anticipate what course an institution is likely to take in the future.

The GoI initiative to open a national institute lent the project the ultimate legitimacy. In the 1960s this legitimacy was necessary to facilitate participation by international organizations such as the FF or HBS. Undoubtedly, GoI concerns and objectives would overshadow any others. The wisdom and the ability of the leaders of Government to support the institutional vision plays a defining role in the long term development of any national institution.

The PPP was founded with the 'stakeholders' agreement' enshrined in the constitution, which also had governance incongruity and a 'big brother' partner. Many future conflicts can be traced to this design parameter, although in many other respects it has stood the test of time. Academic autonomy has remained unhampered throughout the last five decades. Yet, at the same time, many opportunities could not be accessed, real accountability has become diluted, and some unproductive, highly diversionary, and distracting power games have been played. What is remarkable is that such a lopsided structure of governance did not cause much serious harm during the first few decades.

The unbalanced partnership relationship described above actually worked smoothly because of the qualities of the leadership in those initial years. All the parties concerned acted with restraint and wisdom, committed to realizing the mission of the institute based on their shared values. It was this spirit that made it possible for the institute to function smoothly and to make tremendous progress in spite of the GoI dominant structure.

At the same time, cracks began appearing in the structure as soon as stress began to develop. These cracks have led to a few crises. Problems relating to the respective roles and limits of the GoI and the BoG have risen on several occasions, bringing into sharp focus the need to review some of these provisions in the changed circumstances we face today.

Whenever a new institution is founded there is always great enthusiasm at the initial stage. The founders are all absorbed in making their vision a reality. Particularly in the case of a social enterprise like IIMA, a missionary spirit and passion become the driving force. Additionally in the case of IIMA, the choice of location had to be agreed, partner had to change from the pre-arranged UCLA to the 'partner of choice', HBS; these were all exhausting exercises, which stretched out over a period of nearly five years.

It is impossible for any MoA or governance structure to remain optimal for all times and all situations. Even the constitutions of countries have to be amended once in a while as times change. As we will see later IIMA MoA was no exception.

The issues that arise are as follows:

1. Why was such an MoA accepted by the other two partners – viz. GoG and 'local industry'?
2. What are the 'design' flaws in this arrangement?
3. Should we change the constitution, i.e. the MoA, altering the governance roles of various organs?
4. If so, then in what respect?

5. What should be the role of government, the dominant promoter, vis-à-vis the Board and the 'management' ?
6. How should the Board be composed?
7. What should be the accountability mechanisms?
8. What should be the relative roles and limits of the Board and the internal management?

We will examine these issues in Chapter 7.

3

Partnership with HBS

On May 28, 1962, Dr Ensminger of the Ford Foundation, Delhi sent the following cable to Dr Jivraj Mehta, Chief Minister of Gujarat:

'Harvard has approved association with Ahmedabad Management Institute [Stop] Our New York office now proceeding with details'

This brought the complex drama of selecting a partner to a close, opening up a whole world of opportunity for IIMA!

THE SELECTION OF A PARTNER

The story of how HBS came to be selected as a collaborator with IIMA resembles a game of snakes and ladders. The time-sensitive nature of the project along with the asynchronous decision making by various promoters contributed to a drama that could well have wrecked the initial partnership completely. The decision to step back from an initial commitment to UCLA—remember that Dean Robbins, on whose report the decision to create IIM was taken, was after all the Associate Dean there—as also from an innovative idea of a consortium of business schools as partners and to go into partnership with HBS, makes for an absorbing tale.

The FF was committed to involving UCLA even before Ahmedabad came into the picture. Even when the GoI decided to establish two institutes instead of one, all along it was assumed that one of them would be at Mumbai. Ahmedabad was nowhere in the picture. As a consequence, as Dr Jivraj Mehta, the Chief Minister of Gujarat, put it in his letter to Prof. Thacker of June 8, 1961 '... it took some time to finalize the location of the institute.' By then the FF came to an understanding with UCLA for institutional collaboration.

Ahmedabad was determined to find the best school possible as a partner and in their view, HBS was most certainly one of the best. There were also some personal overtones. Shrenik Lalbhai had studied at HBS, and Vikram Sarabhai was a frequent visitor at MIT and had a few connections at HBS. Without a doubt, HBS was far better known in India and was considered by most to be the best business school. However, the FF was the funding agency and the foreign exchange component was underwritten by them; therefore their commitment to UCLA would have been difficult to overcome. On the other hand the local industry as represented by Vikram Sarabhai could not be reconciled with the 'take it or leave it' overtone of Mr John Coleman, a staff member of the FF, in New Delhi. It probably touched a raw nationalist nerve. Vikram's civility, innate acumen, and ability to reconcile differences managed to salvage the situation.

Perhaps unaware that the FF had already committed to UCLA, Vikram made an orchestrated effort to explore Harvard's interest in supporting IIMA. He strongly believed that IIMA should have the best partner and felt in his heart that HBS was the best. If not that, he was optimistic of the idea of forming a consortium of institutions which would include HBS, MIT, and others based on the pattern of the collaboration relating to IIT Kanpur. This is where the misunderstanding between Vikram and the FF began. John Coleman was an advisor based in the New Delhi office of the FF. When Coleman found out that Vikram wanted to go with Harvard, he bluntly stated the FF position of commitment to UCLA. (See Appendix 1– Coleman letter dated April 29, 1961.) Vikram reacted by saying that the GoI, GoG, and local industry were all partners in this national institute and FF a strong supporter. He went on to say that in such a multilateral relationship, no one party should thrust one's decision onto the others. In his letter to Coleman dated May 19, 1961, (Appendix 3) he observed: 'I think it is important, then, that the means that we adopt should be compatible with this objective and that no one party in this cooperative venture goes ahead and makes commitments without prior consultation with the whole group.' Such actions would really run against the spirit of the entire partnership.

John Coleman found this stance a little irritating. He argued that the decision had been made prior to the selection of Ahmedabad. In fact, at that time the assumption had been that the second location would be Mumbai. He also argued that UCLA was an outstanding institution, renowned for its role in the growth of California. Dean Robbins, the author of the report for the establishment of the Institute was from UCLA and he was extremely enthusiastic about collaborating with one of the two institutions. Given the FF's commitment, Coleman insisted on UCLA as partner. He also gave a veiled hint that the entire relationship with the FF would collapse if Ahmedabad refused to go along with it. (Appendix 4, May 31, 1961.)

Apparently this was not known to the Indian side. So, parallely, Professors Kabir, Thacker, and Vikram had engaged in an exploratory dialogue with Harvard. UCLA found out about this through a conversation between Associate Dean Hassler of HBS and Associate Dean Robbins of UCLA. Unhappy with this turn of events, UCLA brought the matter to the attention of the FF. This led John Coleman to speak to Humayun Kabir and Thacker and dissuade them from pursuing the Harvard option. He then spoke with Vikram, saying that both Kabir and Thacker had promised to disengage from this pursuit and would respect the FF's committment. The message was also conveyed to Jivraj Mehta and relayed through Ishwaran, Chief Secretary of Gujarat State, to Kasturbhai Lalbhai. Kasturbhai was seemingly alarmed at the prospect of losing the support of the FF. It appeared that Coleman had won the argument and overcome the opposition.

Vikram apparently was alone but he refused to back down (Appendix 2). For him this was a matter of principle. He argued that in a group everyone's viewpoint must be respected and discussed before arriving at a decision. He even mooted the idea of talking to Ambassador Galbraith in order to arrange aid from other sources. He knew that HBS was willing and had learnt that Harvard's involvement with Turkey was now coming to an end. Nevertheless, he was careful not to burn his bridges or slam the door on either the FF or UCLA. He decided upon two things—to meet with the FF Senior Administration in New York, and to visit UCLA as well. He probably wanted to find out the depth of commitment to UCLA and also whether the decision really was so irrevocable that it would lead to the Foundation's withdrawal from the project. In New York, he met the senior management of the FF, including the Programme Director, Overseas Development: South and South East Asia, George Gant and the Programme Associate, Robert Culbertson. Vikram's magic must have worked because after the meeting, the overall tone of the letter from Culbertson was one of mending fences. There was to be no more of the take-it-or-leave-it attitude. In reply, Vikram mentioned to Culbertson that if HBS was approached by all parties, including the FF, they would explore seriously the possibilities of participating as a partner. Further, if the FF decided to have a consortium to help both IIMA and IIMC, HBS would be willing to consider participating in that as well.

Vikram then visited UCLA. He demonstrated his openness to consider it as a potential partner, while also preserving his right to express his own views on who the best partner for Ahmedabad would be. All of this took place between the months of April and June, 1961. Following his visit, some reassessment appears to have taken place at UCLA.

In a letter dated November 3, 1961, Dean Jacoby of UCLA (Appendix 5) informed the FF: 'It is with great reluctance that I feel obliged to write you that the Graduate School of Business Administration at UCLA must decline your invitation to assume responsibility for the development of the proposed India Institute of Management, Ahmedabad, India'. Subsequently, Dean Robbins wrote a letter dated November 17, 1961 (Appendix 6) expressing his disappointment that the engagement had been broken off. Whether there was something more to it than the letters reveal is difficult to say. The volte-face is hard to understand and the mystery as to why UCLA withdrew from the race remains unresolved.

Between February and November, 1961, while the relationship between the FF, UCLA, and IIMA was unwinding, Vikram had sent out feelers to Harvard. The key players from the Harvard side were Associate Dean Hassler, Director of Overseas Relations John Fox, Harry Hansen, and possibly Andy Towl. Vikram had arranged for both Humayun Kabir and Thacker to meet with this group. Harvard had shown some preliminary interest, without which, these meetings could not have taken place. Someone, possibly Kamla Chaudhary who was at Harvard, played a role in forging this connection. Vikram had not let the HBS trail go cold even while he was engaged in the serious review of the FF's position regarding UCLA.

After UCLA sent in their letter of withdrawal in November, 1961, Douglas Ensminger, who had taken over from Coleman as the FF representative in New Delhi wrote to his friend, John Fox on November 29, 1961, to explore the HBS interest. Between then and December 13, 1961, discussions took place between various officials of the FF and HBS. Then things began moving very rapidly at HBS. As a result, Harry Hansen sent a detailed manning proposal to George Gant in a long letter, dated December 20, 1961. This was based on discussions between Associate Dean Hassler, John Fox, and Harry Hansen. There is a reference to an Ad-hoc Committee at Harvard engaged in examining assistance to IIMA. The same four names mentioned above were the members of this committee. In the meantime, Dean Baker became Acting Dean as Dean Teele had resigned due to ill health. Baker was more energetic and probably more favourably inclined towards the project than his predecessor. The group decided to take things forward.

The FF asked Harry Hansen to visit India. He arrived in Ahmedabad where he attended the Planning Committee meetings on January 28 and 31,1962, as a special guest, where Ensminger was also present. He raised several issues regarding Harvard's role in the selection of Director, faculty, and engaging the business community of Mumbai by establishing a centre there. This came in the form of a memorandum which he prepared and submitted to the FF dated February 7, 1962. There was no commitment to engage in the project as yet but some of these issues needed to be ironed out before Harvard could make its final decision. This memorandum was an important agenda item at the first board meeting of IIMA on February 28, 1962. Dr Ensminger of the FF also attended the meeting. The minutes of this meeting clearly bring out the acceptance of all points of the memorandum. There were a few issues relating to the selection of Director and the commitment to establish a centre in Mumbai, on which some more discussion took place.

It appears that Ensminger, Coleman's replacement at the FF, Delhi, was extremely supportive towards the Harvard collaboration. As it turned out, the shift from UCLA to Harvard did not leave any bitter feelings in the FF despite the earlier posture adopted by Coleman. Ensminger became an enthusiastic supporter of this engagement and played a vital role in ironing out some of the issues in a very practical manner. His major contribution was to delink the establishment of the Mumbai centre from the decision to help IIMA.

At Harvard, the Ad-hoc group was becoming very enthusiastic about the collaboration opportunity with IIMA. Harry Hansen worked hard to gather the support of the faculty and the Ad-hoc group helped. Harvard held a series of meetings in the approval process. A meeting of the Policies and Programmes Committee took place and Hansen submitted a memorandum, which they approved. Following that, a meeting of the tenure faculty was held and they also approved the memorandum. Then, on May 7, 1962, a meeting of the entire faculty took place to vote on the proposal. The memo asking the faculty of Harvard to take a view on this project was addressed by the Ad-hoc committee. It is clear that there was still some reservation or opposition within the Harvard faculty. Sensing and anticipating this, the Ad-hoc group made extensive preparations, and the vote was positive. Subsequently, the formality of getting approval from the Harvard Corporation also took place on May 21, 1962. On May 27, 1962, a cable from Ensminger carried this positive news to Jivraj Mehta, the Chairman of the Board (cited at the beginning of the chapter).

A number of extremely important points need to be noted in these developments. It is highly likely that there was a certain interpersonal tension between Vikram and Coleman. Vikram was unwilling to give up his concern over the principle governing the relationship between partners. A deadlock was encountered. While the other partners accepted Coleman's stand point as the final position of the FF, accepting it as a fait accompli, Vikram focused on the main objective of finding the best partner, stuck to his principled stand on the relationship and far from being deterred he set about winning them over to his point of view. He pursued this by taking matters to the highest level of decision making in the FF in New York.

He displayed enormous self belief and confidence while dealing with high level functionaries within the GoG, the GoG, and at HBS. They all had different organisational backgrounds and therefore different compulsions as well. To navigate through such a maze requires not only a deep conviction and an extraordinary ability to negotiate but also an uncanny sense of priorities and great communication skills. While everyone else wanted to fall in line with the FF position as enunciated by Coleman, he showed the courage and equanimity to examine the issue in terms of principle, persuaded them, and finally brought them all around to his point of view. The leadership qualities and the values which emerged out of this process clearly made a deep impact upon the nascent institution.

When an institution comes through such a testing period during the very moment of its birth, when even the parentage changes hands, institutional culture and character are formed. Values such as self respect, principle over expediency, humility, and transparency combined with tact and a single minded focus on the main objective become etched into the institutional memory. After a difficult and painful labour, a strong relationship was born. IIMA acquired the dignity to speak with everyone as an equal.

This tie-up contributed immensely to the academic development, administrative processes, and values such as faculty autonomy at IIMA. It is a matter of speculation as to what would have happened if Vikram had conceded to Coleman and allowed the partnership with UCLA to go ahead. My guess is that IIMA would not have become what IIMA is today.

Throughout this whole episode, UCLA appears somewhat hurt. The knowledge that the Indian side had approached Harvard deeply upset them. In any case UCLA had not actually committed to assist IIMA. They had only indicated their willingness to consider the matter. Why then this sense of hurt? In terms of preparation prior to the decision making stage there is little evidence of any real effort on their part, not when compared to the efforts Harvard had undertaken. Harvard had formed a strong group to study the matter and chart out the course. All of this is captured in Harry Hansen's letter to George Gant, Director of the FF, dated December 29, 1961. I would like to underline that this was done even prior to the Ford Foundation's formal approach to HBS. After the approach was made, senior Harvard faculty invested a huge amount of time in preparing plans for collaboration and charting out the various steps needed for its successful approval at various stages within the HBS as well as Harvard Corporation.

A study of this entire episode is immensly valuable. Institution builders have to work with many stakeholders and many partners. This episode serves as a case study in handling complex multi-lateral relationships. And who were the players? A world renowned business school, a global Foundation with development agenda, the GoI, the Chief Minister of a State, and two representatives of local industry. Each of them would have their own motives, agenda, working methods, and decision processes. To forge a partnership where the power balance between these partners was so skewed is nothing short of a coup.

So, what do we learn from the perspective of institution building? Dignity and self respect certainly became stamped on the culture of IIMA even when dealing with the high and mighty. This demonstrates the power of clear thinking with principles and focus rather than expediency. A strong commitment to excellence is the driving force behind such an effort. Reinforced by extensive preparation and superior communication skills, this is where the leadership of Vikram left its indelible mark on the culture of the institution. In the face of such turbulence and pressure the faith that Kasturbhai Lalbhai and Jivraj Mehta displayed in Vikram further demonstrates the wisdom of the early leadership. Jivraj Mehta's letter to Thacker dated June 8, 1961, shows the statesmanlike quality of the Chief Minister. The balanced approach and sensitivity to different points of view—all these clearly set him apart as a political leader. As for Kasturbhai, he appears to be saying 'there are minefields but you are the best judge.'

This has left an imprint on the Institute's personality and culture in all its subsequent dealings with other parties—whether it was the FF, HBS, GoI, or anyone else. The Institute does not lecture others like a self righteous moralist, but rather acts like a wise man foreseeing the future of a strong and equal partnership. The ability to walk the tightrope between self interest and self respect has been displayed time and again. The way in which Jivraj Mehta dealt with the HBS proposal for a Research Centre in Mumbai, the issue of the HBS role in the Director selection process, and how the GoI was persuaded to forego the CAG audit—this is all down to the genius of the Gujarati psyche. It is episodes such as this which truly show 'Why IIMA is what IIMA is'.

There is a subtle irony to the episode. As we have seen, there were four partners. The GoI was the prime mover and chief promoter of the idea. The GoG provided the land. The Ford Foundation was a major source of funding and also provided an important link with universities abroad in the USA. Local industry's role was confined to providing funds for the infrastructure. One would expect the FF to emerge as the most influential decision maker when it came to the selection of a US partner. Under normal conditions local industry would have neither the clout, nor the competence to influence this decision. However, in this case, it was local industry who made the choice, overcoming the objections of the FF, orchestrated support from the GoI, and ultimately got Harvard's agreement to enter into partnership. The spectator had become the captain!

THE HBS DECISION PROCESS

HBS must have had some prior interest in joining the project. They had, after all, sent both Professors Meriam and Hurley to India, as far back as 1957, when at the request of the FF they had been asked to study the possibilities of opening a business school. Then, for three years, they faded into the background. Why this happened is unclear, although there is some mention by the FF that Harvard's resources were overstretched, owing to their commitments in Turkey. In any case, Vikram's efforts and the serious interest shown by the GoI succeeded in reviving HBS's interest once again. It is instructive to study the workings within HBS and to trace the process they followed along with the chronology of events leading to their decision.

January, 1962	The HBS Ad-hoc Committee was formed to examine the issue of collaboration.
	(Note: The Ad-hoc Committee's report is unavailable for use, being an internal document belonging to HBS. However, I have used the citation from this report quoted in a Memorandum by a Harvard representative in around October 1962.)
February 7, 1962	Harry Hansen's (HH's) 'Memorandum concerning the institute of management, Ahmedabad'.
May 7, 1962	Faculty of HBS voted for collaboration.
May 21, 1962	The Corporation (namely the Harvard Corporation) approved the School's participation in the development of IIMA (collaboration).
May 25, 1962	Harry Hansen, Project Advisor, sends his memo to the HBS faculty. (Inviting interest from HBS faculty).

January 28, 1963   Harry Hansen appointed Project Director by Harvard
                     Corporation. Dean Baker's memo.

In early 1962, the GoI and the FF formally requested the collaboration of
HBS for IIMA. Capturing the views of the Ad-hoc Committee, the Harvard
representative noted the following:
'The role of the Harvard Business School in relation to the Institute at
Ahmedabad can best be stated in terms of the report prepared by the
Ad-hoc Committee of the Harvard Business School on the Indian Project.
*"The underlying premise is that it is not the School's responsibility to
develop an Institute and turn it over to the Indians, but that there is a
mutual creating, developing, and building of the Institute. The exact
nature of the relationship between Institute and School staff cannot be
stated because it will be evolutionary in form and will depend upon the
particular people involved and the specific problems faced."* In essence,
a cooperative effort is looked forward to, one that depends upon a mutual
understanding of goals and means rather than upon predetermined and
carefully calculated division of responsibilities among contractual parties.
The Ad-hoc Committee has not attempted to draw up a specific
development programme for the Institute. There are undoubtedly a
number of different alternative programmes, each attractive and workable,
and the Committee believes a choice should be made by those individuals
who will be immediately concerned with developing the Institute. *"The
Committee believes that these individuals, Indians and members of this
School's staff, will naturally wish to consult with and draw upon the
experience of many members of the Faculty."'*
This defined the approach and philosophy of HBS in undertaking the task.
They approached it as an *institution building exercise and not just a collaboration
for a programme.* This is a vital distinction. Apparently, the Ad-hoc Committee
defined the broad concept and contours of the relationship which provided
the backdrop to Harry Hansen's visit to India in January to February, 1962 to
develop an operational plan based on his observations of the state of business
education and the perceptions of Indian industry.
No clear mention is made in any of the available documents as to why HBS
decided to enter into this collaboration. Their motives therefore are really a matter
of conjecture. They seem to have entered the partnership based upon certain
considerations. India was a big third world country with an enlightened and
democratic government. Quite a few key Indians had studied at Harvard in the

post-war era and, of course, the stability of the institution was assured by the participation of the GoI. Indian industry also provided a valuable arena to study the management practices of an emerging third world country in. Not only would this provide great research and learning opportunities for the HBS faculty and students it would also be an entirely new experience for HBS itself. No competitive threat existed within the relationship. And last, but certainly not the least, there was the personal relationship struck by Vikram Sarabhai.

An article, titled 'HBS Helps Launch Indian B School' appeared in the February 1, 1963 issue of the HBS campus magazine HARBUS and contained the following observation by their correspondent John Hunt:

'... I think HBS can be very proud to be participating in such a project, and to have the opportunity to pass on to another hemisphere methods and principals developed here.'

HBS were on board! There is a strange irony here. The relationship between IIMA and HBS came to an end in 1969 and HBS did not return to India until 2007! They had played a major role in the creation of an institution founded in their image. That institution had grown up to receive global recognition. After forty years HBS returned on its own initiative for research, case developments, and EDPs to pursue solo an opportunity perceived then!

THE ROLE OF HBS:

Harvard Business School's involvement was based on the concept of relationship spelt out by the Ad-hoc Committee (cited earlier). The spirit behind that concept was reflected in all the actions taken by HBS. They viewed this as a relationship and not just a transaction.

Harry Hansen's memo of February 7, 1962, builds on the broad policy statement of the Ad-hoc Committee noted above. It comprehensively lays the foundation of the scope and methodology of their engagement besides providing a solid activity plan. The memo contained several concrete suggestions along with some discussion points, pre-conditions, governance observations, and decision points. It also clearly spelt out their estimates of resources; both manpower and financial. Manpower resources mention both HBS and Indian personnel. The document is couched in the language of a proposal and predicated upon final formal acceptance by HBS and the FF. At the same time, it lists many important activities to be concurrently initiated. On the whole, the memo expresses serious intent that falls just short of final commitment.

This comprehensive Memorandum covered many points including pedagogy, research, schedules, manpower planning, budgets etc. It also carried out a need analysis. There is an interesting observation in this regard. Hansen suggested that IIMA should begin with a short top management programme of one week. This is the initial germ of the 3-TP Programme. The main difference being that while Hansen viewed this mainly from a marketing angle, Kamla later viewed it from the perspective of organizational change. Further, concern over the quality of the Post Graduate Programme led to a suggestion that the entry requirement should be Master's and not Bachelor's. Finally, Hansen noted that some kind of an entry test should be introduced to assess the quality of incoming students with a Bachelor's degree.

After the collaboration became operative, Hansen filed his first report to the FF in December, 1963. He reviewed many of the views expressed by him in the memo mentioned above. Some of his main observations are discussed below.

CASE METHOD: THE HBS STAMP

In order to dispel a common misunderstanding about HBS teaching methods, Hansen observed, 'It goes almost without saying that the HBS is widely identified with the so called 'case approach' to teaching. What is not as widely known perhaps is that the School uses many other teaching methods as supporting pedagogical devices: readings, lectures, small group exercises, role playing, business games, the incident approach, and others. Because these other methods have not been as widely publicized, many persons interested in education have viewed the HBS as having a doctrinaire approach to teaching by use of cases. This is not so, although the School believes in the primary importance of the case approach and this is indeed the core of the School's teaching.'

'When the first members of the Indian faculty came to the HBS in September 1963, it was clear that their predisposition toward the 'case method' ranged from some scepticism to mild but guarded support. The School's position was to let these men form their own opinions without any attempted indoctrination. It took about three months before the group could dispel their preconceptions through intellectual acceptance of case teaching to real personal acceptance.'

He compared the HBS teaching approach to the methods adopted by medical and law schools. How it deepens the understanding of the students is best captured in his words. He almost sounds evangelical. 'Day after day, these real and specific cases are presented to the students for their considered analysis, open discussions, and final decisions as to the type of action which should be taken. In total, during his two years of study, the student is confronted with close to a thousand cases. As the number of cases discussed increases, the student begins to observe interrelated coherent patterns and, on the basis of these, draw out general principles. Through these cases, the student learns how to differentiate one situation from another and recognize the more important issue.'

'The case method encourages among the students interaction with each other. Instead of a child like dependence on the teacher, the students learn to be independent and self reliant.'

The case method was a great success in the EDPs right from the beginning. The PGP students, however, found it more difficult and took longer to realize its value. The study of science is based on experiment, observation, and analysis. Management studies do not afford that possibility but the case method probably comes closest to it.

PROGRAMME PHILOSOPHY

In planning educational programmes, Harry Hansen noted that four different educational courses were planned. 1. PGPs for young people; 2. MDPs for executives for short duration of about two to sixteen weeks; 3. A doctoral programme; 4. Special programmes for university teachers, cooperatives etc.

All of these programmes would be residential. He further adds: 'Although these programmes differ in many ways, they have several features in common. They all centre on the development of basic skill and knowledge in the field of management rather than on specialized functional techniques. All these programmes are interdependent and sustain each other. There are a multitude of facts and details relating to particular industries and to individual businesses which the students and research workers can learn from the experienced executives. The experienced executive, on the other hand, needs to know new advances in knowledge and techniques. He also requires an understanding of young men and women entering the threshold of business careers. This kind of interaction helps in creating a supportive climate in organizations where the young students hope to find their professional careers. The Institute provides to all of them certain common experiences, ways of looking at things, points of view, and opportunities for sharing values related to business, government, and society.

'Education for business is a dynamic thing sensitive both to the changing character of business itself and to the advance in the field of knowledge on which an understanding of business should be based.' This has, without a doubt, left an indelible mark of differentiation on IIMA.

THE HBS APPROACH TO INSTITUTIONAL ASSISTANCE

When going through the HBS papers—Harry Hansen's reports, HBS Faculty notes on course design, and HBS Librarian Kipp's notes on library planning—one realizes how seriously HBS really did take their role. The systematic approach and thoroughness which they brought to the task of institution building, proved invaluable. Harry Hansen's mild rebuke to the Indian faculty on planning a trip to Washington without stating the objectives also underlines the HBS culture of the value of accountability. HBS had a reputation to defend!

HBS made several important decisions to develop IIMA.

1. Treated it as an institution project and not a side activity.
2. Stationed an experienced faculty member at Ahmedabad for a long period. (Warren Haynes)
3. Appointed a senior faculty at HBS as project advisor for nearly five years. (Harry Hansen)
4. Committed training of five annual batches of eight faculty members each year at HBS.
5. Sent seventeen HBS faculty and research associates to IIMA for fairly extensive teaching.
6. Sent a team of HBS graduates as case writers to India for a period of about a year.
7. Sent a team of professors to teach in the first Senior Management Programme at Jaipur i.e. the programme was predominantly manned by HBS faculty—the only Indian was Kamla Chaudhary.
8. Sent a team of two to three at Associate or Senior Assistant Professor level for developing courses. The two faculty members originally assigned dropped out at the last minute for personal reasons and were replaced by Neil Borden of HBS and K.V. Ramanathan. This was a fumble for HBS but it eventually worked out fine.
9. Even after IIMA had been established for five years it would continue to provide visiting faculty from HBS—one or two each year. In this respect, Harry Hansen added a reverse visiting faculty position for Indian faculty

to HBS.

10. The third grant from the FF provided doctoral and graduate fellowships under which C.K. Prahalad, K. Balakrishnan and others were deputed.

11. Selected participants from IIMA executive programmes to be sent to HBS executive programmes like Programme for Management Development (PMD) and AMP. (This was not in the original plan but apparently inserted later). The FF footed the bill for this.

Not only did HBS play a leading role in the academic planning aspect of the institution, their firm stand on certain governance and policy issues also made an enormous impact on the development of the governance culture and academic ambience. Their stand on consultancy in the face of opposition from the GoI, academic autonomy and accountability, and their tradition of building strong bonds with alumni of LDP (Long Duration Programmes) and EDPs (Executive Development Programmes sometimes referred to as MDPs— Management Development Programmes or SDPs—Short Duration Programmes) had a deep and lasting effect on IIMA.

COLLABORATION IN ACTION

A study of the reports filed by Hansen to the FF over three to four years reveals a continuous evaluation on the part of HBS as to how the development of IIMA was unfolding.

Hansen observed in his first report of December 31, 1963 that 'IIMA was well on its way to becoming a pace setting institution in India with regard to teaching and research in the field of business administration.' He further observed that '... progress of the institute is above all a feather in the cap of India.' He listed the various programmes mounted over a period of twenty two months. He lists the following as the key factors behind this successful launch.

1. Support of local industry
2. Choice of Vikram Sarabhai as first Hon. Director
3. GoG support
4. Outstanding BoG
5. GoI in the persona of M.S. Thacker
6. P.L. Tandon as first industry Chairman
7. Faculty development by sending teams of faculty to HBS for about a year over a period of two to three years. This helped imbibe the unique approach of HBS to research, case writing, teaching, and also the 'culture

of admin'. 'This approach must be seen first hand, and this culture must be lined in and experienced so that it can be really absorbed.'

8. The generous support provided by the FF.

Hansen articulated the issues relating to the recruitment of faculty, compensation and consulting in his first report to the FF of December 31, 1963 mentioned earlier. The strong position taken by HBS (based on their 'Policies on outside activities of senior faculty of HBS' which were adopted at a faculty meeting on December 16, 1946) and equally strongly endorsed by the BoG, finally helped to overcome the initial resistance of the Indian government to income from consulting. Hansen's observations relating to compensation and the changing labour market conditions for faculty proved to be prophetic. The MoA provides that the faculty compensation will have to be approved by the GoI. This meant that the faculty would be treated as Government employees and their compensation would be tied to the GoI system. Hansen could see that this would eventually create a gap between market reality and GoI dispensation. The only way out would be 'to become a private institution completely subsidized by private business with the freedom to set its own salary scale'. He also noted that '...the Board must exercise restraint in the exercise of any power it may hold over academic activities'. Particular reference was made to the freedom to pursue teaching and research in those areas which the faculty considered 'most promising'. The BoG may exercise some oversight through fund allocation in a broad manner. Vikram really believed that this was a 'question of personalities'. However, he himself and Ravi Matthai, the first two Directors (Ravi became Director on August 29, 1965), and the Board members developed strong conventions whereby restraint was exercised, sensitivities respected, and the freedom of faculty protected.

Faculty from HBS came to IIMA for periods ranging from three months to a year. Most of them came to either teach in the EDPs or to act as guides or consultants for teaching, research, and case writing. By 1964, their role and relationship with the Indian faculty came up for review. Vikram felt '... that the concept that the Americans were consultants to the Institute be abandoned and that in the future the Americans join the Institute as members of the Ahmedabad faculty, with the same rights and privileges as other faculty members.' This was in itself a far reaching observation and policy stance which helped to establish both the dignity and confidence of the IIMA faculty.

Hansen also noted the support provided by Unilever under the leadership of Prakash Tandon. Many members of Unilever acted as faculty in the various EDPs, making a lasting impression on all the participants.

HBS attached great value to establishing strong relationships with industry. This is reflected in the introduction of 3-TP Programmes, bringing top HBS faculty to teach in the programme and then following it up with the 3-TP alumni conference. This generated enormous goodwill, established the image of IIMA, and set a benchmark for programme design and delivery for the Indian faculty to follow. It also paved the way for industry aid in designing the curriculum, case writing, consultancy, and to a limited extent obtaining guest faculty.

In matters such as course and faculty development, the main route used was to depute the first three batches of recruits to ITP conducted by HBS. This ensured their exposure to the case method and a certain uniformity in approach. It also fostered a sense of general management orientation.

In planning the infrastructure, the library, and making admissions and evaluation policies, HBS's systematic contribution was very useful. Their methods were, in essence, a complete departure from the classic Indian education system. Interactive classrooms for case teaching, a grade point system for evaluation, multipoint determinants for admission, and the dynamic objective oriented design of courses and programmes were all new to the Indian faculty at the time. The presence of Warren Haynes and other HBS faculty helped to reinforce this learning process. And of course, cementing it all in place was the solid leadership of Vikram Sarabhai and later, Ravi Matthai.

HBS's assessment of the progress IIMA made in those initial years is best reflected in the successive observations of Hansen. In his report of December 31, 1964, he observed, 'There is no question, however, that a new educational force is now operating in India.' In his report for the following year he noted, 'The fact that the Institute after two years and nine months is moving forward with a position of leadership in management training in India, reflects the dedicated devotion to their tasks of members of the BoG, the Officers, and the Faculty and Staff of the Institute.'

STRESS POINTS WITHIN THE RELATIONSHIP

Just as in any partnership, the relationship between HBS and IIMA was not completely stress free. Prior to making their formal decision, HBS had sent Prof. Hansen to India in early 1962. It was his report titled 'Memorandum Concerning the Institute of Management, Ahmedabad' which became the basis on which the HBS faculty and Board made their decision. Hansen met with several Indian industry leaders including many from Ahmedabad itself. Mumbai had a diversified industrial base and it was also the centre of the nation's professional management. Other important amenities such as schools, a large international airport, an expatriate community, and a cosmopolitan culture were all perceived as great advantages for such a venture. But the decision for Ahmedabad was a fait accompli for HBS. However, they wanted to maintain strong links with Mumbai. During the very first meeting of the BoG, they promoted the idea of opening a research centre in Mumbai. Jivraj Mehta deftly disposed of the notion by observing that IIMA is a national institute and it should have such centres in various parts of the country and not just in Mumbai. Vikram pointed out that several leading industrialists from Mumbai were members of the BoG. Ensminger was a practical person and knew better than to insist on this point in the meeting. (Note: The idea of a second campus in Mumbai was later revived in 1995 but was aborted due to the parochial approach of Shiv Sena, a powerful regional political party.)

HBS wanted a definitive voice in selecting both the Director and faculty. Harry Hansen made a strong pitch for this but eventually conceded that the selection would be an Indian choice and that it would be improper for HBS to have the power of veto. He did state, however, that 'The School would request the privilege to advise in the selection of the Director' in view of the long association requested from HBS. In principle, this was recognized, but in 1962, their role was played down as the process had already been initiated. Ensminger was on the Selection Committee. Vikram Sarabhai was in place as a coordinator. When the first search proved unfruitful in late 1963, Vikram was appointed as Honorary part time Director. In 1964, HBS strongly pitched for a full time Director. They believed that Kamla Chaudhary's role as a foil for Vikram Sarabhai was not in the best interests of IIMA. The BoG formed a special Search Committee and eventually Ravi J. Matthai was selected. The Committee comprised of Harry Hansen, V. Isvaran, Vikram Sarabhai, Navnitlal Shodhan, and P.L. Tandon (Convener). Tandon by this time had succeeded Jivraj Mehta as the Chairman of the BoG. Unlike MIT, the partner institution at IIMC, HBS were unable to play a more decisive role in these matters.

For faculty appointments, HBS asserted its right to refuse admission to HBS for faculty training. This was accepted. Vikram underlined that the Director should play an important role. The outcome was that instead of giving HBS the power of veto, they would be involved in an advisory capacity. Hansen noted, '...Harvard has been involved in an advisory capacity on all faculty appointments, and cooperation is excellent.' Later, when Warren Haynes was appointed as

India Project Head, he became a member of the faculty Selection Committee.

On the whole, collaboration with HBS worked well. IIMA certainly benefited greatly. Ravi Matthai noted in the fourth report to the FF dated December 23, 1966, 'The collaboration of the HBS with the Institute in the formative years has been most rewarding'.

HBS was compensated by the FF for both its efforts and expenses (see p. 27). The breakdown of the budget items for this grant is shown below.

TABLE 4.1: FINANCIAL STATEMENT OF FUNDS PAID TO HARVARD UNIVERSITY IN CONNECTION WITH THE INDIAN INSTITUTE OF MANAGEMENT, AHMEDABAD

	Budget (in $)	Actual to Aug. 13, 1963 (in $)	Projected to Aug. 31, 1964 (in $)	Total (in $)	(Over) Under Budget (in $)
Long term foreign advisers	215,000	67,727	97,415	165,142*	49,858
Short term consultants	60,000	18,664	33,252	51,916	8,084
Fellowships	65,000	46,640	36,160	82,800	(17,800)
Books and equipment	75,000	28,919	46,081	75,000	--
Project administration costs	29,000	13,201	20,596	33,797	(4,797)
Overhead	21,700	8,739	11,184	19,923	1,777
	465,700	183,890	244,688	428,578	37,122

*Current plans call for some increase in the projected expense of long term foreign advisers.

The first two grants to the Institute from the FF came to a total of USD 1,541,100 and the third and terminal grant was $660,000 covering three years beginning in September, 1966. A large part of the grant was used to pay HBS for the collaboration project, leaving about $125,000 for use either in rupees within India or to support IIMA staff travel to the US or fellowships to IIMA sponsored faculty or business leaders.

To begin with, the FF issued its grants in two parts. One was given directly to the grantee for its use under various heads. The other was given directly to the supporting agency also under various heads. This was all described in the grant letter. There was no direct financial relationship between the grantee and the supporting agency. Grant utilization reports were therefore filed by the supporting agency directly with the FF.

The process changed with the third grant. The grant letter was issued to the grantee, mentioning heads and amounts to be spent including payment for services to the supporting agency. This letter was supported by Memorandum of Understanding (MoU) between the parties. From then on, the grantee was placed in the centre, and handled the relationships with the FF or supporting agency directly.

Letters dated September 19, 1966 were issued by Joseph McDaniel, Jr Secretary FF, NY to HBS and IIMA; as was the draft MoU. However, the final MoU was signed on different dates. Ravi Matthai of IIMA signed it on August 21, 1967 and Dr Ensminger of the FF in New Delhi on September 2, 1967. Dean Baker at HBS signed later on September 18, 1967. The main objective here was to reduce IIMA's dependency on HBS. Why and how this dependency was to be reduced had been spelt out in the dialogues which led up to the MoU.

'The reduction of the dependence of the Institute upon the School has been expected and desired by both institutions. The timing of a noticeable change in relationships between the two institutions, and the desirable rate of change thereafter are naturally subjective judgements. One could assume that the Institute in order to achieve its independence would wish to reduce its dependency early, and the School wholeheartedly supports that aim. From the School's point of view, the question is not so much independence and dependence, but rather when can it be known whether the administrative point of view in teaching and research is transplanted from the School to the Institute. This was a major reason for the collaboration. We have some reservations as to whether this time has been reached. Nevertheless, the decision being made that the Institute should significantly reduce its dependence upon the School, the question now is how to implement the decision.'

The same letter which forms the basis of the MoU further mentions, 'We believe that the responsibility for manning for the second two years of the grant must rest with the institute. Any other solution would lead to misunderstanding between the Institute, the School, and the personnel recruited. Our role should be limited to that of suggesting candidates for the Director to approach, and to offering advice when asked on possible candidates.'

'In view of Harvard's early close connection with the Institute, it might seem appropriate for Harvard to assume the role of interesting individuals in going to Ahmedabad. But since we will not always be in agreement with the Institute as to the desirability of the work for whom individuals are being recruited; since we cannot assure people that they will do the work for which they are recruited; and since people will not feel they are working for and with us, with the career implications such work promises, but for an overseas institute, we would be poor convincers. To this we add that since negotiations will be between IIE (under instructions from the Institute), our work as an intermediary would be frustrating and redundant.'

In conclusion: 'We look forward to this transitional period which will further the development of the Institute as a sister institution.'

COMING OF AGE

The third grant covering the period 1966–69 really signals IIMA's coming of age and taking charge. From now on, IIMA was to be the prime mover and ultimate authority. IIMA was free to widen the search for faculty development, and for visiting US faculty, by going beyond HBS. Budget control and the allocation of funds were now squarely placed in IIMA's hands. The umbilical cord to Harvard had finally been cut as IIMA was granted sister institution status.

The attitude of the FF was aptly described in an internal memo dated September 20, 1967, from Rey Hill of the FF's New York office to John Bresnan of the Delhi office. 'If there is a difference of opinion with the supporting agencies, and I doubt if there is, it is one of individual motherly reluctance to permit the child we all helped train to move out into the world on his own. It is now time for the child to make his own mistakes and to correct them.'

'We are now entering into a two-way MoU with IIMA, one which provides that IIMA will make separate arrangements with HBS & IIE (International Institute of Education) as desirable. This has some advantages ... And it gives IIMA the leadership role in developing its outside relationships, which is as it should be.'

By 1969, the relationship began tapering off. Initially it was thought that the collaboration would be extended for a further period of five years. It was also envisaged that faculty exchange might continue, and indeed, for a while it did. There was a section of opinion at IIMA that had this collaboration been extended, IIMA would have developed faster and arrived on the international scene many years earlier. In their view, Ravi should have shown a greater initiative. Today, fifty years after the relationship was first forged, many IIMA graduates have received faculty appointments with HBS. You could say that IIMA is paying back with gratitude!

ASSESSMENT OF HBS COLLABORATION FROM THE PERSPECTIVE OF IIMA

It is difficult to make this assessment and know exactly what can be ascribed to the collaboration with HBS. This is mainly due to the early academic leadership of Vikram Sarabhai and Ravi Matthai. Both men were educated in leading foreign universities and had already developed insights into the processes that build great academic institutions. Even so, some observations regarding the contribution made by HBS can be made.

1. For the first three years, Indian faculty was sent to HBS in teams each year, for ten month periods. This helped bring about a great homogeneity of approach. The faculty imbibed several important academic values. It gave enormous confidence to the Indian faculty, and made them aware of faculty autonomy in academic administration. They became zealous guardians of faculty autonomy. It is safe to say that this would not have happened if the collaboration with HBS and the resulting deputation of Indian faculty to HBS had not taken place.

2. The second important contribution was the programme design philosophy absorbed from HBS and the pedagogy of the case method. The Indian faculty began thinking in terms of market need and programme objectives, and designed courses with relevant teaching material, pedagogy, and assessment. Programmes began to be viewed as education products. The framework to do this all came from HBS.

3. The third most important factor has been HBS's great emphasis and demonstration of links with the practicing world or, as they say, client system. This was forged through case writing, consultancy, and executive development programmes. After being exposed to this at HBS, the Indian faculty mustered the necessary confidence to approach businesses and engage in these activities with them.

4. The fourth factor was the demonstrative impact of the HBS faculty teaching and working in India. Their handling of class, their handling of assessment, their interface with Indian businesses—all these had a demonstrative effect on the Indian faculty. Besides, the presence of HBS faculty exercised a great brand pull with the Indian students and executives. From the very beginning, people perceived IIMA as a high quality school. They recognized that the faculty could contribute to improve and develop their own practice. They were knowledgeable and capable. They had an understanding of businesses and possessed the insights into how academic

knowledge can be used to improve business practices. This helped to raise the profile of both the faculty and the Institute.

5. Reinforcing all of these was the programme of sponsoring Indian faculty for higher studies at HBS for their DBA programme under which people like C.K. Prahlad, John Camillus, K. Balakrishnan, and others went. The FF also financed the sponsorship of selected executives from the executive development programme offered by IIMA to attend HBS's flagship executive programmes like AMP and PMD. This helped networking within India and across the world. It also created an enormous sense of goodwill for the Institute and forged a closer bond between the Indian business world and IIMA.

In the above assessment, the role played by Hansen needs to be appropriately acknowledged. Hansen was the prime mover at HBS before the collaboration decision was made. He persevered and skillfully navigated the collaboration proposal through the various approval forums at HBS. It was 1962. HBS was recognized as the world's best business school. Many in the US did not know India, nor cared. Ahmedabad was not even a recognizable speck on the map of India from the US perspective. HBS was wedded to faculty governance in academic matters. Why go to India? Why to Ahmedabad? Why to a new grassroot institute? Why devote HBS resources to such a risky, distant enterprise? Are there no other good options to extend HBS's global reach? Why not Europe or the neighbouring Americas? These would have been the natural questions and concerns. Hansen managed to quietly steer through them.

Till the HBS faculty and the Harvard Corporation had approved the collaboration proposal in May 1962, he was designated as the project advisor. After that, he was appointed Project Director. His job was to keep an oversight on the progress of the collaboration, persuade HBS faculty to participate, mobilize other faculty resources, guide and mentor Indian faculty who went to HBS, manage budgets and finances, smoothen out HBS's relationship with BoG, Chairman, and Director, establish policies and processes at the fledgling institute; in short to imbue IIMA with HBS culture—an extremely tough job considering that all this had to be done through persuasion as there was no formal authority. What was achieved is a tribute to his skills and commitment.

Professor Mote observes:

'At HBS, Professor Hansen was our friend, philosopher, and guide. He organized meetings with the IIMA team every Friday afternoon. He got us interested in the case method as an effective tool for teaching. We spent enormous amount of time discussing with him the pros and cons of the case method. He patiently heard our doubts and offered clarifications. It took me quite some time to appreciate that cases were more than a practical example of a theory. More importantly, he ingrained in us the importance of faculty freedom. I frequently told Carolyn (Hansen's wife) that Harry gave us "tiger's milk".

When Sarabhai visited us in HBS, we were reluctant to speak. Harry got miffed with us and said that you must speak and then the ice was broken. It is no exaggeration to say that Harry played a very important role in grooming the first batch of faculty for teaching in IIMA. Probably, the outside world does not realise Harry's important contribution in preparing the faculty.

When we returned to India and were planning for the first PGP, we (Namboodri, Karim, and I) were proposing a five day week so that we could review the week that had gone by and plan for the coming week. Probably Harry misunderstood the reason for observing a five day week. He thought that following the Indian traditions that teachers do not work hard, we were following a "soft option". He sent us strongly worded note and admonished us for being lazy. When we explained to him our rationale for a five day week he was considerably relieved. He said, "Oh you mean that Saturday would be a non-teaching day".

From that day, Saturday in the IIMA was labelled as a non-teaching day. Such were the people who built IIMA as an institution and laid a strong foundation for its growth, development, and prosperity.'

To this process, he brought great passion and commitment. He was deeply moved and got emotionally involved in the 'great enterprise'. His speech at the first convocation which we note at the end of this chapter demonstrates this.

It did not end in 1966 or 1969. He carried this with him for the rest of his life. I had gone to IMEDE in Lausanne (the precursor of the present day IMD) in 1978 to meet my friend Mote who was a guest faculty there. Hansen was an HBS representative there. Over a cup of tea at his place, I mentioned the idea of joint EDPs between IMEDE and IIMA. Mote supported the idea. Hansen's face lit up. I was leaving the next day. He implored me to stay back for a day and meet some leading members of the faculty, especially Professor Taucher, to discuss this idea. I could not resist his enthusiasm. I changed my plans and met Professor Taucher the next day. Based on this discussion, Taucher came to India. I reported back to Dr I.G. Patel who was the director then. IIMA organized executive/faculty seminar in Mumbai and Ahmedabad. I.G. Patel, Mote, and I had planned to take it forward and expand it into a collaborative relationship for EDPs in India and other third world countries. Before it could be concluded, Patel left for LSE and this initiative ran into a dead track. Had this been followed up properly, IIMA might have emerged as a global management school far ahead of many others around the world.

Hansen felt deep involvement in the welfare and development of IIMA. There is no doubt about this. IIMA has not fully understood or recognized the contribution of a distant US don!

My overall assessment is that without this collaboration, it would have taken many years for IIMA to become a leading management education institution. Whether collaboration with any other institution would have worked to the same extent, is an open question. There are not many comparative studies available of either HBS collaborating with other institutions or Indian institutions collaborating with other foreign institutions during that period. The only other example is of IIMC. The progress of these two institutions—IIM Ahmedabad and IIMC—does provide some understanding of the differences in approach. IIMA even today bears the stamp of HBS philosophy—whether it is the case method, live contacts with businesses, or faculty autonomy; the influence of HBS is clear for all to see. Combined with the talents of the early leadership, the collaboration really did help build a strong academic foundation at IIMA. I do not know whether HBS's Turkish foray yielded quite the same dividend.

Harry Hansen expressed the warmth of the relationship and the bond that had developed between IIMA and HBS when he addressed the first convocation on April 10, 1966.

'To you who created this institute, we send greetings: here is a dream given reality in this class, in the guests assembled here, and the magnificent buildings that arise around us. What finer reward is there than to see the fruits of one's labour before one's eyes.' To the faculty he said, 'You had a thankless task in which you could not escape criticism: you were asked to teach, to research, to administer, to come to know each other, to forge new concepts of faculty behaviour, and to do all of these things yesterday. To you, speaking of my colleagues, I bow and offer my hand; you were asked to do the impossible, and you did it.' To the students he said, 'Be reminded by your senses that you are more than the class of 1966; you are part of the class of the twentieth century and that of the twenty-first and beyond. No one has been before you; there is no end to those who follow after you. ...If there be stars in your eyes, don't brush them away.'

4

The Selection of an Architect

'As one enters the temple, it is as though a hand caused it to be. The details, with all this effort, recede in the light of the glorious over all conception. It is only after the wonder of the spaces in their music of light becomes real and settled that the marvelous carving of the details takes over. It is all truly a marvel of architecture and spiritual expression.

Louis Kahn

January, 5, 1964

Philadelphia, USA'

(From the visitors' book of Ranakpur Temple)

Buildings not only create spaces for activities, they also provide an identity and an image. Up until 1962, very few institutions of the IIMA type were being built in India. IIMA wanted to be different. A campus covering various facilities—classrooms, discussion rooms, faculty offices, library, and residential accommodation for all categories of residents—with students at the centre, needed to be created. The use of space was considered in minute detail. For example, students were expected to engage in lively discussions in small groups after the classes came to an end. Students living in groups in dorms needed a venue for socializing in the evening. Classrooms needed to be acoustically isolated. The number of students, faculty, and staff all had to be taken into account. Every little detail needed visualizing. A precise architect's brief had to be developed.

THE SEARCH FOR A WORLD CLASS ARCHITECT

With HBS on board as partner, both Kasturbhai Lalbhai and Vikram Sarabhai set their sights on building a world class campus. Even before HBS decided to join as collaborator, Vikram had discussed the matter of an architect for the campus with Kasturbhai. He wrote to Jivraj Mehta on March 2, 1962, after the first BoG meeting on February 28, 1962. 'The Institute may come to a formal arrangement with the National Institute of Industrial Design for the latter to undertake the total designing of the project. The Design Institute may appoint Mr Doshi as the local architect and associate with him one outstanding architect and a structural designer in the USA. Some brainstorming sessions could be conducted at Harvard with the Indian and foreign architects who have been chosen by the Design Institute and designers such as Charles Eames and Professor Kepes of MIT. These sessions would clarify the total needs of the Institute and suggest alternative solutions related to the social structure of the Institute in the wider community. It would be good if the preliminary site planning can be completed by July, 1962, and plans for the first buildings be completed by October 1962.' After this Doshi was consulted. He has noted, 'My suggestion to have Lou (Louis Kahn) design the IIM campus was accepted on the condition that I should represent both the client and the architect. In short, it would be my responsibility to see the project through to completion.' (*Architectural Legacies of Ahmedabad: Canvas of Modern Masters* by Doshi, p.17)

All concerned parties had faith in Doshi and therefore asked him to contact Louis Kahn, one of twentieth century's most renowned architects. Doshi had met Kahn during his stay at the University of Pennsylvania as a visiting faculty. He says of that initial discussion, 'This contact led me to suggest Vikram and Kasturbhai to assign the IIM Ahmedabad project to Lou. Kasturbhai was a man of great judgement and trust. He just asked, 'would you select him for your own project?' That concluded the proposal.'
(From Doshi's monograph, July 2007)

Doshi possessed all the humility of a truly great professional. He says, 'I promised to represent Kahn as associate architect. I preferred to see in India another historical campus than undertaking this project myself.' It took some persuasion on Doshi's behalf but finally Kahn responded by saying, 'If you say so, I will do what you desire. Doing a campus in Ahmedabad fascinates me.'
(Doshi's monograph, July 2007)

Kahn came to Ahmedabad to meet both Vikram and Kasturbhai. Initially the work was being carried out at NID. When he arrived at NID, Kahn did not understand why he was needed as the buildings for NID had already been designed. Then it became clear to him that he was to create an entirely new campus. The first drawings and plans were all prepared at NID. Kahn spent a great deal of time with Vikram and Kamla Chaudhary trying to understand the functions and aims of the new Institute. Kasturbhai was interested in architecture and contributed to the process with some important practical suggestions. A wonderful dialogue developed between Kahn and Kasturbhai. While he respected Kahn, he was not overwhelmed by his reputation. Once both of them were reviewing Kahn's plans for the main academic block; Kahn had provided for a canteen in the same block. Kasturbhai immediately reacted by saying that they couldn't have it there. Indian food is spicy and has strong aromas. Having the canteen nearby the classrooms would 'pollute' the ambience. Kahn accepted this. Such insights were noted by Kahn, who observed, 'Mr Lalbhai (Kasturbhai) is one of the greatest natural architects I have encountered'. Each believed in mutual commitment as the true basis of a relationship rather than elaborate agreements. Kahn observed, 'Contracts on paper only mean disputes. It is not what is signed on paper but it is what you see in the eyes of the clients'. (From 'Louis Kahn' monograph by Doshi)

Not only was Kahn an architect, he was a philosopher of space. 'It was the rotation of sun, direction of wind, and nature of rain that started to move Lou's pencil', Doshi noted. His design gave a sense of grandeur, purity, and harmony to the campus buildings.

Kahn was a great believer in achieving harmony with nature through his designs. The soothing sight of plants, a cooling breeze, the flutter of birds, and the tranquility of water were important to him. His imagination seized upon the Indian values of trust, tolerance, gentleness, and peace. He wanted to create a seamless flow between living and learning. The values of simplicity, austerity, frugality, functionality, and accountability greatly influenced his vision and geometry.

Doshi says of Kahn, 'His rigour of geometry, his austere plans or elevations, his frugal but well defined masses, and his monochrome built forms were a whole new world. His conversations resembled our traditional ashram discourses. With his grey hair, thick glasses, and thoughtful pronouncements, he became for us an ever patient teacher, a yogi of architecture.'

'I see in these built forms an attitude to architecture, that of fusing life in totality, a life which is not only in constant flux, but is also like a flowing river searching ways to meet the ocean of eternity.'

(Excerpts from *Architectural Legacies of Ahmedabad: Canvas of Modern Masters* by Balkrishna Doshi, Vastu-Shilpa Foundation for Studies and Research in Environmental Design, Ahmedabad)

Some other observations about Kahn are worth noting here.

'Kahn's mythic stature in American architecture is matched only by that of Frank Lloyd Wright; and even Wright is less likely to be spoken of with such reverence. The architectural historian Vincent Scully, Kahn's most ardent promoter, once claimed that he was "the hinge on which Modernism turned." His pure geometric forms were infused with an aura of silence, and they had as much to do with Roman precedents as with the late Modernist period he worked in. Far from mental abstractions, they were meant to be touched; their solemn surfaces of concrete, stone or brick carried the weight of history.'

—NYT Art & Design Nicolai Ourousoff,
May 26, 2010

THE ROLE OF THE LOCAL LEADERS

It is not enough for a building to provide efficient space for activities, it should also evoke thoughts and emotions. A building needs to create an identity and assume a personality. This is what makes the IIMA campus really stand out. It bears the stamp of these outstanding minds—the rationality of a scientist, the practical wisdom of a home grown entrepreneur, and the spirituality of a 'philosopher of space'.

Both Kasturbhai and Vikram had an innate sense of architecture. Both had already established several institutional buildings. For ATIRA, A.P. Kanvinde, an outstanding architect of his time was invited from Delhi. Vikram's home, Chidambaram, was also designed by him. Kasturbhai had built many AES colleges and renovated several Jain temples. He had called upon Corbusier, the celebrated French architect, to design the Millowners' building. At the request of his nephew, Chinubhai Chimanbhai, the Mayor of Ahmedabad, Corbusier had also built the 'Sanskar Kendra', the city museum. A family which had built many temples steeped in traditional architecture and another which had a great sense of modern design and architecture came together. Here they were not building for themselves, they were building for the institution, for the city, and for the entire nation. They knew they were making history and they had the confidence and ability to see this through to the finish.

The pioneering leadership of Kasturbhai and Vikram, and the harmony with which they worked not only with each other but also with the world's greatest professionals, contributed to the creation of a unique institution that will remain aesthetically and intellectually appealing to people of all times.

It should be noted that the main promoter of the Institute was the GoI. Generally, GoI buildings follow a strict procedure when it comes to selecting an architect. Most of the time, they end up with lowest quotes and lowest quality. IIMC ended up with Public Works Department (PWD) type buildings. Why didn't this happen in Ahmedabad?

To begin with, Kasturbhai had pledged funds for building construction as part of an agreement with the Government. The amount committed was Rs 30 lakh, the initial estimate of the cost of buildings as quoted in the Dean Robbins report. This gave Kasturbhai the freedom to choose his own architect and not follow GoI rules. Kasturbhai and Vikram then decided to enlist an internationally renowned architect. Again, this marks the vision of these two sagacious industrial leaders. Let us rewind to the early 1960s—the resource crunch, the stress on Swadeshi (our own)—buildings meant enclosed spaces with walls and doors. To even dream of a professional architect let alone an international architect was at least a quarter century ahead of the times. Funds were short. Industry's fortunes had plummeted with the Chinese invasion of 1962. It took nearly six years for a substantial part of the promised funds to trickle in. Pressure for funding escalated as the earlier estimates had fallen woefully short of the actual costs needed. Both Vikram and Kasturbhai explored various avenues in order to raise money. Finally, Vikram managed to muster some help from the FF. Throughout this struggle, the plans were altered and priorities reset time and again, but the vision was never abandoned. The campus took more than twenty-five years to complete.

There remained yet another hurdle. Foreign exchange was extremely tight. Paying an architect's fees in foreign exchange would have certainly been a dampner, given the extreme control exercised by the Reserve Bank of India (RBI). Lalbhai and Vikram remained undeterred and continued to pursue their vision.

Doshi noted the following exchange between Vikram and Gautam Sarabhai, the Chairman of NID. 'We have little foreign exchange. We can perhaps fund some staff and stationery expenses for Prof. Kahn's conceptual work in Philadelphia. The rest will have to be done here.' Luckily, the conversation was in Gujarati. Then Vikram said to Kahn, 'We will have a special office set for IIM under Doshi's leadership for you at the NID. We will provide travel expenses. Five trips—would that be enough? The FF will fund it.'

They enlisted FF support for foreign exchange payments, but eventually, Louis Kahn responded by doing it *pro bono*, all as a result of the great bond that had developed between himself and Kasturbhai. An insight into the development of this relationship is provided by an observation by renowned architect L.M. Pei. 'Talking about Louis Kahn architect L.M. Pei said that Kahn would strongly push through his view discussing with the client unlike him who showed great patience. But once he found a sympathetic client he would be a "client for life". The result—a monument of an institution, a destination for architectural pilgrimage, and an awesome structure—an inspiration for all those who pass through its portals.

Kasturbhai: Chairman of the Building Committee

Building costs turned out to be far higher than previously estimated as there had been such a long time gap between the date of the estimate and the actual execution of the project. With HBS as a collaborator, nothing less than the best was acceptable. Finding funds may have been a struggle, indeed, it would have been easy to lose heart, cut corners, and settle for a compromise; but instead they chose to explore other options for funding altered the construction schedule, and performed a rigidly tight balancing act. This was the stuff that the early leadership was made of.

Kasturbhai chose Gannon Dunkerley (GD) as the contractor to execute the project. GD, with headquarters in Mumbai was the only contractor led by professionals in those days. It had British lineage and operated all over the country. It had maintained extremely high standards of quality and integrity. H.M. Shah and Dastoor, who headed the Ahmedabad office, were both qualified civil engineers. Kasturbhai evolved his own unique method of dealing with the contractor.

Initially, he fixed the rate for two buildings after consulting Doshi. However, many more buildings followed and work continued for many years. Kasturbhai retained GD for all the building work. He would check every bill himself and settle it after allowing a reasonable escalation in consultation with Doshi. He was watchful, knowledgeable, and thorough. At the same time, he was also fair. No one ever argued once he had made his decision. GD was happy to work with him. Kasturbhai's involvement ensured that the work was of the highest quality and was also executed on time.

Kasturbhai was the Chairman of the Building Committee for a total of seventeen years. It is difficult to imagine how a man of his stature, who headed such a large industrial empire, and ran so many public institutions accepted this position, found time, and discharged the responsibilities with such efficiency and effectiveness. He could not have performed his duties with greater passion and dedication if he were supervising the construction of his own house!

5

Issues of Governance

'Keeping in view that the IIM Boards can govern effectively only if *they are the ultimate repository of all authority within the Institute*, we would recommend that the Director be appointed by the Board without any reference to the Government.'
Committee to Review the Functioning of Indian Institute of Managements, July 1992

GOVERNANCE STRUCTURE AT IIMA

We have discussed earlier how IIMA was formed. Although the GoG, local industry, and the FF all contributed initial resources, the basic features of the Constitution reflected the dominance of the GoI. This gave shape to a unique and complex governance structure, which was not without internal tensions.

In any institution, structure of governance is central to its functioning. It starts with interpreting the purpose and objectives, translating them into activities, ensuring its alignment with the original purpose, defining the basic values, raising and managing resources, and discharging its accountability to resource providers both initial and subsequent, tangible and intangible. Governance encompasses an arrangement of operational organs and decision makers, their relationships inter-se, and with the outside and inside stakeholders with a view to best realize the institutional objectives. The governance structure defines the authority and the accountability of the various organs and decision makers of an institution and, ideally, enshrines a system of checks and balances.

Governance structure has three layers. The basic layer is composed of the resource providers. Depending on the form of organization adopted, these can be members of a Society or Trust, or shareholders. The second layer is the BoG or Directors who are put in charge of the organization and its resources. The third layer is an executive or executive group to whom the BoG delegates the management of the organization.

In most cases, the resource providers will place certain broad restrictions or approval requirements on the authority of the Board of Directors. This would relate to limits on borrowing, the issue of capital, types of activities or business to be pursued, the remuneration of the Board members, and the process of accountability. In varying degrees, the MoA provides for certain managerial positions, their functions, accountability, and their inter-se relationships. The Board in turn empowers the executive group to carry out these activities within certain boundaries, with a review and reporting requirement. This three layer approach is designed to ensure that the original aims and purpose of the organization is realized effectively and efficiently and within the boundaries of 'risk' stipulated by the members.

Three factors are at the root of such a structure. Decisions in a complex, dynamic environment require expertise and speed. Multilayer accountability in the achievement of objectives and use of resources is vital. Large groups with diverse interests may provide resources and define the boundaries of risk but the actual day to day management has to be undertaken by a smaller group.

In this Chapter, I am going to deal with the governance issues relating to the first two layers, namely the dominant promoter viz. GoI and the BoG.

THE ROLE OF THE BOARD OF GOVERNORS

In any form of organization, some limits will invariably be placed on the authority of the Board. The Board is generally required to obtain specific approval from the general body of shareholders. Although these shareholders in case of IIMA included the GoG and local industry along with the GoI, the GoI was given overriding authority on several basic decisions including some which would normally fall within the authority of the BoG. The selection of a Director and the fixation of employees' salaries were two such decisions. It seems as if the principle of checks and balance was skewed! A laudable early experiment in PPP was tinged with the GoI colour.

When it came to appointing a Chairman and Director, the reins were handed over to the GoI. There is no evidence of debate or discussion on this issue, despite the far reaching departure from the draft prepared by Vikram as we saw in Chapoter 3 on Constitution. Based on faith in GoI possibilities of future problems around these issues did not figure in the discussions at that time. As a result despite the basic conception of IIMA as a PPP, the dominance of the GoI was conceded without a murmur. It could well have been either an act of faith or a sign of exhaustion. Whatever the case, quite possibly the potential for future mischief was completely underestimated. Despite the basic conception of IIMA as a public private partnership, dominance of the GoI was evident.

The BoG is the main organ through which an institution is administered. Out of the twenty one nominated members twelve (including the ex-officio Director) would be appointed by the GoI either directly or indirectly (through one of the GoI organs like AICTE), two by the GoG, four by the IIMA Society, two from faculty and, one from professional body. Maximum four could be appointed by the BoG itself. Chairman and Director were effectively appointed by the GoI. In Chapter 3, the composition of the BoG has been described in detail.

From a current perspective, the above scheme appears clearly lopsided in terms of the decision making powers of the GoI in critical matters. Indeed, the rights of the other partners were dwarfed by it. In contrast, the role of the GoG was limited to providing land for the campus and consultation on the selection of Chairman and Director. The GoG had two representatives on the BoG. The role of local industry was confined to raising funds for the infrastructure of the organization and providing links with industry for the various educational and training activities of the Institute.

Structure is an important element of good governance, but at the end of the day, it is its practice which is crucial. Conflicts in practice and interpretation are inevitable even within the best designed and drafted governance structure and rules. In fact, they define and clarify the ambiguities, the vagaries and generalities, inherent in any written 'legislation'. In the case of IIMA, such defining moments and conflicts arose on quite a few occasions. But, trust and goodwill between the initial stakeholders, coupled with sagacious leadership and unity of purpose helped to build a culture of governance.

Whatever drawbacks there may have been in the overall governance structure, academic autonomy was by and large secured. The Institute functioned well, achieving academic excellence in its programmes. The Institute broke new ground in admission policy, programme design, and delivery. IIMA, maintained practice orientation through case writing, research, and consultancy right from the start. In the classroom, students got to wrestle with real life management problems. Admission policy was strictly merit oriented and designed to be free from bias. A sophisticated and refined method of testing merit with proper checks and balances was put in place. Administration was supportive and result oriented. Evaluation was transparent. IIMA took special pains to build bridges through the client system and delivered value to its students and participants of the EDPs. IIMA graduates were in great demand and performed exceedingly well within a short span of time. In other words, the programme made them 'corporate ready'.

That the unbalanced nature of this partnership described above worked so smoothly, was due to the effective leadership in those initial years. All the parties concerned acted with restraint and wisdom, committed as they were to realizing the mission of the Institute based upon their shared values. In spite of the balance of power remaining firmly in the hands of the GoI, the selection of Chairman and Director remained largely depoliticized and yielded some of the best possible choices. It was this spirit that allowed the Institute to function so smoothly and it continued to make tremendous progress.

At the same time, fault lines in the structure soon became apparent, especially in times of stress. Problems arose relating to the respective roles and limits of the GoI and the BoG. Some of these problems not only underline the basic flaw in the initial arrangements, they also bring into sharp focus the need to review those provisions.

Whenever an institution is founded, there is always great initial enthusiasm. The founders are absorbed in their vision. Particularly in the case of a social enterprise like IIMA, a great missionary spirit and passion are the driving forces. Sometimes the cold logic of governance arrangements become clouded and the flexibility to adapt to the new realities of an ever changing world may get overlooked.

As noted in the Chapter 3, Constitution has to be adapted to the emerging context. Allowances should be made to review and modify it as needs arise.

Over the course of the last few years, management education has undergone and continues to undergo, far reaching changes, right across the globe. Slowly but surely, business education is becoming a globally traded product. Consequently, it is subject to the same pressures as felt by manufacturing and other service industries. With the expansion of professional education in the developed countries, their business schools are aggressively marketing their education around the world. In 2011, the GoI has introduced the Foreign University Bill in Parliament. Global competition in management education has spurred governments in various Asia Pacific countries such as Japan, Australia, China, Singapore, Hong Kong, and South Korea to strengthen their premier management schools to be in the top twenty-five on an international scale.

IIMA legitimately aspires to be an important and recognized global player in the field of management education and to achieve high ranking in all respects. Given the high priority attached to education in the country's development strategy, IIMA can and will play a crucial role in this endeavour.

Some of the earlier arrangements of governance as enshrined in the MoA require a certain amount of revision in this context, especially with respect to its effectiveness in realizing the mission and objectives of the institution, along with its continued growth and development.

The issues that arise are:

(i)   Why was such a governance structure accepted by the other two partners, namely, the GoG and 'local industry'?

(ii) What are the 'design' flaws within these governance arrangements?

(iii) What have been the 'practice flaws' in governance?

(iv) In general, how the GoI has exercised its dominant authority.

The first issue is a matter of speculation and I do not propose to deal with it. The 'design flaws' and the 'practice flaws' relate to:

(i)   Composition of the Board

(ii) Selection of Director

(iii) Salary fixation of faculty

(iv) Acquisition of real estate

Arising from the discussion of these 'flaws' we need to consider the following questions:

1. Should we change the constitution, i.e. the MoA, altering the governance roles of various organs?

2. If so, in what respect?

3. What should be the role of government, the dominant promoter, vis-à-vis the BoG and the 'management' ?

4. How should the BoG be composed?

5. What should be the accepted mechanisms of accountability?

6. What should be the relative roles and limits of the BoG and the internal management?

I am highlighting a few of the issues around which Governance dissonance arose. The recommendations of various review committees will be examined and in the process pointers to change will emerge.

ISSUES RELATING TO BOARD OF GOVERNORS

The main issues relating to the BoG are:

1. Size and composition of the Board

2. Role of Board Committees

3. Tenure and Nomination

4. Functions and Accountability

The BoG is normally constituted in order to ensure that all the various stakeholders have fair representation. As we have seen, in the case of IIMA, there were three major partners, the GoI, the GoG, and local industry; although as chief promoter, GoI clearly played the dominant role. In the initial constitution, decisions regarding the composition and representation on the BoG were mainly taken by the GoI. The Ministry of Education, now known as the Ministry of HRD, was the department of government directly responsible for the Institute and GoI wanted to ensure that this Ministry was represented on the BoG, along with other representatives of various interests such as industry, commerce, trade unions, and professionals. Of course, representation is also provided for the GoG and local industry as representatives of the IIMA Society. The initial composition of the BoG certainly reflects this.

With regard to the composition of the BoG, in the wake of the Mandal Commission, a very tricky situation emerged. The GoI suggested reserving places at BoG Level for SC/ST. The Board felt that there were other ways of achieving this. As we will see in the next chapter on Leadership, the matter was referred to the highest level in the GoI, and eventually the wise decision to selectively use the GoI's own nominated seats for this purpose was taken.

At the time, this original composition was appropriate in many ways. While the BoG appeared to be large, it also accommodated various direct and indirect stakeholders. Furthermore, it had to provide for representation from practicing managers and other professionals. The provision of co-option of up to four members by the BoG in the MoA made it possible.

During those initial years, attendance at BoG meetings ranged from nine to thirteen which, as there were no co-opted members at the time and given that the total size of the Board was twenty-one, was perfectly reasonable. In later years, the size of the BoG grew fully to twenty-five members. It was noticed that the average attendance at meetings still remained around nine to eleven. Local Board members always registered much higher attendance than those from outside.

At IIMA, the BoG mainly functioned as one large entity. It did not constitute many committees. In fact, the Finance and Building Committees were the only permanent ones to be constituted. For some years, there was a Personnel Committee for appointment of the faculty. This was discontinued in December 1999. The Finance Committee was constituted as required by the GoI and as the building activity was more or less continuous, a permanent Building Committee was also established. These committees mainly constituted local members. All other matters were placed before the BoG directly. This way of functioning had its advantages as well as disadvantages. The advantage was that all members of the BoG had an equal opportunity for involvement and participation in every issue that was raised.

Also it has been observed that whenever there is a committee, the BoG tends to become divided between committee members and the rest. This can lead to the various members adopting very defensive positions.

The main disadvantage here comes down to the lack of time given over to study the issues in depth and also the insufficient involvement of the BoG members. A large BoG, can frequently dilute individual involvement. This also created another problem. When various members of the BoG are absent from meetings, it takes a lot of time to update them. This can also lead to remarks or observations which are repetitive in nature and can often be quite contrary to the decisions already taken by the BoG. Issues such as these can only be avoided in cases where the BoG is very compact. Yet, while some argue for a smaller BoG, the representation of various stakeholders and other wider points of view require a relatively bigger BoG.

In spite of this, at IIMA, the general feeling of most BoG members, as well as Directors and senior faculty members over the years has been that our BoG has functioned well, providing support while never infringing upon academic autonomy.

Discussing this composition, the Nanda Committee appointed by the GoI to review the working of the IIMs in 1979 made a practical observation. They suggested that the Chairman may appoint a local member as Vice Chairman, under whom there will be a Committee of Board which will meet more frequently and thereby help the Director whenever issues arise. The Director then has no need to call the entire BoG. However, this suggestion was not followed. Subsequently, the Kurien Committee also reviewed the size and composition of the BoG in 1992. They felt that for optimal functioning, the BoG should be reduced to fifteen members. Later, in 2009, the Bhargava Committee also suggested a smaller and more compact BoG. Based on my own experience, I believe that a Board of about sixteen people with representation from the various direct and indirect stakeholders would work well and effectively. At the same time, I do see some merit in the earlier suggestion of the Nanda Committee to have a local Board or a Committee which could help the Director deal with issues as they arise without wasting any precious time.

With regard to the issues of selection, change and succession of the BoG membership, the process adopted by the GoI has worked reasonably well. The GoI nominated leading members from among the various direct and indirect stakeholders, who, while not being able to attend many meetings, did provide crucial support on several important issues. Many of them were eager to pull their weight and were available for advice, and shared their insight both in and out of meetings. Later on, with the advent of video conference facilities, it has become possible for many of them to contribute to the deliberations of the BoG from afar, during the actual meetings.

In more recent years, two Chairmen brought about some important changes. I.G. Patel believed that local leaders brought stronger and more abiding commitment to the BoG. Elaben Bhatt and Anil Bakeri were both inducted during his tenure. Narayana Murthy introduced a wider representation from our alumni. He believed that alumni would have a very high level of emotional bonding with the Institute and therefore would act as champions and guardians of the Institute's key interests. During his tenure, three or four members of the alumni were inducted onto the BoG.

Normally, those BoG members nominated by the GoI were changed after one or two terms. However, whenever the BoG felt that the contribution of an individual member was of a high order, the Chairman would strongly recommend that the GoI reappoint him. In some cases the Chairman and the Board would even co-opt such people. In most cases, the GoI officials on the BoG changed frequently, their attendance was low, and their involvement in BoG deliberations limited.

While some members of the BoG have shown less involvement and commitment than desired, in most cases it can be truly said that IIMA's BoG members have taken their responsibilities seriously, devoting time both at meetings and behind the scenes while continuing to provide much needed support to the Director and faculty.

FRACTURED AUTHORITY

Right from its inception, IIMA's BoG has worked under fractured authority. Although it was the apex body of the institution, it had no decision making authority in the following matters:

1. Selection of the Chairman
2. Selection of the Director

3. Term of appointment and compensation of faculty and other staff
4. Reappointment, succession, and change of the BoG members except for co-option
5. Acquisition of real estate

These powers were retained by the GoI. In some cases the BoG had a recommendatory role but without the ability to make the final decision. The Bhargava Committee looked at the governance issue in considerable depth. They were quick to realize the fragmented nature of the governance structure, yet at the same time, their basic premise was that these were public institutions.

Taking note of the dysfunctional impact on the accountability of the BoG due to this fragmented nature of authority, they made some far reaching recommendations. They suggested the creation of a PAN IIM Board above the individual IIM BoG. Such a Board would coordinate between all IIMs, approve their plans, and allocate and shift resources. The constitution of the PAN IIM Board was to be professional. They would be nominated by the GoI and the Chairman of the PAN IIM Board would be appointed by the Prime Minister. Thus, they placed their faith heavily in the PAN IIM Board, which would of course be strongly influenced by the GoI.

They also recommended that the BoG of each IIM should become more compact, and should include as many alumni as possible. It should be self perpetuating except for one nominee each from the GoI and the GoG. The Director would be selected by the Institute BoG though not the Chairman.

The Bhargava Committee fell short on several points. They did not recommend that the faculty salary should be finally determined by the BoG. Instead, they suggested making some faculty appointments contractual. In such cases, the BoG would have the freedom to determine the terms of the contract. In the case of choosing a Chairman, they felt that the Board should recommend the name but that the final decision should lie with the PAN IIM Board. They dispensed completely with the representation of the local industry through the IIM Society.

This dispensation ignored the specific circumstances of IIM Ahmedabad. IIMA was the only institution where local industry had played a crucial role and provided significant funds for building the infrastructure. Over the last fifty years, the local members of the IIMA BoG and, more particularly, the representatives of the Society have played an active role in building the client system, in providing links to the local community, and in taking up issues with various authorities such as the Municipal Corporation or local government. When natural disasters such as earthquakes struck, they were the ones who provided support to the Director. Time and again, the Director always found support from the local BoG members. The Bhargava Committee did not recognize that IIMA Society, unlike other IIM Societies, had a large number of active members and the proposed changes would require their approval. It is true that Ahmedabad is a unique case but one would have expected the Committee to come up with a differentiated solution rather than painting every institution with the same brush.

While Dean Robbins had originally conceived of a PPP, the Bhargava Committee pronounced the institutions as public institutions. As noted earlier, this PPP structure—even though lop-sided—had worked reasonably well. Given the changing reality of management education, both in India and globally, this shift in the basic form would emaciate the individual IIMs by limiting their flexibility and adaptive responses. Instead of strengthening the PPP structure, they recommended suspending it completely. In the context of this and the other issues which will follow, the Bhargava Committee missed out on a golden opportunity of aligning governance structure with the changing reality.

THE APPOINTMENT AND THE TERM OF BOARD MEMBERS

Nearly all the review committees—the Nanda Committee, the Kurien Committee, and even the Bhargava Committee—have taken a view that the term served by a member of the BoG should be around three years and that BoG members should have a maximum of two terms. The major concern appears to be that no one develop a vested interest in the institute and that fresh viewpoints be sought. To ensure some degree of continuity, they have recommended that Board members retire in batches. In other words, between a half or two-thirds of members will continue while a third or half of them retire. Certainly, there is some merit in the argument that Board members should not become a permanent or semi permanent fixture. However, it has to be said, that in my experience at IIMA, many of those members who have served for longer periods of time, mainly as representatives of the Society, have provided a degree of continuity and given a time perspective on various decisions which would not have otherwise been possible. In any institution, many decisions play out over long periods of time. Some of these decisions have links with past discussions and actions. It is not always feasible to refer to all the previously recorded decisions relating to a certain issue each time the need arises. In any case, recorded decisions often omit the logic and debate leading up to them. The presence of long serving members can provide both a memory bank and a binding force that can be very handy in such circumstances. Significantly, in 2011, Harvard University voted for a 7 year term of office to be repeated once for Board members, in order to provide for continuity. A better possible solution would be to stipulate that in order for a member to continue serving beyond two terms, the BoG should be required to reach a unanimous decision through the holding of a secret ballot.

THE ISSUE OF THE SELECTION OF THE CHAIRMAN

At IIMA, the GoI selects the Chairman in consultation with the GoG. A healthy convention emerged here. Nearly all the Chairmen nominated by the GoI came from an industrial background, with the exceptions only of I.G. Patel and S.K. Khanna. The Nanda Committee had little to say on this issue except that the Chairman should be a person of outstanding merit who has proved himself in the field of management, and has express interest in the field of management education. The Kurien Committee recommended a change. They said that the Board members should recommend the name of the Chairman to the GoI who would then take the final decision. If the name selected was not acceptable to the GoI then the BoG could suggest another name. The GoI decided that a Committee should be formed in order to recommend a panel of names to the Government for their nomination. The Committee comprised of a representative of the GoI, a representative of the GoG at the level of Chief Secretary, and the outgoing Chairman and two members of the BoG. This Committee of five would then recommend a panel of three names from amongst whom the GoI would select the Chairman. This plan was put into practice and survived one or two rounds. In 2002, the GoI dispensed with the Committee and took over the role of the sole authority to nominate the Chairman. That practice continues to this day. The Chairman normally serves a single term of five years, although Keshub Mahindra was re-nominated for a second term.

The MoA defines the role of the Chairman very clearly as a non-executive position, whose duties are to preside over BoG meetings and to act as the spokesman for the Institute. It is also the Chairman's role to take up issues regarding the institute with the GoI. While he has no formal authority, except as Chairman of the BoG meetings, on an informal level, by setting the agenda he can guide discussions and influence the direction of the Institute.

Recently, some confusion has arisen over the role of the Chairman. A feeling was expressed that the Chairman's duties go beyond what was formally mentioned in the MoA. The GoI was asked to form a committee in order to clarify this point. The Bhargava Committee considered the issue and finally confirmed that the Chairman's role is non-executive and without any formal authority. The Committee, however, suggested that the Chairman be nominated by the BoG for consideration by the PAN IIM Board for their final decision. In other words, the appointment of the Chairman would remain more or less the prerogative of the GoI. The nearest it came to being a nominee of the BoG was through a process of consultation adopted by the empowered Committee on the basis of the Kurien Committee recommendation.

The Bhargava Committee recommendation has not been accepted by the GoI. So, currently, it is the GoI which nominates the Chairman. Looking at the functioning of various Chairmen over a period of time one can say that with just a few exceptions, the Chairmen have remained both positive and neutral and have also provided necessary leadership to the BoG and the Institute.

The role of the Chairman came under enormous pressure when the fee controversy emerged in 2004, as described in detail later in this chapter. Narayana Murthy was nominated by the Government and yet he had to take a stand against the GoI on the fee issue. Despite the enormous stress inherent in such a situation, Murthy decided his position on merit and his interpretation of the MoA. It came under pressure once again when Singhania took over. Somehow he felt that the Chairman's role should go beyond just chairing the BoG meetings. He felt that more formal authority was needed and should be provided for. He suggested to the Ministry that there should be greater clarity on the role of the Chairman and his authority and asked that a Committee look into it.

My own feeling is that generally IIMA Chairmen have functioned in the best interest of the Institute. They have provided leadership, direction, and ensured accountability. They have acted as effective gatekeepers; from the external environment meddling into institutional affairs and insulating academic management from the undue reach of the BoG. Going forward, I feel that the best way would be the way the empowered Committee formulated. That process would generate good outstanding names, take into account the contextual factors, would be free from bias from any one constituent, and reflect the consensus of Government, industry, and the current BoG.

SELECTION OF THE DIRECTOR

The first instance of stress within the structure of governance came up when the first full time director had to be selected and appointed. The clauses in the MoA and the rules framed by the BoG governing the selection of the Director are reproduced below:

Clause of MoA:

3(i)(j)   to create administrative, technical and ministerial and other posts under the Society other than the post of Director of the Institute and to make appointments thereto provided that the posts so created are in the cadre and scales of pay as approved by the Central Government from time to time. The *appointment to the post of Director shall be made on such* **terms and conditions** *as may be decided by the Central Government in* *consultation with the State Government.*

Rules:

12(ix)   to create teaching, administrative, technical, ministerial and other posts under the Institute other than the post of Director and to make appointments thereto provided that the posts so created are in the cadres and scales of pay as approved by the Central Government in consultation with the State Government from time to time. The *appointment to the post of Director shall be made with the* **approval** *of the Central Government* on such terms and conditions as may be decided by the Central Government.

The problems inherent in this and potential conflicts were underlined as early as 1964 in the selection of the Institute's first full time Director. Vikram Sarabhai was the first part time Honorary Director but this was going to be a temporary arrangement. Appointing a full time Director became a top priority. A search for a candidate to fill the post was mounted in 1963. A former government official, J.M. Shrinagesh, ICS (Retd), was selected after a round of discussions and interviews. The appointment was finalized and the letter of appointment issued. The remuneration was fixed in parity with Mr K.T. Chandy, the Director of IIMC and Mr Gupta, Director of Administrative Staff College, Hyderabad. This was then sent to the GoI for their approval. However, the GoI did not give their approval. The Financial Adviser for the GoI informed Dr Sarabhai, in his letter No.62-CA(P) dated January 8, 1964 to Vikram, '...The pay drawn by J.M. Shrinagesh at the time of retirement was Rs 3,500 pm. According to Government decision, the pay of re-employed pensioners has to be so fixed that together with the pension and the pension equivalent of gratuity, if any, it does not exceed the last pay drawn, subject to the ceiling of Rs 3,000 per month. This decision is also applicable in the case of posts in autonomous organizations, etc.' The Directors of the other institutes were receiving more than this figure but the GoI would not relent on their decision in spite of the efforts of both Vikram Sarabhai and Kasturbhai Lalbhai. Consequently, Shrinagesh declined the offer. He strongly felt that the lack of parity with the other institutes was wrong and unfair. In his letter dated February 6, 1964, to Vikram Sarabhai, he said, '...You will appreciate the fact that in your letter of the 15th January and in Dr Jivraj Mehta's letter of the 26th January, the Institute of Management had put forward certain terms which I had duly accepted and this fact you had intimated to the HBS. However, in view of the Government decision to change the scale to Rs 2,000-100-2,500 and thus to create a difference in the standing of the Director of the Institute of Management, Ahmedabad, as compared to the Principal of the Administrative Staff College Hyderabad, and Director of the Institute of Management, Calcutta, I see no alternative but to regret that I cannot join Ahmedabad in the circumstances.' After that, the BoG had to look for another candidate. A fresh Search Committee was formed. Vikram was asked to be a member. He was so upset with the GoI approach that he initially refused to take part and only later, after a great deal of delicate persuasion, did he become a member.

Vikram Sarabhai's observations on this episode are worth noting:[1]

'After discussion the Board decided to appoint a Committee consisting of the following persons to select a suitable person as Director of the Institute:

1. Shri V. Isvaran
2. Shri Navnitlal Shodhan
3. Professor Harry L. Hansen
4. Dr Vikram A. Sarabhai
5. Shri P.L. Tandon: Convener'

'The Hon. Director mentioned that he was unhappy with the manner in which the last recommendation for the appointment of a Director had been disposed of. He felt that an important matter of principle was involved when the GoI had exercised their right of independent assessment of the merits of a proposed candidate which was at variance with the judgement of the BoG. He did not question the inherent right of GoI as per the Constitution of the Institute; but felt that the BoG should have taken this question more seriously. He was also not in favour of a definite time limit being stipulated by which a Director must be found. This step was fraught with dangers taking the realities of the

---

[1] As recorded in the minutes of the BoG meeting dated March, 1, 1964

situation into account. While thanking the BoG for including him as a member of the Selection Committee, he wished to reserve his acceptance till he had more time to think over the matter.'

In the above case, Vikram Sarabhai was aware of the provision of the MoA and the Rules but he was underlining the potential for governance dissonance in this regard. It is a sad commentary that when it comes to the appointing of a Director, the GoI has progressively usurped even the limited right of selection by the BoG over the years, as we will see in what follows.

It should be noted that the MoA states that the 'appointment to the post of Director shall be made with the **approval** of the Central Government on such terms and conditions as may be decided by the Central Government' but is silent on the actual selection process.

There have been three distinct processes for the selection of Director followed at different times.

Inception to 1994:

> Initially the Chairman of the BoG was the Chairman of the Search Committee for the Selection of Director and the BoG constituted the Committee. Invariably one GoI representative either from the State or the Central government was nominated to the committee.

1994-2002:

> The *Committee to Review the Functioning of Indian Institutes of Management (Kurien Committee, 1992)* in their report observed:
>
> 'The IIM Directors are at present appointed by the Board but with the approval of the Central Government. ... **Keeping in view that the IIM Boards can govern effectively only if they are the ultimate repository of all authority within the Institute, we would recommend that the Director be appointed by the Board without any reference to the Government.**'
>
> They then recommended 'The Director's appointment should be by the Board and not by the Government.'

The GoI then constituted an internal (Government's) empowerment committee to consider the various recommendations made by the Review Committee and to decide the methods and actions to be taken for their implementation. The Empowered Committee did not accept the recommendation and went ahead to lay down a process as well as the constitution of the committee. This in itself was a step backward as far as the autonomy was concerned. Even so, it should be noted that the Empowered Committee retained the primacy of the role of the BoG in so designing the constitution of the Search/Selection Committee that the majority members were from the Board and the Chairman was the Chairman of the Board. This committee gave the following direction in this regard:

'With regard to the appointment of Director, a 5-member Search/ Selection Committee, consisting of the Chairman of the Board, a Representative of the Ministry of HRD at the level of Education Secretary or Education Adviser (T), a Representative of the concerned State Government, at the level of Chief Secretary and two members nominated by the Board may be provided for in the Rules of all four Indian Institutes of Management.'

The Search Committee was expected to recommend a panel of three names (a panel and not a prioritized list of three names) to the GoI from which the GoI would select the Director. This fine distinction became clarified when Jahar Saha was selected. The Search Committee had suggested names in order of preference but the GoI insisted that it be only a panel of names. As the role of the BoG and its Chairman was given primacy in this process, it was adopted by IIMA de facto.

2002 onwards:

In 2002, the process changed yet again as the constitution of the Search Committee became as follows:

1.	An eminent industrialist/educationalist/scientist /technocrat/ Management specialist etc.	Chairman
2.	Chairman, BoG of respective IIMs	Member
3.	Two experts to be nominated by Government of India from among leading industrialist/ technocrat/ educationalist etc.	Members
4.	Secretary to the Government of India in the Ministry of HRD, Department of Secondary & Higher Education.	Member
5.	Special Secretary (Technical)	Special Invitee
6.	Joint Secretary in-charge of Technical Education, MHRD, Department of Higher Education	Member Secretary

The Search Committee's mandate was to provide a panel of three names from which the GoI would select the Director. This was followed when the Director was appointed in 2002 and 2007. The matter of this change in the process in 2002 was taken up with the GoI though no formal protest was registered. At that time, no formal communication was received asking the IIMA to amend the relevant clause in the MoA and a rule under the Rules. The GoI realized that the process notified by the GoI was not envisaged in the MoA nor was it consistent with past practice. Therefore, in 2008, the GoI asked the

IIMA to make this amendment. However, the BoG and the Society have refrained from proposing the modification in the Rules. The 'ultra vires' nature of the notification continues and has yet to be formally challenged.

Instead of moving forward to provide autonomy in this respect, the GoI is over a period of time, actually abridging it. From the initial formulation as mentioned in the MoA and the Rules, of getting the approval and sanctioning the terms and conditions for the appointment (and not the selection) it has moved to specifying a process and also laying down the constitution of the Search Committee in a manner so that representation from the Board was eliminated and the Chairman of the BoG reduced to just an ordinary member of the committee.

The GoI is progressively usurping the autonomy of the Society and the Board in this regard. Such moves fly in the face of good governance, especially in the context of the following points:

1. The Director is the Chief Executive of the Institution. The Society is an independent body which functions through a Board which has wide representation from all sectors including the government. A process to select the Chief Executive outside the structure of an independent Society, superceding the provisions of the MoA is antithetical to the basic tenets of governance.

2. The current committee of the BoG has more than adequate representation of the government and its nominees. The members represent various constituencies and are all eminent people from industry, business, the public sector, NGO, and other important sectors. The members of the BoG are well informed and involved in the governance affairs of the Institute. They carry the responsibility for the working of the Institute and its development. They bring with them a wider perspective of an external environment and are aware of how the Institute works. This puts them in the best position to judge and select the appropriate person as the Director.

3. There is a deeper issue of accountability. When an outside committee on which the BoG has no representation selects a Director, the accountability of the BoG goes out the window. Similarly, the accountability of the Director becomes greatly diluted when the appointment is made by an external body. This is equivalent to having the CEO selected by an outside body in a Company. No sound governance or management process can ever have this kind of mechanism.

FACULTY COMPENSATION

Another major crisis centred around faculty compensation. The MoA stipulated that the pay scale and benefits of faculty and staff require the approval of the GoI. The relevant clause of the Rules reads as follows:

'Subject to the provision of the Memorandum, the Board shall have the powers to create teaching, administrative, technical, ministerial and other posts under the Institute other than the post of Director and to make appointments thereto provided that the posts so created are in the cadres and scales of pay as approved by the Central Government in consultation with the State Government from time to time. The appointment to the post of Director shall be made with the approval of the Central Government on such terms and conditions as may be decided by the Central Government.'

This was done with a view to keeping a check on operational costs as faculty salary was a major component of total costs and the GoI was providing the backstop. It was also done to maintain 'parity' with other employees in the government system such as government employees, other university staff, etc.

Harry Hansen anticipated problems with regard to this and prophetically observed:

'There can be little doubt that in the years immediately ahead, many members of the faculty of the Institute will receive attractive offers to enter business, and faced by the hard economics of providing for families, being increasingly aware of their own futures, the best of them may well sacrifice the amenities of academic life for challenging work in industry.

It is important that the fact be recognized in India that by developing an Institute as closely attuned to industrial, commercial, and financial life as is the Institute of Management, Ahmedabad, members of its faculty are entering a new labour market. A market, made up of academic people who can only perform in academic life, though the operation of supply and demand factors leads to one price for teachers. But if the teachers are part of the market for business managers, a completely new market for teachers exists, and the price for teachers is bound to be higher.

Since the salary scale seems unlikely to be revised or to have much flexibility, at present there is only one practical way to anticipate the problem and that is by facilitating the individual's ability to offer his talents in the consulting market. In the long run, there is an alternative of uncertain availability and that is for the Institute to become a private institution completely subsidized by private business with the freedom therefore to set its own salary scales.'

Stipulations such as the adherence to government pay scales which hamper the pursuit of IIMA's vision and objectives in the current global educational environment need to be amended. The Government of India's powers to decide the compensation package of the faculty and staff has created huge problems. Because of this, IIMA has been forced to find other ways to supplement compensation and this has created distortions and led to many unintended consequences.

Times changed. Institute progressed. Global benchmarks became relevant. International mobility became easy. Globally academic talent became scarcer. Pressure on faculty compensation increased. Faculty strength stagnated. New recruits were difficult. Older members of faculty stayed on because of 'inertia' and the social roots they had put down and the flow of new talent dried up. The next table shows you this.

FACULTY STRENGTH FROM 1991 TO 2010

Year	Faculty	No. of Students (LDPs*)
1991	83	427
1992	81	410
1993	74	452
1994	77	453
1995	74	443
1996	75	445
1997	77	440
1998	77	453
1999	81	443
2000	83	427
2001	84	448
2002	80	462
2003	80	525
2004	76	608
2005	79	605

2006	81	672
2007	83	741
2008	86	798
2009	94	846
2010	92	900
2011	90	955

PLACEMENT SALARIES AND FACULTY COMPENSATION

In the first few decades what drove most faculty was the pioneering spirit. Material compensation was less important. The whole country was imbued with a zeal for nation building and financial compensation across all sectors was low. The GoI exercised considerable control over executive pay levels and caps were prescribed on managerial remuneration which broadly were within the ratio of 10:1 compared to the lowest paid employees. The economy was inward looking and remuneration caps coupled with high taxation led to distortions and value erosion. Gradually talent began to migrate. Those who were 'trapped' became highly dissatisfied.

The only relief available for some came in the form of consulting income. The primary purpose of consultancy was to remain in touch with practice and try out theoretical formulations in the real world in order to learn from it. Instead, it had now become a valuable source of top-up income. Even this source of relief came about only after prolonged struggle. Right from the very first meeting in 1962, the GoI representatives on the BoG were opposed to this. However, HBS as a valuable collaborator insisted upon it. Fortunately, the GoI relented on this issue and consultancy was taken out of the purview of GoI authority to decide compensation packages. Consultancy was subject to two conditions. It was to be cleared with the Director so that he can determine the educational value of each such assignment. A ceiling was placed on the number of days of consultancy as was the practice at HBS.

A small yet irritating rule related to foreign travel especially in the years up until the late 1990s. Foreign travel by faculty members had to be cleared and approved by the GoI. Often this soured relations between the Institute and faculty. One case in particular upset the faculty a great deal. Labdhi Bhandari, a bright alumnus of the second batch and an outstanding faculty member was not allowed to visit Columbia to receive the award for best dissertation. The matter was taken up with the education secretary and the minister. Even though the expenses for the trip were to be taken care of by the foreign university the request was still denied. In the early years of the Institute, this approval process created enormous problems. To what extent it made the faculty more inward looking and the institutional benchmark horizon narrower is difficult to assess. Had the faculty been allowed greater international contact it is possible that shortcomings in research would have been much less evident.

The economic effects of the command and control model are well known. Some liberalization started in 1986, but it wasn't until 1991 that major ideological change came into being. Manmohan Singh launched a series of economic reforms. Central planning had failed and he started the process of greater reliance on markets. What followed was nothing short of a revolution.

As enterprise was freed and the doors were opened to competition, domestic and global, industries began to restructure. The shining example of the IT industry was a constant reminder of the potential talent and entrepreneurial skills of Indian businessmen and executives. Companies finally realized that it was talent and not license that would help them survive and thrive. The era of the talented executive had arrived.

This is reflected in the placement salaries of IIMA graduates. The table for the period 1991 to 2010 underscores this point.

TABLE 6.1: AVERAGE STARTING SALARY DETAILS OF IIMA GRADUATES (1991–2010)

Year	Domestic-INR (PA)	Overseas-USD(PA)
1991	54852	NA
1992	62400	NA
1993	76200	NA
1994	92784	NA
1995	117600	NA
1996	216000	NA
1997	252000	NA
1998	322000	USD 68941
1999	370000	USD 74000

2000	600000	USD 83000
2001	671889	USD 97533
2002	588681	USD 76421
2003	6,20,000	USD 70,000
2004	7,10,000	USD 58,000
2005	7,90,000	USD 80,000
2006	9,70,000	USD 92,500
2007	13,70,000	USD 100,000
2008	17,81,000	USD 120,000
2009	12,17,000	USD 83,000
2010	14,94,000	USD 110,750

This had a ripple effect on the whole economy. Overall salary levels rose and the IT sector became the number one choice for most talented people, followed by finance and consultancy.

All of this created more pressure on faculty compensation. When freshers began commanding salary levels, which were between 25 to 50 percent higher than veteran faculty members of up to twenty years' experience, the murmurs became a shout.

Pressure mounted as schooling, housing, and vacation costs all went up. The wives of faculty members felt increasingly that their husbands were being under paid. Constant arguments over alternative employment broke out in many homes. The system was rattled but the clause in the MoA was a dead weight.

When Narayana Murthy became Chairman in 2002, 'Vindi' Banga and K.V. Kamath joined the Board. The BoG now had a strong presence of successful alumni who had become CEOs. They were aware of executive pay scales and the shortage of talent in the real world. They were also conscious of the modest standard of living and the financial pressures on the faculty. They strongly advocated generous compensation for their 'gurus'. They were well aware of the competence of the people who were working with them and also knew the competence of those who had built their talent. When comparing the faculty salaries with executive levels of pay, the chasm glared them in the face. They wanted faculty salaries to reflect those of modern day executives.

Narayana Murthy formed a committee to look into this and find ways to redress the issue. Rather than focussing on executive salaries, the Committee decided to benchmark faculty salaries with academic salaries in the top business schools in the US. The committee also noted the huge legal constraint (MoA clause referred to earlier) under which they had to work. The easiest solution seemed to be finding ways to top up their salaries. The basic recommendation can be summarized as under:

1. Follow up with the Government on the proposal for autonomy in the fixation of pay scales.
2. Until this is achieved, revise the rules with regard to consulting, research, healthcare, etc., and also introduce a performance incentive scheme to compensate the faculty for their poor salary scales.

Of course, this device being 'artificial' in nature, the inevitable happened. The academic management tried to create some indicators to find the value of contribution and tried to link reward to that. For example, teaching in 'in-company' programmes was treated as consultancy. An extra teaching load above the norm became incentivized.

The seeds of such a crisis in internal governance were lying in the MoA but remained dormant for long. Things had happened just as Harry Hansen had anticipated. Crisis led to 'circumvention' and circumvention led to distortions and unintended consequences.

CRISIS IN GOVERNANCE—NEW CAMPUS

In 2001 it was proposed that IIMA set up another campus. On the one hand there was a burgeoning need for professionally trained managers and on the other there was a huge constraint of creating a new institution with an adequate infrastructure and world class faculty. IIMA was running short term programmes for Indian Oil Corporation (IOC) staff at their Delhi campus. IOC, a GoI enterprise, proposed that IIMA set up another campus in Delhi on their land. The primary purpose for this was to have a permanent arrangement with IIMA for long duration programmes for their own staff. As a policy, IIMA did not want to become an in-house training institution for IOC. IIMA felt that in order for an educational programme to be more effective it would be more desirable to have students from diverse backgrounds. The Institute therefore proposed that if it were to start such a campus in IOC premises it would have to be broad-based. IOC found the proposal agreeable, but the GoI prevaricated. As a result, the project was shelved and then buried.

A parallel proposal came for establishing a campus in Navi Mumbai. Mr Ranganathan, the Chief Secretary of the Government of Maharashtra, was very keen on the idea of setting up such a campus in Maharashtra. The matter was discussed by the Board and Mr Sanjay Narayan, Finance Officer for the GoI, was extremely supportive of the idea. He was a Maharashtra cadre officer and he urged the Board to pursue the project. He also promised full support from the Finance Ministry. The Board decided to explore the matter and Professor Jagdeep Chhokar and I went to Navi Mumbai to look at the various sites offered by CIDCO. We chose the site which was on a hillock. This was earlier offered to Indian School of Business (ISB). IIMA BoG's recommendation was to move forward immediately.

Mumbai is the commercial and financial capital of the country. Many of the IIMA alumni work there and most leading organizations in the area have taken advantage of executive training at IIMA. They had been urging IIMA to establish a centre in Mumbai for years. Not only would this help with short duration executive programmes it would also help in research and consulting. There was a huge market for both short and long duration programmes in innovative formats like weekend or evening programmes for working executives. Faculty had long sensed this and were eager to establish a base in Mumbai. Ironically, what HBS wanted in 1962 was now being proposed. The Board accepted the recommendations and the Director wrote to the GoI for its approval. Once again, the GoI didn't come to any kind of a decision regarding the proposal. As time passed, changes took place within the Maharashtra government, and there was also a new Director at IIMA. The new State government raked up the issue of domicile reservation. The IIMA Board stuck to its core values and turned it down. The proposal collapsed.

In both these cases IIMA was denied the opportunity to spread its wings. The irony is that just a few years later, the GoI and the Bhargava Review Committee strongly recommended that IIMA should take up the task of mentoring other institutions. This is yet another example of how some of the innocuous looking clauses, which were initially inserted in the MoA by the GoI for a different purpose, defeated the very objective for which these institutions were established. This underlines a governance failure to adapt the Constitution to the changing times.

THE FEES ISSUE, 2004

In 2004, Shri Murli Manohar Joshi was the Minister of Education. At the time, IIMA was charging Rs 1.30 lakh per year as fees for PGP programme. Right from its inception, IIMA had been following an admission policy by which no one with merit would have to forego admission for want of funds. IIMA had worked out a support system to enable economically disadvantaged students to complete their studies. Furthermore, with an average starting salary of Rs 8 lakh in 2004, the value of this education was very well established in the minds of students, parents, and others. In other words, everyone knew that financing IIMA education was a no-risk bankable proposition. However, the Minister claimed that he wanted to provide access to a wider class of students and made an announcement stating that he would like to reduce the fees from Rs 1,30,000 p.a. to Rs 30,000 p.a. This came as a shock.

By this time IIMA had dispensed with the GoI grant. It had managed its financial affairs to become and remain self reliant. Such a hefty reduction in fees would have punched a huge hole in IIMA finances. It would have driven IIMA to approach the Government in order to cover the short fall because of the drop in fee revenue. Dependence reduces the degrees of freedom and increases its vulnerability.

There was also the matter of important policy principle. For delivering education at such a high value, should there be a subsidy? For those who can afford it, it is obvious that such a subsidy is regressive and for those who cannot afford it, arrangements were in place for scholarship support or by which their future income could be used to pay for their tuition fees without creating hardship. The matter was discussed by the Board and the unanimous view was that IIMA should register its protest against the Minister's directive with the reasoning described above.

The Ministry, however, remained adamant. Some of the alumni took up the issue against such a unilateral decision by the Ministry. They went to the Supreme Court with a Public Interest Litigation (PIL). Representatives of the Society on the BoG also became agitated. The Institute took a careful look at the MoA which under clause 3 (i) (h) specified, that the right to decide the fees rests with the Society through the Board. Legal opinion from an eminent counsel also supported this contention.

A raging public controversy emerged. The constitutional stand adopted by the Board was unacceptable to the Government.

The Director took the lead and responsibility of organizing the various stakeholders such as the faculty, administrative staff, State Government, and the Board of the Society. He was the only paid employee spearheading the campaign to resist governmental pressure over the fees issue.

On March 9, 2003, a meeting of the Society was held with Shrenik Kasturbhai in the Chair. About 40 members attended the meeting. All efforts to alleviate the situation had failed. I was the first speaker to point out to the Society members and the GoI representatives that as per the MoA the right to decide the fees rested with the Society as per clause 3(i) (h). The GoI representatives, V.S. Pandey and Vinod Pipersania, took the extremely aggressive posture of threatening to remove the Director and to take over the administration of the Society. All the 40 odd members of the Society who were present on that day were stunned by the bullying tactics that the GoI was resorting to. However, they refused to back down. They reiterated their right to decide the fees which they had delegated to the BoG.

On March 10, 2003, a press conference was held on behalf of the Society. I briefed the press on the legal aspects over the right to decide the fees and also the general view of the Society on this point. I pointed out that the BoG had always exercised this right with great circumspection. I also mentioned that the Society and the BoG took this decision about fees whilst bearing in mind the access to be provided to students coming from economically disadvantaged families. When the value addition is so substantial there can be no justification in providing subsidy to students who can afford to pay the costs of their education. For others, financial aid by way of scholarship and student loans had already been put in place.

At the Board meeting, representatives of the Ministry of Education continued to take the same extreme stand but they received no support from any other member of the Board. The BoG reaffirmed its right to decide the fees as a management organ of the Society and refused to submit to the pressure tactics of the GoI. As this ugly confrontation developed, all the stakeholders of the IIMA rallied round the Society and the Board. The Chairman, the Director, independent Board members, members of the Society, faculty and staff, students and alumni were all solidly together. The situation was nasty and far too close for comfort. IIMA was tested. It came out unscathed.

Narayana Murthy as Chairman had originally been appointed by the same Minister he was now arguing against. Dr Bakul Dholakia as Director, was under serious personal threat. He assessed the situation carefully, realized the covert agenda, skillfully mobilized the opinion of the stakeholders, tactfully sequenced the events and designed their setting, while coordinating on many fronts— opinion building, legal challenges, PR, etc.—and orchestrating the whole theatre of a very elaborate battle. The atmosphere around the IIMA campus was that of a 'war zone'. That this could be accomplished in an organization which worked within a collegial culture speaks volumes about the commitment to the cause, the organizing capability, and the qualities of leadership. The whole academic community around the country was watching this spectacle. One misstep and the game would have been over.

As we saw earlier, IIMA was founded as a PPP institution. The Constitution specifically provided that the right to decide the fees and manage the finances was the responsibility of the BoG as an organ of the Society. This arrangement had run smoothly for forty years. Periodic internal assessment had also been practiced in the form of the Committee for Future Directions (CFD) to ensure that IIMA's mission and objectives continued to be fulfilled. The functioning of the Board required dialogue and discussions between the various stakeholders represented on the Board. None of the stakeholders had acted unilaterally. The interests of all the stakeholders were balanced in all the decisions taken.

The faculty spoke with one voice against such unilateral infringement and so did the student body. The industry and the trade representatives of the Board also spoke with one voice. The absence of the representatives from the GoG in the Board meeting was significant!

Having met with this unexpected response from the opposition, the GoI representatives were seething. They contemplated taking further action along the lines of the threats they had already issued. In the meantime Parliamentary elections were announced. As per the constitutional provision, no major decision could be taken after the announcement of the election. The attention shifted to the constituency of Allahabad from where the Minister was contesting. In the election campaign this whole issue was also highlighted. Whether it had any impact or not is debatable but the Minister lost his seat. Mr Arjun Singh, the new Minister of the Congress-led Government declared that he did not want to pursue this kind of policy. He went even further, stating that he would not like to disturb the autonomy of the Institute.

The crisis which had engulfed the governance structure along with the culture of the Institute had been averted. The culture of the organization, the unity of the stakeholders, and the huge good-will of the Institute helped IIMA to escape the attack on its governance structure. It must be noted that it was mainly IIMA, among all the IIMs, which stood up so firmly against this encroachment from the government. To a considerable extent, this strength was rooted in the basic PPP arrangements, the constitution of the Society, the culture of excellence and of course, the awareness of the stakeholders.

RECENT DEBATE ON GOVERNANCE

The Bhargava Committee was very critical of the fractured governance of the IIMs. They observed that the Board does not engage themselves fully in the functions such as strategizing, setting future directions, mobilizing resources, carrying out detailed assessments of the working of the institution, etc. These are the functions of the Board and implementation has to be carried out by the academic management. They should have qualified their statement by stating that IIMA was an exception. IIMA had devised its own process to discharge these functions.

At IIMA academic management took the lead in initiating discussions on the future directions of the Institute, starting new programmes in response to emerging market realities, objective evaluation of its activities, and even resource mobilization. Throughout its history, its directors have taken initiative for these functions. The Board was used as a forum for brain storming. Take for example the practice of periodically constituting a CFD. To begin with, this committee was composed only of faculty members, however, the last two CFDs have included Board members and alumni also. The reports of these Committees covered future challenges and how to deal with them. In other words issues of strategy, organizational structure, and all aspects of implementation were covered. The Board discussed and approved the recommendations of the CFDs.

Good governance practice requires adroit management of the boundary relationship between the Board and the academic management. This encompasses the alignment of the vision and mission adopted by the Board and the academic values and activities as well as the relationship issues between the Director and the faculty within the ambit of the academic culture. The former has been discussed above. How the latter was handled and tested is best illustrated by the following incident.

During Pradip Khandwalla's term as Director, a dispute arose between him and Prof. V. Raghunathan. Raghunathan earlier had gone on a teaching assignment to the University of Bocconi. The same university invited him to return for a period of about three months. The Director turned down Raghunathan's request and refused him permission to go. Raghunathan insisted that the Director had no right to denied his request. The issue degenerated into a personal conflict between the two men. Pradip Khandwalla insisted on taking action against Raghunathan by not only withholding his permission but also demanding that the Institute take a share of Raghunathan's earnings. A protracted dispute ensued. The situation became ugly and when the press got a wind of it, a media storm broke out.

Raghunathan had approached various board members hoping for their intervention. When he approached me I advised him to take up the matter through the faculty council. For some reason this did not happen. He then wrote to the Chairman, S.K. Khanna, and all the members of the Board. One of the Board members was a member of the ad-hoc grievance redressal committee in an earlier matter. When the matter came to the Board, he wanted to form a new grievance committee to look into this matter. My view was that the board members should not get involved. I believed it would only serve to set a wrong precedent. I pointed out that we had a process by which any grievance against the decision of the Director can be handled. The concerned party should forward his grievance to the Chairman through the Director. At the Board meeting the members accepted this. Another member, while agreeing with this position, added that good governance requires that the Board should not look over the shoulder of the CEO when a conflict arises between a faculty member and the CEO. If the Board is dissatisfied with the CEO he should be replaced but the Board should not meddle in such issues. The Board asked the Chairman to inform the faculty concerned that he should follow this process.

This incident brings out the need to maintain a delicate balance between internal governance and the Board's responsibility as the final custodian of institutional values and fair dealings within the institute. The process worked well; it is based on trust and natural justice and provides a reasonable system of checks and balances. Many argued that there is a great danger of the Director acting arbitrarily in an unfair manner. Of course, this is possible, but redressal is always available. The alternative scenario of Board members meddling in various matters relating to the faculty and the Director is dangerous.

Two other conventions adopted by the Board need to be mentioned. At almost every Board meeting there is a presentation of an activity/programme covering both the strategic and operational aspects. The Finance Committee of the Board looks at the finances in considerable detail, asks probing questions, and provides valuable input. The IIMA investment portfolio has consistently earned the best returns within the statutory limitations on investment avenues. The GoI financial advisors on the Board have cited this as an example to other institutions. Nevertheless still greater involvement by the eminent Board members can certainly add even greater value.

In short, the functions of governance have not been neglected, but they have evolved thanks to the adoption of innovative processes which in no way dilute the accountability.

One of the main reasons such strategic initiatives got effectively implanted is the personality of earlier leaders such as Vikram Sarabhai and Ravi Matthai. These were men of wide vision, unquestionable commitment and integrity, and deep sensitivity to the academic community and members of the Board. As a result, they initiated many of these functions internally and generated a dialogue with the Board before giving their final approval. This practice has been carried forward by the Directors who followed in their footsteps.

Another reason has to be that the calibre of the Directors and faculty was such that the members of the Board not only respected them deeply but developed implicit faith in them. Within ten years IIMA had achieved iconic success. This only served to reinforce the confidence of the Board members in the academic management. What may appear as an abdication of the role of the Board to an outsider is in fact an innovative approach, which enhanced the effectiveness, developed the faculty, and instilled a greater sense of self reliance.

WHAT NOW?

For many years the conflicts described above remained latent and the institute's progress was not stalled. There was, however, always a lurking fear that some day the role of the government may be so exercised as to hamper the development of the Institute. The danger that the government could be swayed by some narrow political end, bureaucratic control, or other extraneous considerations is ever present. At the same time, it must also be noted that there have been many thoughtful, supportive bureaucrats who have valued the contribution the Institute makes and have been quite protective.

Bureaucratic pinpricks are inevitable when working within a government system and IIMA has to put up with them. The real issue is the dissonance between the objectives and aspirations of the Institute in the emerging global environment and the systemic government controls facilitated by some of the clauses of the MoA. A great deal has been achieved but a great deal still remains to be achieved. Successes have come through wise leadership across sectors, enormous dedication, a unique culture and values, and a certain amount of crafty subterfuge. The resultant public image has become a protective shield, albeit a fragile one. Having to deal with a very large number of institutions, bureaucracy has to resort to standardization. Policy makers change every few years. In the process the involvement cannot be deeper, sensitivity to individual institutional situations suffers, and the scope for differentiated solutions becomes non-existent. That apart, the danger is ever present that someone in the government might tend to overreach or exercise authority in a dysfunctional manner. I believe, the scope of such 'muddling through' has been exhausted apart from the huge cost associated with it in terms of time and effort. Now, the structural albatross has to be tackled. The time has come for a review and a recast!

PS: The IIMA Society has adopted amendments to the MoA in March 2011 mostly to address the issues raised here. As of September 2011 they are awaiting approval from the GoI and GoG.

6

Early Leadership

'What chance gathers she easily scatters. A great person attracts great people and knows how to hold them together.'

Johann Wolfgang Von Goethe

'The prestigious institutions like the Physical Research Laboratory, the ATIRA, the Indian Institute of Management and the National Institute of Design—all bear testimony to Kasturbhai's vision and foresight.'

Vikram on Kasturbhai

'He had a great heart. He could talk with Governments, he could build institutions, but he could concern himself with the problems of individuals. His heart was big because he gave and asked nothing for himself in return. Those who met him were better for meeting him because he was concerned for them. He had the patience and the rare gift of listening to understand. A great mind can be cold but his was warm.

He had a beautiful soul because he saw the good in others. The trust he gave was trust returned and we felt cleansed by having worked with him.'

Ravi on Vikram

Pioneering leaders give personality and character to an institution. This personality is an indefinable mix of the traits, attitudes, values, and skills of not just one individual, rather, it is a composite of a group of people. Certainly, in many cases where there is one strong and passionate leader, the institute will bear the imprint of his character, but in the case of IIMA, there were several leaders and the Institute took on a composite personality. At IIMA, the personality of the institution was not formed by just Vikram Sarabhai or Kasturbhai Lalbhai or Dr Jivraj Mehta, or Ravi Matthai, but rather it became a blend of everything these individuals had to offer. Rather than becoming fragmented and schizophrenic, this composite personality was integrated and harmonious. It was not designed. It just happened.

Although each of these men were strong, outstanding leaders in their own right, they also shared a common set of beliefs, purpose, and mutual respect, along with a spirit of tolerance and accommodation. This lies at the root of IIMA's homogeneous personality, and it has been consolidated and carried forward by the leaders that followed in their footsteps. In fact, it had such abiding value and relevance that even after fifty years we can still see their imprint. Of course, over the years there have been tumultuous events and situations, even leadership divergence, and yet the core of that institutional personality remains intact. While exploring this abstract proposition I think it is best to look at the qualities of these early leaders.

KASTURBHAI LALBHAI AND VIKRAM SARABHAI: THE PIONEERS OF IIMA

Kasturbhai Lalbhai and Vikram Sarabhai both came from two of the oldest business families of Ahmedabad. Both were Jains. Kasturbhai was more devout and Vikram more modern. At the same time, both were profoundly humanist in their outlook. They were troubled by what they saw all around them; great poverty and deprivation, social evils such as casteism and untouchability, religious bigotry and anti-humanist attitudes. They saw blind faith and an unquestioning attitude. At the same time they also saw a great heritage and craftsmanship, along with an inspiring equanimity and composure, even amongst society's most disadvantaged.

Both men were deeply concerned by the plight of these people. They did not view them as a political tool to be used for gathering votes, nor did they see them as an economic opportunity, ripe for exploitation, or social scum to be ignored and avoided. Instead, they viewed them as ignorant, toiling, suffering humanity—tolerant and fatalistic, skilled but unresourceful. Their response was not to create a platform of activist reform or the distribution of welfare but rather an institutional innovation. This was no empty emotional response it was a constructive commitment.

Here is an example of their progressive approach. After ATIRA was established, the mills of Ahmedabad became members by paying contributions. Initially it was proposed that each mill would pay a uniform fee. Vikram

Sarabhai suggested that instead, the membership fee should be calculated on the basis of spindles and looms. This method was seen and accepted as a much fairer formula. The contribution from Calico Mills did not arrive, even though Vikram was its MD. In his official capacity as Honorary Director of ATIRA, Vikram wrote a letter to his father, Ambalal Sarabhai, Chairman of Calico Mills, requesting the contribution. His father replied that he would contribute his share on the condition that ATIRA set up a Human Resource Development (HRD) division. This was back in 1948, when few in India talked about it. Vikram accepted the proposal and Dr Kamla Chaudhary became the first head of the HRD division.

Earlier Kasturbhai had harnessed Vikram's talent in building ATIRA. Apart from Vikram's close family connections why did Kasturbhai Lalbhai provide him with such unwavering support? His own son, Shrenik Lalbhai, was also educated at prestigious institutions such as MIT and HBS. Certainly, Vikram had been making a name for himself for some time, but even after Shrenik came on the scene, Kasturbhai turned to Vikram for major initiatives. Kasturbhai Lalbhai was free from the kind of dynastic bias that afflicts so many leaders. Today, meritocracy is a value lauded by all professionals and modern organizations, but in an environment where familial bonds were considered natural, where the founding families had contributed so much, where most others had not outgrown a culture of feudalism, such support based on an assessment of talent was remarkable.

There is another aspect worthy of note. Kasturbhai Lalbhai was an undisputed business and social leader. Because of his financial clout and social standing he held an enormous innate authority. That said, he never tried to maneuver himself or his family into positions of power. Whether it was the Chairmanship of IIMA or FICCI, or any of the powerful GoI committees he sat upon, he was never interested in the pursuit of personal glory. When the GoI awarded him the Padma Bhushan in 1969, he remained unmoved. For him, he was only concerned with the job at hand, and his mind was fully focused on how best to do it. Self-aggrandizement never entered the picture. Adulated and respected as he was, there was almost an unself-conscious presumption of authority. His own conscience was the touchstone. He would do whatever it took in his best judgement to complete the task in hand and that was the end of the matter. In every initiative he took in both education and the social field he invariably involved the community. AES, ATIRA, and Anandji Kalyanji Trust (a Trust which looked after the management of many Jain temples) are all good examples of this. Instead of creating these institutions by funding from his own private charitable trusts, as he could have done, he formed broad based organizations and involved other members of the community.

He would meet with other leaders and persuade them to join the organization and contribute funds and resources. There were other rich families who established institutions from their own funds and managed them without help from any outsiders. Kasturbhai's approach was more difficult. Differences of opinion were sure to arise and these would all have to be reconciled. His vision would have to be accepted by the other contributors. It also meant accountability to the community. He chose to subject himself to this discipline. These attitudes were rooted in the traditions of Nagarsheth and Mahajan and his own family lineage.

One can also find similar character traits in Vikram Sarabhai. Self-effacement, reluctance to pursue or exercise authority, steady focus on how best to do the job—these values were invaluable and left their imprint on all the institutions with which he was connected, whether it was AES, ATIRA, PRL, or IIMA. It is not just professionalism, it goes way beyond that. It is detachment, it is the 'sthitapragna' of the Gita, it is Gandhi's 'Vaishnavjan', it is the 'aparigrah' of the Jains. Both men knew the power of science and technology, and the professionalism of the West but they were also deeply imbued with Indian values and culture. That Ravi Matthai, coming from an altogether different background, also had similar character traits is no coincidence. Intuitively Kasturbhai and Vikram must have perceived these values in Ravi when they selected him. That such a leadership came together in the establishment of IIMA tempts one to label it as a historic constellation and almost an affirmation of the hand of destiny. Omit any one of these three leaders and IIMA phenomenon would not have happened!

Three religious minorities—Parsis, Jains, and Christians—appear to have played an out of proportion role in the creation of great social institutions in India. The first two have come largely from business backgrounds. They have helped to bring the core business characteristics of 'value for money', 'accountability', 'getting things done', 'result orientation', and 'team work' to such institutions. Many of the social institutions with which these communities have been associated have made far-reaching contributions and have created lasting structures. On the other hand, the Christian community have brought values of deep empathy, humanism, discipline, and dedication. These values, when combined with the brahmanical traditions of learning, have delivered outstanding results. IIMA is one such case.

The locational impact on institution building came about as the result of two things—the macro culture of the region and the quality of its local leadership. Each one by itself could not have made such a positive impact. IIMA benefited greatly from the macro culture of the region which in turn impacted upon the micro culture of the institution. The Gujarati attitude of 'getting on with the job', the emphasis on constructive action, and mutual accommodation instead of ideological positions helped assimilate people from diverse backgrounds, religions and even other nations, such as the USA. Of course, not all institutions with local leaders have succeeded. Some have become mired in local squabbles. Therefore, it is plain to see it is not merely the involvement of local leadership that is important, it is the quality of the local leadership. Kasturbhai's leadership provided resources, laid down accountability, and avoided nepotism. Vikram complemented him with his commitment to the pursuit of excellence, a global vision and the ability to attract talent. The combined force of this duo along with the Chief Minister Dr Jivraj Mehta's political support set IIMA apart. Gujarat politics was a product of Gujarati culture and it reflected an ingrained respect for local trade and industry—the 'mahajan'.

KASTURBHAI LALBHAI: THE VISIONARY INDUSTRIALIST

In one of the early meetings of the BoG, the issue of MBA degree granting status was being discussed. At that stage, the issue was of great importance to the Institute. Without a degree, students would naturally shy away from an education programme that involved two years of study. HBS had raised the issue of degree conferment right from the beginning. Attracting good students was absolutely essential to the building of a good institute. Vikram Sarabhai and later Ravi Matthai, pressed for the degree granting status in the Board meeting but the GoI members were becoming defensive. They attached many conditions to it. The University Grants Commission and AICTE conditions and supervision would have to be accepted. A special Act of Parliament would be necessary to avoid this. This would have led to the direct political oversight of the Institute. The BoG debate was serious but inconclusive. Kasturbhai Lalbhai stated that we should make do without the degree granting status and there was a finality about his position. The matter was settled. It was a bold decision, one which only a few would have dared to venture. In fact, only Kasturbhai Lalbhai was capable of it. Instead, attention turned towards building the image of IIMA and the PGP as a brand.

Kasturbhai was offered the Chairmanship of IIMA on several occasions. Each time, he steadfastly refused. He was then offered the Chairmanship of the Building Committee of the Board, which he accepted and served with singular distinction for seventeen years. The contrast in his response is difficult to understand. In the first place to decline the Chairmanship of IIMA even in those days was an act of great 'self denial'. No one would probably pass it up. At the same time, his decision to accept the Chairmanship of a Committee of the IIMA Board was intriguing. During the same period he had accepted the Chairmanship of IIT, Mumbai and served for nearly ten years. This only made his non-acceptance of IIMA Chairmanship even more puzzling. Both his values and attitudes are revealed in his response.

Kasturbhai was deeply committed to IIMA. He had a passionate interest in architecture, buildings, their aesthetic aspects, and costs. Therefore his accepting the Chairmanship of the Building Committee had a purpose. On the other hand, he reasoned that coming as he did from Ahmedabad, his acceptance of the Chairmanship of IIMA would make IIMA appear more like a local institution than a national one. That is why he declined the offer. He put the Institute first, and himself second.

It is interesting to note that Nehru had also appointed him as a member of the governing body of the Council of Scientific and Industrial Research (CSIR) and the Chairman of its Finance Sub-Committee. This body was responsible for allocating and approving funds for various research projects. Kasturbhai Lalbhai was neither a scientist nor a technologist. Whatever knowledge and understanding he had of science and technology, he had picked up during the course of managing his industries. True, he was one of the few industrialists who understood the need for research in industry and was the prime mover in establishing ATIRA and starting an R&D department in Arvind Mills. He was also the pioneer in founding Atul Ltd in Valsad, an industry that was driven by both knowledge and research. Shrenik Lalbhai recounted a conversation with Verghese Kurien of Amul. Kurien told Shrenikbhai that he had asked for a research grant to produce cheese from buffalo milk at Amul. Most of the members of the Committee had doubts over whether this could be done and were therefore not inclined to support it. Luckily, Kasturbhai prevailed, and approved the grant. The final result? 'Utterly butterly' Amul cheese!

One often wonders why Kasturbhai Lalbhai did not choose to start a medical college. Shrenikbhai says that Kasturbhai believed that while establishing a medical college was a relatively simple task, running it successfully was extremely difficult. On the one hand there would be poor patients who could not afford to pay and on the other, medical technology was changing fast and required considerable and constant funding. Therefore, the viability of a medical college through private funding had serious limitations. His sound business sense told him that such a project would be a fund guzzler and so he kept away from it. Self-reliance and long term viability were always uppermost in his mind when it came to institutional survival.

Likewise, he refrained from establishing a law school, even though the legal profession was extremely popular. The Law Society had already set up a fine college of law in Ahmedabad. In fact, he had served on their governing body since 1927 and was its Chairman from 1958 to 1978. He saw no need to establish another law school, besides it would only have presented a serious conflict of interests.

As the leader of the Ahmedabad textile industry he had sparred with Gandhi in 1919, when Gandhi led the textile union to a strike. Gandhi went on hunger strike, but Kasturbhai reacted by saying that Gandhi was shaming the Ahmedabad textile industry and thereby pressuring it to agree to his demands. Finally both of them decided to appoint an arbitrator in order to resolve the issue. Ambalal Sarabhai was a little closer to Gandhiji, in fact, he used to secretly fund him. Kasturbhai also gave his support to Gandhi, passing funds through Ambalal Sarabhai.

Kasturbhai had a legendary reputation for brevity and directness. He was a quick decision maker, a man of action and few words, renowned for the short duration of the meetings he chaired. Even when important decisions were at stake, his decisiveness helped the Board to deal with the issues quickly. His brief comments were always completely unambiguous, direct, and to the point. One particular episode comes to mind.

Kasturbhai was to chair the 20th meeting of the IIMA BoG on December 17, 1966, for the first time in the absence of Prakash Tandon, the Chairman. As part of the preparation for this meeting Ravi Matthai met Kasturbhai in order to brief him. After the briefing Ravi half-seriously remarked, 'Kasturbhai, this is an IIMA Board meeting and not a meeting of the Board at Arvind Mills. There will be discussions and debate. I hope you will bear this in mind.' Ravi was on the Board of Arvind Mills and had seen how Kasturbhai used to speed through the agenda of the meetings and conclude the meeting in fifteen minutes. Kasturbhai sat through the meeting which lasted two to three hours. As Ravi noted, 'His ability to absorb this punishment was remarkable.' After the meeting Kasturbhai looked at him for a while and said with a quiet smile, 'You professors talk too much.'

Kasturbhai had a wonderful relationship with Sardar Patel, the first Deputy Prime Minister of independent India. Both were action oriented, decision makers, and problem solvers. Whether it was developing the city of Ahmedabad, the founding of AES, the funding of an engineering college, or even raising funds for Congress, they always worked together in harmony.

Kasturbhai Lalbhai embodied frugality. Any ornamentation, which did not add to function, he would strike down. He found beauty in simplicity and could accept ornamentation and decoration only in monuments and temples. Kasturbhai used to travel by Gujarat Mail from Valsad twice a month. Once in 1974 I was travelling from Mumbai to Ahmedabad and he boarded the train from Valsad at midnight. Both of us were in the same compartment. The next morning when I got up I saw him and greeted him. He began telling me what had happened at Valsad station the previous night. People were distributing sweets in celebration of the fall of the Chimanbhai Patel Government in Gujarat over the issue of corruption. Later, we talked about the state of the textile industry. While we were talking about all this, he was folding the sheets and blanket provided by the railways. I was amazed. This simple act revealed many values about the great man. It implied simplicity and the dignity of labour. Although the sheets and blanket were railway property he handled them with as much care as if they were his own property—an embodiment of the trusteeship principle. It also signified his aesthetic sense; crumpled bed sheets and blankets heaped in a pile are not a pleasant sight. At the same time it revealed his concern for neatness and tidiness. This combination of simplicity, frugality, conservation, trusteeship, and aesthetics defined him as a man. Was Louis Kahn, the architect, influenced by these values? This simplicity and frugality almost bordering on asceticism are clearly visible in the design of the IIMA buildings.

VIKRAM SARABHAI: THE HUMANIST SCIENTIST

Vikram Sarabhai's studies at Cambridge University were interrupted by the outbreak of World War II. He returned to India where he researched under the Nobel Laureate, Professor C.V. Raman. Cambridge gave him permission to complete his research in India and to submit his thesis to the university. His upbringing, his interest in science, and the research work he had undertaken for his PhD instilled in him a spirit of scientific inquiry. He believed that the use of this spirit in business and institutions would contribute towards building India.

While pursuing his research interests he also took charge of the family business in Baroda, which dealt in chemicals, pharmaceuticals, and machinery among other things. He developed the business further with many foreign tie-ups and Sarabhai Chemicals became a research-driven company with modern facilities and all the latest products. Ciba-Geigy became a major collaborator. He started an innovative market research outfit called Operations Research Group (ORG). He attracted outstanding talents to lead all these institutions.

As mentioned earlier, Kasturbhai Lalbhai had spotted him for an initiative he wanted to undertake in the field of research and education. When he went to take the final exam for his PhD at Cambridge, Kasturbhai asked him to visit research labs like Shirley before returning home to India. Shirley was one of Europe's leading Textile Labs. After his return, and after the establishment of ATIRA, he was invited to step in as its first Director in 1948. He continued to attract young and outstanding talent. Dr Kamla Chaudhary was a fine example of this. He wanted young talented people like this, rather than older hands with more experience. Other millowners found this approach reckless but Kasturbhai Lalbhai gave him his full support and backing.

There are two things worth noting about his approach. At ATIRA he established the HRD division in order to effectively influence practice in technology application and to improve productivity. He integrated various disciplines in order to solve practical problems. He brought the same approach to IIMA when he became the first Director.

This approach was probably rooted in his exposure to the US model of research, education and training. Although he studied in England, most of his subsequent contacts and work were with US universities. This association, along with his being born into a leading business family and heading a fledgling branch of the family business, probably led to his strong bias towards problem solving. He was in tune with the open, democratic, non-hierarchical experimental culture of US universities such as Harvard and MIT. Their methods appealed to him and he adopted their way of working in Indian institutions. He was also a research scientist. He continued his pure research interest even after the completion of his PhD at Cambridge. PRL was his creation, his baby and he continued his study of cosmic rays there—and all this while running a successful part of the family business empire and heading a research organization like ATIRA. Combining this pure research bent of mind with his zeal for nation building, he pioneered the approach of harnessing global education and research in order to solve local problems in a contextual way.

During his life, Vikram Sarabhai was associated with a number of research and educational institutions like ATIRA, IIMA, and PRL, to name but a few. The wa y in which he worked with these institutions has made a deep and lasting impact on their culture. He always put institutions above himself and emphasized merit above everything else. While looking over all the recruits he enlisted to these causes, we cannot find a single one with even a semblance of nepotism.

He created these institutions and left them without even a shadow. It was his firm belief that when leaving an institution, one should not make the life and work of your successor difficult. He therefore completely removed himself from the institution. This was in stark contrast to the 'empire building' and 'zamindari' approach of most institutional leaders. Most people believe that the institutions which they once led should remain beholden to them. Vikram, on the other hand, did not want to leave even a lingering trace, except with regard to the values, culture, and working processes.

It is also worth noting the dignified and principled manner with which he conducted negotiations. Take for example his response to Mr Coleman of the FF during the disagreement over selecting a partner for IIMA. I have referred to this earlier in Chapter 4. This was a matter of principle. He shunned expediency, defined the principle of partnership clearly, and then conducted the negotiations in a deft, delicate, and dignified manner. Underlying this was his scientific temperament and deep self belief. This resulted in cool confidence, devoid of aggression or abrasiveness. He achieved his objective without causing any collateral damage.

I have often wondered how Vikram Sarabhai could switch his thoughts so easily from science to management, and then to the arts. He worked on many fronts, setting up diverse goals for each of the institutions he worked with. He had a rare sensitivity to people and his conceptual ability was unparalleled. That was the reason why he was able to work successfully across such a broad spectrum of institutions. As he was completely purpose oriented, it was possible for him to work for each institution at the same time. This created a huge impression on the people who worked with him. They felt valued, empowered, and important. He instilled self belief. Whether it was the former President Dr Abdul Kalam or Chief Election Commissioner Mr Seshan, or Dr Ensminger of the FF, or Professor Harry Hansen of HBS, or the entire faculty he recruited at IIMA; they were all influenced, charmed, and charged by his leadership.

His initial faculty recruitment policy proved not only to be bold and experimental, it was also sagacious. He avoided recruiting academics from the established university system because he realized that business education was different from conventional higher education. Emphasis was to be placed on applied subjects and practice, and Indian universities had no tradition in these fields. He believed that the Indian university system was conventional and not open to experimentation. His own experience of the political and bureaucratic functioning of Gujarat University had been dismal to say the least. Vikram's understanding, insight, and foresight worked to IIMA's great advantage. He had already done the same thing while recruiting scientists and technologists at ATIRA and this served to reinforce his approach to faculty recruitment at IIMA.

Throughout the history of IIMA, one is often struck by the faculty's deep commitment and great sense of belonging. One of the reasons for this is that unlike the policy pursued at IIMC, Vikram recruited faculty who were not well known academics but rather from a diverse variety of backgrounds. Rather than pursuing established names, he gave importance to people who were keen and eager to teach. His emphasis was on people with potential, deep commitment, and a spirit of adventure. The faculty was young, keen, and ready to learn. They were inspired to take up the challenge. HBS was a great institution, being sent there and working with their faculty was a great privilege and opportunity and most of the Indian faculty rose to the challenge.

This is where IIMA differed from IIMC, becoming not only more experimental but also more innovative. This approach has stayed with IIMA and has continued to contribute to its strength over a period of five decades. In retrospect, it looks like the obvious policy to follow, but when one reflects on the risk of adopting such an untried policy in a fledgling institution we realize the boldness, innovation, and analytical judgment of a great leader. Jahar Saha, former IIMA Director observed, 'The faculty selection process followed by Vikram Sarabhai was the key determinant in the development of IIMA.'

Another outcome of this approach was that because the faculty was not made up of established names, they did not have an agenda of their own. The Institute was not identified with the faculty and as a result they all shared the same vision, values, and operational philosophy. They were all living the shared adventure of building a world class institution and this became a driving passion. As individual characters got submerged in these ideals and dreams, the Institute emerged.

Just as it had been at research institutions like ATIRA, at IIMA, Vikram's emphasis lay in the solving of practical problems. From the very beginning he advocated that each faculty member should carry out all the four activities, namely, teaching, research, consultancy, and case writing. This gave the faculty insights into real life business, provided a practical bias, and produced live contacts with the business world. Here he was in sync with the HBS approach. This added great value to the development of the faculty, the design of the programme, and the pedagogy adopted. The final result was that in the corridors of business enterprises, IIMA was considered not to be an ivory tower but an academic mansion and a problem solving partner.

Although he was a trained research scientist, Vikram was not himself a specialist. He was not an expert in any field in a narrow sense, but he was an expert and a specialist in integrating talent to build an institution. He was a 'specialist' in deriving an action programme from his deep understanding of the purpose and its interface with reality. Prakash Tandon summed it up like this:

'I do not think he added anything himself to physics, industrial research, or management—he had not the time—but he widened the horizons in those areas, and of the men who trained and researched in them. It is significant that in the plethora of institutions we have built in India since Independence, his were among the exceptions that flourished; textiles, management, space. Into whatever he built he also conveyed his own characteristic refinement and excellence, whether a personal relationship, a building, or its landscaping. You could see his hallmark.'

(Prakash Tandon, 'Return To Punjab 1961-1975' page. 111 to 135)

Coming as he did, from a business family, it was surprising that Vikram Sarabhai was neither narrowly focused nor had a 'what is in it for me' attitude. On the contrary, like Kasturbhai Lalbhai, he displayed a rare public spiritedness and avoided the self absorption that generally afflicts leaders coming from big cities. This public spiritedness was what distinguished both him and Kasturbhai from industrialists from other parts of the country. Who else would have struggled so tenaciously for IIM to be located at Ahmedabad and furthermore, who else could have gone to the FF with a very weak bargaining hand and succeeded in securing HBS as a partner instead of UCLA? This unique combination of values and skills are deeply ingrained into the DNA of IIMA.

RAVI MATTHAI: THE SELF-EFFACING LEADER

I attended IIMA's first Programme for Young Executives (PYE) in 1964. I was selected from this group of PYE participants to go to HBS for the PMD. This was part of the FF grant to develop faculty and a few select groups of Indian managers.

After finishing the training programme at HBS, I returned to India and began working in the industry. One day, in 1966, Professor V.L. Mote approached me to find out whether I would be interested in teaching a course at IIMA on a visiting basis. I knew Mote, as he was a faculty member in the PYE I attended and prior to that he had been my boss when I was working in Calico Mills in 1961–62. Mote was the PGP Chairman. The culture at IIMA was to empower people in order to help them achieve their goals. Vikram Sarabhai and after him Ravi Matthai, built that culture. Mote was empowered to recruit faculty. This was somewhat urgent, as Professor K.V. Ramnathan who was handling the Management Accounting course had resigned in order to go to North Western University, USA for further studies. Mote's proposal came as a surprise and a challenge. I accepted.

After a couple of years, we were discussing a programme for small and medium companies with Ravi. I was invited to join the Management Development Programme Committee. I made a few suggestions about the profile, attitude, and constraints of executives from small and medium sized companies. Based on that I made observations about the location and design of the programme. A sixteen-week Management Development Programme (MDP) was to evolve out of this. At one point in our discussion, completely out of the blue, Ravi said, 'Prafull, you should coordinate this programme'. I was taken aback. I was only thirty years old, had only two years' academic experience, and even that was only part time. I was still working as a full time executive. Ravi was taking a big risk. This was probably only the third important MDP that IIM had launched. It was reaching out to a new sector of the market. Not only was there a great financial risk, there was also a risk to the organization and reputation of the institution. To hand over such a risky project to a part time green horn was a massive gamble. But it was Ravi's nature to rely on his judgement and to empower the people he believed in. I am sure he must have devised some damage limiting strategy in case the decision misfired. But to this date, I still don't know what it was.

Ravi Matthai relied on personal judgement and intuition. He never put great emphasis on CVs or references. Personal judgement based on a few critical observations at work was sufficient for him to make a decision. He then empowered, supported, and created owners of ideas and projects. Thereby he created an acute sense of responsibility self accountability. He had charted a road to personal growth!

In 1974, I had the idea of starting a management consultancy. I was engaged in running a textile company. I was the President of the AMA. Management consultancy in India was in its infancy and IIMA professors in teams were offering consultancy. Prof. Mote and Prof. D.D. Trivedi, another friend who was a senior Professor at H.L. College of Commerce, and I formed a consulting company. I was only a visiting faculty member at IIMA, still, I thought that I should bring the matter to the Director's attention. I talked to Ravi about the idea. I did this as I felt that consulting was also an IIMA activity and I was conscious that I was setting up a company, which would work in the same field. Besides, I was asking an IIMA professor to join me as a promoter and director. When I spoke to Ravi about it, he made a very simple remark. He said 'Prafull, there can be a conflict of interest but I know, if and when it arises, which interest you will put first. So, I have no objection.' These words of faith and trust were far more binding, far more effective and touching than any sermons, questions, or conditions. There was no other way he could have created a sense of deeper commitment to IIMA. The relationship was inviolable!

Vikram Sarabhai and Ravi Matthai may both have come from industrial backgrounds but they both had a deep sense of the appropriate structure in an educational institution. They were aware that for an educational institution to thrive, a flat peer driven structure is required, rather than a strict hierarchy as in a industry. Kamla Chaudhary greatly reinforced this. In contrast, conventional universities in India all have a strict hierarchical culture; there are Full Professors, Associate Professors, Assistant Professors, Readers, Lecturers, etc. Everyone is conscious of their position in the hierarchy. But at IIMA, there was no such hierarchy although 'payroll' differences did exist. In fact, a new faculty member would have no idea who enjoyed what kind of designation. Everyone was called 'Professor'. In terms of responsibility, at IIMA an Assistant Professor may be given the Chairmanship of a Committee and a Full Professor might be a member of that Committee. For example, Professor Dwijendra Tripathi was made the Chairman of the PGP while he was still an Assistant Professor. Also, unlike the practice at other universities, if a faculty member did research work he was not required to send it through Professor in his field.

In the internal working of the Institute, Ravi practiced certain values and followed certain processes which have stayed with IIMA ever since. Some of the core values he inculcated in the early years proved to be a strong foundation base for the future. One such value was that the Institute should remain student centric. At IIMA, right from the beginning, student assessment was always viewed differently. If students failed it was considered to be wasteful and examined as an issue of admission policy, or design and teaching inadequacy not accepted as normal. The question always lurked whether it was a student's failure or the failure of the institution.

Ravi Matthai insisted that once a schedule of class sessions had been drawn up, and the faculty had approved it, then no further changes should be permitted. He also insisted that the grades must be turned in on set dates. Once, Udai Pareek was coordinating the 3-TP programme and Vijay Vyas was one of the faculty members. Vyas' sessions for two days were drawn up after discussions with him. The programme was then frozen and announced. Subsequently, a very important meeting at the World Bank required Vijay Vyas' presence. He asked Udai Pareek to change the dates of his sessions but Udai stuck to the tradition of not changing the schedule. Vijay Vyas then went to the Director, Dr Samuel Paul, who said that he would not like to intervene in the matter, and faculty should take the view. Vijay Vyas, sensing the likely faculty decision in the matter, did not press the issue further. Finally, the World Bank accommodated by sending him back for two days to take his session and even paid his travel fare.

Ravi Matthai was always loathe to resort to rules. He preferred to work on trust. For him, an academic institution was a place where people worked on mutual trust and not through bureaucratic rules. He favoured faculty freedom above anything else. Tripathi narrated an interesting incident. In the early years, great emphasis was placed on case writing. At that time, most of cases used were HBS cases. The Institute had set itself a stiff target to achieve fifty percent Indian cases in its programmes. Faculty members were furiously engaged in developing these cases. An open line of funding was available for this and there was no prescribed limit on the amount that could be spent for this purpose. One particular instance of misuse of the fund came to Tripathi's notice, who in his capacity as PGP Chairman was in charge of the case unit. He took the case to Ravi, explaining how the funds were being misused. He also recommended that a limit of Rs 3000 be placed on the amount that could be spent without prior approval. Ravi agreed with this suggestion, signed the note, and marked it to his Secretary. The system was that once he marked a note to the Secretary, it would then be circulated to the faculty. Tripathi believing the decision had been taken, awaited the circular. When no circular came, Tripathi asked Ravi about what had happened. Ravi said, 'I changed my mind. I felt that just because one person has possibly misused the trust, I would not like to make a rule for everyone and vitiate the atmosphere of trust in the faculty.'

Ravi realized that the recruitment of talented faculty was a pressing institutional need. He started an intensive, and for the time, unconventional campaign in order to achieve it. Making regular visits to US academic institutions, he would interview large numbers of faculty prospects and then make them an offer on the spot. He relied implicitly upon his own personal judgement and did not follow the formal process of constituting a selection committee and asking the prospective faculty member to give a seminar. I myself had personal experience of this approach. I was a visiting faculty member at IIMA, as mentioned earlier. Ravi and Kamla would often drop hints to me that I could probably consider joining IIMA as a full time member of faculty. Kamla even mentioned that I would find a greater fulfilment in life if I pursued a full time academic career. Incidentally, around that time I had received a letter exploring my interest for a faculty position from IIMC, on the recommendation of Prof. Baxter who had been my Professor at the London School of Economics. I believed that Ravi and Kamla's words had been more an expression of good will than a well considered offer, and I was in two minds. Then due to personal circumstances, the moment came when I felt that I would like to opt for becoming a full time member of faculty. I mentioned quite casually to Ravi that I may consider joining IIMA full time. Soon I received a letter of appointment from Ravi. I went to him straight away and told him, 'you have issued this letter of appointment to me. Do you realize that I don't even have a Master's degree?' He paused for a while, looked at me and with typical brevity asked, 'So what'?

While freedom of faculty was a mantra for Ravi Matthai, so too was professional integrity. One of the Professors had written an article as part of a backgrounder for a prestigious lecture series. The bulk of the article was picked verbatim from a German journal to which he had access. Tripathi noticed that this was a clear case of plagiarism. He drew the matter to the attention of the faculty and Ravi. The faculty felt that Tripathi had blown things out of proportion and protested to Ravi. Initially, he was inclined to not take any form of strict disciplinary action, keeping in mind the overall feeling among the faculty. However, later he reconsidered the matter and dismissed the person concerned. This, incidentally, was the first case of dismissal in IIMA.

In his value system, IIMA was a temple of learning, and the students looked up to their faculty. Intellectual integrity must be a fundamental value in such an institution. Any leniency, let alone compromise, would hit at the very foundation of the Institute. It would be a scar, a stigma. He deeply believed in this and his strong clear-cut action made that value all permeating, ensuring that it became part and parcel of the very atmosphere at IIMA.

Ravi did not believe in issuing value statements on glossy brochures, or catchy slogans on placards and hoardings; he had little patience for grand mission or vision statements. He chose, instead, to simply live the institutional and personal values that he believed in. He would provide all the freedom to the faculty to pursue whatever it was that they wished to pursue. He would allow them to discuss and debate the institutional tasks. Often decisions were delayed and his attitude and authority questioned. He was the target of attack and corridor sniping. He had no problem with that. But plagiarism was completely intolerable. He exercised his authority, simply and directly. Living a value like this has helped to make IIMA what it is today.

It is true that when an individual relies so heavily upon his intuition and personal judgement, he can often unconsciously develop biases. People may well begin to interpret his decisions as undeserved favours or ill-considered rejections. Ravi Matthai may also have had his favourites, yet when it came to decision making he always remained objective and rational. Tripathi narrated the following incident to me. There was a discussion over the promotion of a certain member of faculty. The general impression was that the person concerned was close to Ravi on a personal level. However, in spite of this closeness, Ravi made it clear that in his view the individual did not deserve the promotion and as a consequence, he blocked the proposal. Many were surprised by this decision, but a true leader will cast aside personal likes and dislikes, often paying an emotional price, as he detaches himself and unwaveringly places the institution first. Institution building really is an exercise in asceticism!

Ravi brought both discipline and a student centric culture. He lent enormous dignity to the faculty as a whole by inculcating processes based on mutual trust, accountability, and discipline. This imparted not only great dignity and confidence to the Institute, it also established a huge sense of pride. As a result, a faculty body developed which was neither arrogant nor servile; neither snobbish nor conformist; neither bureaucratic nor arbitrary; neither overly conventional nor totally maverick; neither ivory-towerish nor just expedient practitioners. As a group, the faculty developed a great balance of values, attitudes and competence; ever jealous to guard their freedom while taking care to not trespass upon the freedom of others. These core values have defined IIMA as a centre of learning.

In 1972, after serving as Director of IIMA for seven years, Ravi told the BoG that he would like to step down. This request took the BoG by surprise. Under his pioneering stewardship, the Institute had taken great strides. The BoG would not accept his resignation and insisted that he continue. Again, after sometime, Ravi brought up the issue and this time he insisted that a change was necessary. His resignation (See Appendix: Ravi's letter of resignation) is a unique exercise in self denial.

Brushing aside his objections, the Institute organized a felicitation after he stepped down. At the function, he elaborated upon the reasons behind his decision to resign.

1. He had always maintained that the Director's role is first among equals. He wanted this to become deeply embedded in the culture of the organization. He, therefore, decided to step down *within* the institution.
2. In the life of an institution there are different phases where different kinds of leadership is required. He led the institution in the start up phase. Now someone else with a fresh viewpoint should become the leader in order to take it to the next level.
3. In India, people in office use the institution as a stepping stone for career advancement. He felt that this was not in the best interest of the institution, so he wanted to set a different precedent at IIMA by stepping down *within* the institute.

To my mind, this was a major landmark in the development of IIMA. It firmly established a new tradition of continuity and change. It outlines the proposition that it is the collective will of the faculty, which is the final authority in the institution in academic matters. It also demonstrated that within an institution no one is indispensable and that the institution is bigger than any single individual. Above all, it underlined self effacement. He was there, and yet he was not!

Under normal circumstances, Ravi would have preferred to leave the Institute at the end of his term, so as to not leave a distractive shadow looming over his successor. But he also wanted to establish the principle of 'first among equals' and to register his belief that the Institute should not be treated as a ladder for self promotion. He therefore deliberately chose to step down within the Institute and continue as a faculty member. Such actions were unheard of in India. A new value had been implanted in Indian institutions.

When the MBA programme was launched at IIMA, Vikram Sarabhai was the Hon. Director. He was there for the first year of this MBA programme, before Ravi stepped in and took over the reins. Both men played a stellar role in the development of IIMA. But their roles were markedly different. Vikram's main contribution was to ensure that IIMA was located in Ahmedabad and that HBS was enjoined as a partner. In terms of laying the foundations for the internal workings of IIMA, two or three points that he introduced were absolutely crucial. To begin with, he made the decision to send the first few batches of faculty, around twenty five, over to HBS for induction. He set in motion the process of faculty consultations on all academic matters. He also saw to it that new concepts such as 3-TP were developed and implemented with the joint efforts of HBS and the Indian faculty. He insisted that the HBS faculty come as regular faculty members and not as consultants. His stature and views were greatly respected by the BoG. This equation and empowerment of the Director was of key importance to all future Directors. Vikram was also instrumental in the selection of a foreign architect, namely Louis Kahn, and he ensured that the campus plans were prepared. He also laid down the dictum that each member of faculty would undertake all the four major activities, as mentioned earlier.

It was up to Ravi Matthai to strengthen the foundations laid by Vikram Sarabhai. He empowered the faculty and encouraged them to guard it zealously. Not only did he give freedom to the faculty, he also gave it autonomy. This autonomy of faculty is one of IIMA's greatest strengths. For the most important and basic decisions, the Faculty Council is the final arbiter. Providing free space for faculty to pursue their interests is critical in stimulating creativity. At the same time, there is a also a need to ensure accountability. In my conversation with him, Udai Pareek expressed the view that this should be done based on individual and group accountability. The criteria for which would be decided by the faculty. Unlike at Calcutta, Ravi ensured that the academic management was insulated against ingress and interference from the BoG. Ravi's goal was to make the MBA programme the best in India and to ensure that upon graduation, IIMA's students were 'corporate ready'. To this end, he fine tuned the placement policy and nurtured an atmosphere where teaching in the classroom by members of faculty became an important parameter in their performance appraisal. In short he made the institute absolutely student centric.

Another of Ravi's major contributions was to keep all the processes informal. He did not demand formal planning from his faculty. He encouraged experimentation and innovation as long as it was all oriented towards the goal of churning out better graduates. He also kept a keen eye on feedback from the students as well as the client system, assigning the best resources for building relationships with industry.

Ravi's commitment to faculty freedom ran deep. Take for example the area of research. Seed funding was available to any member of faculty for a good research proposal. This was not controlled by hierarchy. And yet at the same time, accountability was ensured. The Chairman of Research would pursue the faculty member for the submission of his paper and its presentation at a faculty seminar. In other words, accountability came not in terms of money spent, but in terms of the output of the research and its presentation and evaluation by faculty colleagues.

There was complete freedom to develop the design of courses, the assessment criteria, and the pedagogy to be used. The only requirement was that the course should be so designed that it helps the student master the subject. Indirect market accountability came in the form of a student feedback survey and the views of clients. In 1967, I was teaching Management Accounting II course. Professor K. Balakrishnan was assisting me. I used to give several quizzes during the course and two exams. When it came to awarding grades— quizzes, examinations, and classroom participation were all considered. On one of these quizzes, Balakrishnan suggested that we shuffle the order of questions in two different sets. He suggested we mix up the sets so that the students in the classroom would each have different sets. This would help in catching out those students who copied from their neighbours. When we designed one quiz in this fashion, a student was caught because the answers he had given were completely absurd. It was clear that he had copied the answers from his neighbour. I thought of giving the student an 'F' for the course. I went to Ravi and narrated this incident and mentioned that I was thinking of giving him an 'F' grade. This would probably have resulted in the student being asked to withdraw from the Programme or to repeat the whole year. Ravi reacted by saying that, 'it is up to you what grade you want to give, but see that the punishment is not out of proportion to the lapse'. I thought things over and finally awarded the student a 'D' for the whole course irrespective of what he had secured in the other quizzes and examinations.

Ravi ensured that in important academic matters, the views of the Faculty Council were ascertained. Processes were developed in consultation with faculty.

Under Vikram Sarabhai and Ravi Matthai, IIMA had accepted two basic operating decisions—teaching and research should be practice oriented, and IIMA should be responsive to the client system. This meant that in order to deal with real life problems, an inter-disciplinary approach had to be adopted. Ravi reflected this basic idea in his approach to case writing and research. Writing 'integrated cases' became one of the highest priorities of the Institute.

His emphasis on research came mainly from the practice angle. In other words, he was more attuned to action and actionable research rather than theoretical research. His approach to research was based on intuition and validation through action rather than through the collection of data and conducting surveys. Both of these activities called for an inter-disciplinary approach and required collaboration between faculty members coming from different specialist backgrounds. This fostered a sense of teamwork and helped to develop new insights for faculty members. It helped to build a culture of collaboration in a setting of extensive individual autonomy and provided a desirable balance within the institute.

By the time the first five batches of students had graduated from IIMA, its reputation as the best institution had been established. The graduates were in great demand and the executive education programmes were completely sold out. Internally, the faculty cherished the informal processes along with a sense of freedom and autonomy. It is true that some faculty members were initially confused, lost, and bewildered, but eventually they came to appreciate the positive aspects of faculty freedom and soon settled down. This emphasis on faculty freedom and the informal process built a culture, which has continued to foster self renewal and rejuvenation throughout the various phases of the life of the institution. This is Ravi Matthai's lasting contribution.

Udai Pareek summed up his association with IIMA by saying, 'if I had been self employed, instead of being on the roles of the institute, I would have done the same that I did at the Institute.' This only shows the academic atmosphere that IIMA provided. Or, take the observation of Pankaj Chandra— currently the Director of IIM, Bangalore—who joined IIMA in the year 1989. He had studied in the USA and Canada and was a professor at McGill University, until 1989, when he decided to come to India and join an academic institution. IIMA was his choice. In 1995, a CFD was formed under the chairmanship of Dr Amar Kalro. Both Pankaj Chandra and I were members of the committee. One of the observations that Pankaj Chandra made then is very pertinent. He said, 'Joining IIMA and settling in was never a problem. It was as smooth as it would have been had I chosen to join any of the North American Business Schools.' Academic freedom, the intellectual community, the infrastructure, and the internal governance structure, which were all built over the years by the early leaders have fostered this kind of culture. Our local leaders had built a global culture.

Despite the fact that IIMA's academic programme and pedagogical philosophy was hugely influenced by its collaboration with HBS, and the enormous academic dividend it produced, Ravi Matthai could see beyond that when the time came to renew the relationship in 1967. He observed in the fourth report to the FF in the latter half of 1966: 'The collaboration of the HBS with the Institute in the formative years has been most rewarding.' He then added, 'The objectives of the Institute have been broadened gradually in *response to felt needs* and this practice continues. The original thinking was in terms mainly of business administration. Since then management in agriculture has been introduced as a substantial activity. Institutional growth can be regarded as a function of environmental response. *The primary objective is in relation to Management Education, but there is a wide range of activities to which this education is relevant.* We have planned to extend our range of activities according to what we consider are the *important needs of the country* which we can help meet and to which the environment is ready to respond.'

He then concluded, 'It is hoped that the relationship between HBS and IIMA will develop into one of *mutual functional interests of the two faculties.*' Here is someone who sets his agenda, vows by the basic value of faculty autonomy and quietly asserts the need of the country to which the Institute has to respond, without being overwhelmed either by the reputation of the world's greatest business school or the largesse of a well meaning benefactor. The confidence, dignity, self belief, and a firm sense of destiny have all been ingested into the very fabric of IIMA.

We noted earlier how the nature of the relationship took place during the third FF grant which covered the period of 1966–69.

If one were to define the central value which set IIMA apart from other institutions, it would be faculty autonomy. To accept it as a core concept for designing the institutional policies and processes is a paradigm shift but to actually put it into practice was a Herculean task. India had no long tradition of democracy. It was only just undergoing a slow transition from the feudal to an egalitarian social ethos. Democratic culture had not taken root in either society or its institutions. People were used to either giving orders or receiving them. The boss was the master. He was supposed to have all the answers. Culturally also, respect for elders and gurus meant an unquestioning acceptance of their views, wishes, whims, and directions. The superiors and the subordinates were mentally conditioned to function in that mode. To attempt to firmly plant the seeds of an egalitarian culture can be viewed as an act of supreme self sacrifice for the person in authority. For the subordinate, it was completely disorientating and at first it was also enormously frustrating. It was an epic struggle which generated friction, heartburn, and confusion. What eventually emerged was dignity, self respect, confidence, and self belief. A way of working had evolved which ensured self renewal and self correction, and which also helped the Institute deal with the trials and tribulations flowing from the many subsequent clashes of cultures. This is where the wisdom of leaders like Vikram Sarabhai and Ravi Matthai helped define the personality of IIMA and ensure that it became established as an icon of internal governance.

LEADERSHIP 'CAPITAL' OF IIMA

As I have observed earlier, Kasturbhai Lalbhai did not accept the Chairmanship of IIMA. The Chairman is a non-executive position but at the same time it is an extremely important role. The Chairman provides direction, acts as the public face of the Institute, provides counsel to the Director, sets the agenda for BoG meetings, and oversees all the affairs of the Institute. The Director as well as other BoG members would all look for guidance from the Chairman on many important issues. Almost all the Chairmen of IIMA—with the exceptions of Jivraj Mehta, who was the Chief Minister of Gujarat; I.G. Patel, the economist bureaucrat; and S.K. Khanna, an educationist—came from industry. Many of them played an exemplary leadership role. Special mention needs to be made of Prakash Tandon who succeeded Jivraj Mehta, Keshub Mahindra who was the fourth Chairman and the only one to enjoy two terms, I.G. Patel, and Narayana Murthy.

Prakash Tandon was the Chairman of Hindustan Lever Ltd., an icon of professional management. He took active interest in all the affairs of the Institute, including academic matters. From the initial stages, his association helped IIMA acquire visibility in the eyes of the professionally managed companies in India, spearheaded by Hindustan Lever. He brought the values of professionalism in management to the Institute. Many excellent guest faculty came from Hindustan Lever and Unilever, London. Prakash Tandon himself acted as guest faculty for many EDPs. It was unfortunate that for some inexplicable reason, during the final two or three years of his term, he was not very active at IIMA.

Keshub Mahindra succeeded S.L. Kirloskar as the Chairman in 1973. Kirloskar was very subdued and somewhat inactive. He refrained from getting too involved in the affairs of the Institute and did not bring any strong views regarding the direction the Institute should take. Instead, he allowed the Director to run the Institute with the minimum amount of involvement. Keshub, on the other hand, was a suave, practical, and result-oriented hardcore businessman.

Keshub played the role of the Chairman ideally. He provided leadership to the BoG. He came up with ideas. Temperamentally, he was more active and therefore interpreted his role in leading the Institute by providing direction, ensuring accountability, acting as its spokesperson, and handling top level relationship issues with the major stakeholders like the GoI. He provided a fine blend of accountability and support. As Chairman, he played the key role in the process of the succession of the Director (during his tenure three changes of Directorship took place) and provided courageous and tactful leadership whenever dark clouds hovered over the horizon.

When it came to critical issues with the GoI, he handled them deftly and ensured that the Institute remain insulated from any detractive influence from the government. Time and again this was needed, and time and again he demonstrated his mature relationship management skill. His term overlapped with some momentous political changes. During his term the, Congress Government's days of dominance came to an end and the experiment of the Janata Party took place. Activism on the part of the government in matters relating to the Institute began and IIMA was forced to deal with a new political environment. Keshub understood, endorsed, and respected the values developed in the Institute, and carefully insulated them from some of the negative fall-out that was inevitable in such a time of external change.

He was a firm leader and played a crucial role in the selection of the Director. He maintained that the Director must be left to run the Institute but selecting a successor was an important function of the BoG. Courage of conviction, supporting the Director and yet holding him accountable, understanding the values of academic culture—these were the qualities displayed by Keshub Mahindra during his tenure.

Keshub Mahindra arrived during the first important change of Director. Samuel Paul had just succeeded Ravi Matthai and Keshub provided wise counsel and support to the new Director. He was a keen observer and highly perceptive. Through informal chats and casual conversation with the faculty, he managed to sense various under currents at IIMA during his tenure.

Vijay Vyas's term ended in 1982 and a new Director had to be chosen. Keshub Mahindra was the Chairman; when a Search Committee was constituted, Keshub was its Chairman. He began the process of consultation, meeting with BoG members, faculty members, and possibly staff members too. Keshub did not mince his words nor did he allow himself to be swayed by the views of leading faculty, BoG members, or others who favoured the idea of looking for an internal candidate from within the Institute. He had a different idea and firmly argued for bringing in a leader from outside who would be prepared to shake things up.

While consulting with members of the BoG, Keshub spoke with me. I was acutely aware of the unique culture of IIMA. Faculty autonomy was at its core. No other institution of education in India practiced it to the same extent. In my judgement, this lent enormous resilience to the Institute. When I heard that Keshub and the Search Committee were pursuing the idea of bringing in an outsider, I became deeply worried. I told Keshub about the need to protect and preserve this culture of autonomy. I elaborated and mentioned that the person concerned need not necessarily be a full time faculty member, but that an alumnus, or an EDP participant could also be considered. The idea was to ensure sensitivity to the unique culture of the Institute and acceptability to the faculty. He listened to me quietly and carefully. He then said, 'We want some one like you for an outsider–insider perspective but you are not available. We need someone new to challenge the status quo. IIMA faculty is getting very self centered and even condescending. The time has come to get an outstanding outsider to shake them up. Continuous inbreeding can be harmful. I would like to induct someone from outside.' I came away feeling disturbed. I could see a certain determination and decisiveness, and yet I did not know why he had reached this conclusion. The brief interaction did not leave time for me to probe that question. But he had his reasons, maybe they came from feedback from some source in the Institute or outside, or some other source of information. He had sensed something that I had not and wanted to shake up the atmosphere. In a subsequent meeting, he asked me how I felt about I.G. Patel. I.G. was the governor of the RBI and he was due to retire. This made me think for a while. I had met I.G. on a couple of occasions at the RBI in connection with some policy issues relating to working capital norms. He certainly had a formidable reputation. Still, I was not fully convinced, although my initial reservation about bringing in an outsider had been chipped quite a bit. Someone like I.G. Patel coming to IIMA would certainly overcome the issue of acceptability. The real question that lingered in my mind was what it would do to the Institution's unique culture. As it turned out, I.G. had a brief but effective tenure.

When I.G. Patel received an invitation from LSE to accept its Directorship, he discussed the matter with Keshub. I.G. had felt honoured and excited to become Director of IIMA and had made a commitment to stay the full term of five years. This invitation from LSE created a dilemma for him. Keshub told him that the offer was not only a great career opportunity but an honour for the country as a whole and that he should therefore accept it not allowing his previous commitment to IIMA to stand in his way.

Then came the issue of reserving places on the BoG for SC/ST. The GoI sent a communication asking the Board to reserve two seats for SC/ST on the BoG. The BoG discussed the matter and suggested that the idea of the reservation of places at Board level was ill conceived. The directive was understandable at the level of staff positions because the Mandal Commission, which first recommended reservation, had meant it to create job opportunities for the backward classes. When it came to the selection of faculty or BoG nomination, merit should be the criterion. The BoG suggested that the Institute write to the Government asking them to reconsider the directive. The BoG minutes for that meeting are very brief. They are drafted with a view to not sounding confrontational nor do they attempt to define how the issue should be tackled. That would have tied the Chairman's hands on how to handle it. Instead, the words are couched in general terms. The real story however, is very revealing.

Some BoG members observed that to implement the GoI directive the MoA of the Society would have to be amended. If the Society members did not agree with this, then it would create an invidious situation. The GoI replied that as the matter had already been placed in the Parliament papers nothing further could be done. The matter came up before the BoG in the next meeting. Again the BoG expressed their unease on this point. After listening to everyone, Keshub proposed an approach. He said that we could tell the GoI that they could nominate SC/ST candidates to take two out of the four seats allotted to the GoI under the MoA. In this way, the GoI could fulfil its purpose and IIMA would not have to amend its constitution. Keshub concluded by saying that he would discuss the proposal with the Prime Minister, Morarjee Desai.

He made an appointment to meet with the Prime Minister but before seeing him, he called on the Education Minister. It was more of a courtesy call, but when he called on the Minister, he was not available. He waited for a while and then informed him that the matter related to the reservation of SC/ST seats on the IIMA BoG. He conveyed to the Minister that he foresaw a lot of problems and a tricky situation. The purpose of his visit was to keep him in the loop about the developments before he met the Prime Minister.

Afterwards, he met the Prime Minister. Morarjee Desai accepted the position, checked the situation, and found that this was not the recommendation in the Mandal Commission Report, which had been placed before Parliament, but in the cabinet note. This particular point had been inserted by the Education

Secretary. He assured Keshub that he would accept the solution proposed by him and that he would have the order suitably revised. Thus, a complicated and sensitive situation was skilfully resolved.

Vijay Vyas noted about his relationship with the Chairman, 'When I took over as the Director, the first thing I did was to go to Mumbai and meet Keshub Mahindra who was then Chairman of the IIMA Board. I told him that I had taken over as Director, and I would need his guidance and advice. He said "Vijay, don't expect any guidance or advice from me. If you have any problem you are most welcome to come and discuss it with me. You can see me at any time." He then called his secretary and said "Whenever Prof. Vyas comes to meet me, give him the top priority." Then he said, "It is for you to decide when you would like to meet me and ask for help. I am not going to tell you how you should run the Institute. It is your job, you have been hired for that". This was the type of Chairman any Director would look forward to work with. One who not only had high standing and was approachable, but also non interfering.

The nature of this relationship made it possible for the Director to adhere to certain important processes. IIMA faced a major challenge with respect to student admissions in the late 1970s. Vijay Vyas was the Director at the time and he has noted:

'I did not have the problem of some one pressurizing me for admission from the GoG, or industry because IIMA had already built a reputation that nothing could be done to facilitate someone's admission without due process. But once I got a call from the Prime Minister's office, and a senior officer from the PMO said that they would like to have the son of the Speaker of the Assembly of a friendly country admitted to PGP in IIMA. I said that to get admission, foreigner or Indian, everyone had to take an examination. The officer held a high position in the PMO and was also close to the Prime Minister. He said that what he was asking was in our national interest. I told him, "Sir, there are several ways by which we can serve our national interests. Giving admission in PGP to someone who has not completed the process is not the best way to serve our interests." I was quite firm but he continued to argue. Then I said, "Alright, give me in writing what you would like me to do and I will put it before my Board. I will request the Chairman of the Board to call a special meeting of the Board to discuss the matter." Of course, nobody gives such instructions in writing. And that was the end of the story. The Director should have the courage to stand firm, however influential the person is.'

This is how Keshub emboldened and provided unobtrusive support. I understand from Keshub that behind the scenes, he met with the ministry officials and succeeded in smoothing the ruffled feathers.

When I met Keshub Mahindra in August, 2008, and we discussed his IIMA years, his face lit up. After going over the episodes just described, I asked him for his views on what he felt IIMA should be doing now. He had two main suggestions. He felt that management of technology should be a thrust area. He agreed whole heartedly with me that management of R&D would become very important for Indian industry over the next decade or so. Industry is beginning to realize this. They want to learn and prepare their organization for this. His second point deals with government relations. He was fully aware that the government has become quite meddlesome in its approach and observed that this requires some deft handling. The Chairman and the BoG should handle this and continue to insulate the academic side of the Institute from outside meddling in academic matters. When dealing with government, it is always necessary to walk the thin line between capitulation and confrontation.

...AND THE LEADERSHIP 'DIVIDEND'

I have chosen IIMA's pioneering leaders for a somewhat detailed description. This is not meant as a comparative assessment. As mentioned before, these leaders built the culture of IIMA and left deep imprints. One can trace many subsequent developments to the culture, values, and operating philosophy adopted by these men. Throughout the years, our subsequent leaders have consolidated and developed the Institute on this foundation.

While all the Chairmen and Directors contributed immensely to building this unique institutional culture, we may note some landmarks. I.G. Patel pushed for expansion and brought in greater involvement from the local community. Narayana Murthy campaigned for greater autonomy and vigorously defended it. He also brought about greater alumni involvement. Pradip Khandwala started the process of financial self reliance. Jahar Saha protected the life and property of the IIMA community during the time of the massive earthquake in 2001 and consolidated the Institute's financial position. With I.G.'s help, he resolved the issue of the title of the adjacent plot of land and began constructing our second campus. Bakul Dholakia started new programmes, completed the construction of the second campus, and also dispensed with grants from the GoI. Samir K. Barua boldly exploited the 'value surplus' in the PGP programme and provided for a huge contingent liability of pension, and also weathered the enormous cost inflation unleashed by the Sixth Pay Commission. All of these leaders controlled costs and contributed to IIMA emerging as the first national institution to be completely self reliant and based almost entirely on internal resources.

As we have seen, a varied amalgam of values were implanted by each of these leaders. Kasturbhai Lalbhai brought frugality, trusteeship, and self-reliance. Vikram Sarabhai personified excellence, dignity, innovation, and experimentation. Ravi Matthai built trust, empowerment, academic integrity, and autonomy. Keshub Mahindra excelled in the management of boundary relationships. All of them built a sense of meritocracy, 'institute first', transparency, public spiritedness, and peer culture. Over the years, all these core values have helped IIMA to survive several crises and stand out as an institutional beacon in India. This is the unique DNA of IIMA.

7

Policies and Processes

In order to fulfil its mission and to ensure that matters of administration run smoothly, an institution needs to formulate a series of policies and processes as it develops. The core areas for an academic institution engaged in professional education are admissions, programme design, delivery, assessment and review, placement, and faculty recruitment and development. Of course, there are many more sub-areas such as faculty travel, leave and sabbatical, consultancy etc. In this chapter we will be focusing on the core areas.

THE ADMISSIONS POLICY AND PROCESS

IIMA has always been steadfast in its policy of admitting students strictly on merit. However, the definition of merit differs, with each programme. Merit has never been defined by any one single parameter. For the PGP, an admission committee of faculty members is formed and the members of this committee are rotated periodically. The admission process involves a close scrutiny of all applications, looking for conformity to shortlisting criteria, a common admission test, group discussions, and personal interviews. The minimum qualification is graduation from any branch. All applicants are required to take an admission test. This test used to be different for each IIM; it was first conduced as a common admission test (CAT) for all IIMs in 1977. CAT has been conducted online as a computer based test since 2009. CAT is held on multiple dates. Computerised CAT has ensured reliability, integrity, and convenience. It can now rank as one of the biggest online tests in the world. It has three testing components; quantitative, reasoning and logic, and language skills. Group discussions used to be a part of the process but they were dispensed with four years ago. An offer of admission is made based on application rating, test scores, a review of academic performance, and the candidate's performance in the interview.

Over the years, the value and prestige of the IIM PGP has skyrocketed. These days there is always a stampede of hopeful students desperate for a place on the programme. The number of students applying for IIMA has grown from 700 for the first batch to nearly 200,000 by now. Starting with a ratio of 15 applicants for every available place, now between 500 to 700 candidates apply for a single place. In a survey of various international business schools, The Economist of London rated IIMA as the most difficult place to get in. Throughout the last fifty years, there has not been one instance of any compromise in the admissions process. Whether the applicant is the son or daughter of one of our founding leaders or of a faculty member, no individual applicant is given preferential treatment. This has been one of the strong pillars on which IIMA has built its reputation. Of all the IIMs, Ahmedabad has always been the students' first preference.

This process has been tested several times in many high pressure situations. Take, for example, the case of an Irrigation Minister at the Centre. He wanted to award IIMA a consulting assignment on the Ukai Dam Project Management. He visited the campus in order to discuss the assignment. While he was closeted with Ravi Matthai, many faculty members waited around to meet him. Suddenly, he emerged from Ravi's office and left the Institute in a huff. Everyone was surprised. What happened was that he wanted admission for his son, and Ravi had responded by saying, 'let your son apply, and if he is good enough he will get in!'

I often used to get calls from leading industrialists asking for members of their family to be admitted. My response was always the same, 'admission to IIMA is strictly on merit. There is no "other" way. There is massive competition and only the best get in. If someone with less merit were to come in, it would destroy his own future. He wouldn't be able to cope with the studies. His relationship with the other students would also be warped. That would place him under tremendous psychological pressure and could lead to permanent damage to his personality or withdrawal due to a sub standard performance.' In the early years, these people thought this was a cock and bull story and believed instead that I was not prepared to help them. They were unhappy and angry, but over time these people have realized the importance of the sanctity of the process and such entreaties have been a thing of the past for many years.

A fairly recent example relates to one of the long duration programmes for executives. In one such programme, a close relative of a very high and powerful government functionary was interested in enrollment and the Director came under enormous pressure. He stated that he was trying to build an Institute based on merit and transparency. Although it was Executive Education, it still meant that it adhered to the norms that the Institute had announced for admission. He defied pressure, gave some tactical replies, and at the end of the conversation made it very clear that no matter what happened he would not compromise. One such instance of compromise, and the whole culture of merit and transparency would have evaporated.

While this merit based admissions policy has served the Institute well all these years, there is a need to take a deeper look at the socio-economic and regional profile of the students. Broadly speaking, most of the students come from urban English medium schools, often convent schools, from middle to high income families, and generally, at least one parent tends to be a college graduate. Children from such families tend to be highly motivated, the parents take keen interest and force their children to work hard in order to crack the CAT. They send their children to various coaching classes that provide training in cracking the CAT through an intensive drill of exams based on similar questions. It is an open question whether it is this motivation and practice which helps them to score highly in the CAT test. Statistically, it is hard to believe that all the talent would be concentrated only in this particular class of society which constitutes not more than ten per cent of the Indian population. I believe that the test reflects only the performance on that given day rather than a real potential for learning. The Institute therefore needs to take a few initiatives by way of extention activity. One possibility is to seek out good students from mofussil colleges, give them some orientation in soft skills, in English, and then set aside three seats based on this criteria rather than the CAT ranking. Such an experiment may reveal new insights in the merit testing exercise and the potential for learning.

FINANCIAL AID POLICY

Right from the beginning, IIMA followed the policy of providing financial aid to students coming from economically disadvantaged families. This was funded from the industry scholarship fund initially. It continued in a low key manner as the fees were low and the value kept on growing. No one found it difficult to finance it once an admission was secured. In the last five years, however, the fee increased nearly five-fold. The cost went up to Rs 12 lakh for the two year

PGP. The element of subsidy was eliminated as the Institute planned for financial self reliance. Despite the value of education, this would create a psychological barrier for many families. In keeping with our original policy, the Director proposed a liberal scheme to provide financial aid. The BoG were initially concerned about the high fees but when the details of the scheme were explained they endorsed it. In the year 2010, the total fee waiver came to Rs 10 crore and nearly 40–45 students admitted got full fee remission. Those who could afford did not need or get subsidized education.

PROGRAMME POLICY

Any institution engaged in professional education needs to have a policy on programmes. An institute may begin with a flagship programme, such as the PGP in the case of IIMA. The economic environment continues to change with the times, and as it changes it throws up new opportunities. At the same time, it also means that some programmes will either become obsolete or, at the least, may need extensive design changes. A policy on programmes therefore should cover a review of existing programmes, the exploration of the possibility of line extension of the existing programmes, and the design and development of new programmes.

New programmes have to be relevant to the needs of the client group which could be the corporate sector, the public sector, the social sector, or their subsegments. For example, in the case of the corporate sector, it could be start ups or small and medium enterprises. It could also be industry specific sectors such as health care or urban planning, etc.

It is also important to have a policy on the financial side of the programme. Some programmes take time to establish but overall, each programme has to be viable over a period of time. Some programmes may not be viable in the sense that the beneficiaries cannot fully bear the cost of the programme or the market is very narrow and specific. In such cases, the funding sources of the programme need defining before it is finally authorized. This funding could come in the form of donations, sponsors, or the general development fund available within the Institute. The costing of each programme should be independent of the funding sources. Unless this is done, the accountability and valuation of the programme will become steeped in confusion and ambiguity.

Looking at viability, the development phase of the programme has to be considered. Most programmes go through a period during which the market responds and then stabilizes. During that period, the programme design also evolves. Viability, therefore, needs to be assessed with reference to the expected stabilization period.

A process of authorization has to be established. A new programme passes through various stages. First, comes the conceptualization of the idea and its market assessment, then comes a detailed design and the bench testing of the programme model, followed by marketing and finally, execution and review. At each stage, there is a loop back into the earlier stage or stages. Authorization process can be devised in different manner for each of these stages. The most important being the first stage.

IIMA began with two programmes. The programme for business executives, which soon evolved as the 3–TP programme and the two year PGP, equivalent to MBA. These flowed from the Institute's core mission of professionalizing Indian management. They were oriented towards the business sector. As a part of the same mission, a Teacher's Training Programme was started to create a ripple effect. Short duration programmes were designed and offered in response to the perceived need of the market based on a 'gap' analysis. The earliest of these was a Programme on Managerial Economics (PME). All these programmes were designed to be practice oriented. The case method was the dominant pedagogy. This was based on the perception that most Indian academia focused purely on theory and as a result, was disconnected from the real world. The HBS method was expected to address this shortcoming. It was enthusiastically adopted and almost became a credo of the Institute. All the programmes and academic activities were designed around this.

Social Sciences offer analytical frameworks and Engineering Sciences provide solutions. Management as a discipline falls somewhere in between. It recognizes that each business situation is different and unique in terms of both context and time. It is dynamic and interactive. It realizes that the problem cannot be simulated in a laboratory. The best one can do is to take a snapshot of a problem situation, build various possible scenarios, and then develop possible solutions. The case method evolved as a pedagogical approach out of this recognition. The case method was more akin to clinical analysis than theoretical model building and as a result it was completely new to the initial faculty group. The method was not and could not be definitive, and ambiguity was always at its heart. To begin with, using the method was difficult and required training through exposure. The danger lay in developing simplistic solutions, or in becoming cynical and regarding every given solution plausible. However, after a year's exposure at HBS in the ITP, many members of the faculty became sensitized to the method and afterwards adopted it enthusiastically. Observing the HBS faculty in action both at HBS and IIMA, helped in developing insights and skills in handling the case method. This has stayed with the IIMA system in spite of several periods of doubt. In fact, healthy scepticism has only served to deepen the understanding of this method and refine its usage.

IIMA's programmes evolved through a periodic debate on the mission of the Institute. IIMA began with business oriented programmes. Soon, programmes aimed at the agricultural sector were developed in response to GoI initiatives, especially driven by enlightened ministers like C. Subramaniam. This happened also because both Vikram Sarabhai and Ravi Matthai believed that the Institute should always respond to the needs of the country and should refrain from looking at the environment through the HBS lens only. The development of the Teachers' Training Programme and agriculture sector programmes were an outcome of this perception.

Before Ravi decided to resign, he constituted a reorganization committee to look into the possibility of streamlining the various processes at the Institute. He perceived a certain amount of confusion and unease on the part of the faculty with the existing processes. As noted earlier, Ravi operated very informally. As the number of faculty increased and activities expanded, he began to see a need to formalize these processes. In his letter of resignation, he had mentioned the need to take a new look at the Institute's development. Given this context, the committee also deliberated on the mission of the Institute and the profile of the Director.

This Reorganization Committee provoked introspection and reflection on the direction that the Institute should take. The faculty felt that such an exercise was useful and should be periodically repeated. From this came the notion of establishing a Committee for Future Directions (CFD). This committee was supposed to be constituted once every ten years in order to review the mission, the activities, and chart out the direction that the Institute should take in response to the emerging environment. The first CFD headed by Dr Rangarajan submitted its report in 1977. The idea of sectoral specialization and institution building emerged from its recommendations.

Later, by the time the second CFD report came in 1983, the emphasis shifted a great deal to public policy issues. The next CFD in 1997, wanted to correct that tilt by reemphasizing the prime focus on economic enterprises and internationalization. Recently, in the last CFD formed in 2008 (Report date 2010), the emphasis shifted again towards self reliance focusing on size and scale.

While different views can be taken on the positioning of IIMA, the important thing is the convention of having periodic CFDs providing a transparent, deeply introspective process of review, generating a healthy debate and a directional path; tortuous and messy but in the final analysis self correcting. It also serves as an instrument for internal accountability.

My views on the positioning and programme policy are discussed in the final chapter of this book.

PROGRAMME DESIGN

At IIMA, the model of a pyramid of objectives is well entrenched in the Programme Design. Starting with the objectives of the entire programme, the design relates those objectives to the target audience, working down to course objectives, and then session objectives. This has always been a key element in the design of the programmes. This is reinforced by feedback from the programme participants. This discipline is a key factor in the IIMA system. I believe it originally came through the exposure of the initial group of faculty members to the methods and processes used and followed at HBS. It has stayed with the Institute ever since. It has provided protection against the design of programmes driven solely by dominant faculty interest. It has also provided protection against either an absence of objective or an unintegrated programme design. In other institutions, many programme failures can be traced to these shortcomings, but the system of programme review has enabled the IIMA to address such issues.

The Institute formed a policy to review each of its programmes. A comprehensive review was carried out for its PGP and 3-TP flagship programmes. At the end of the course, the Faculty Committee of the programme would meet and take stock of the situation from the perspective of defined objectives, problem areas relating to the courses, sequencing, topic selection, pedagogy, assessment, and administration. Student/participant feedback was an important element of this process. It helped to progressively refine these programmes. For example, the top tier of 3-TP was reduced from two weeks to one week and the second tier from four weeks to two weeks. This came in response to the increasing time constraints faced by executives at top and senior levels. Another example is the introduction of the capstone case. The faculty group realized that in an executive programme, the capstone case stimulates deep involvement of the participants and integrates their learning from all the subjects. Knowing this, the faculty decided to develop several major capstone cases which resulted in the development of two major case series on SBI and Larsen & Toubro.

The development of a new programme needs a long lead time. PGP X (Post Graduate Programme for Executives) took two years, from the day a Committee was formed, to go into the concept and design of the programme. The PGP-PMP (Post Graduate Programme in Public Management and Policy) programme took the same lead time. Generally, the idea for most medium to long duration programmes comes from either the Director or a senior faculty member. Then, the Director and a group of senior professors with strong external links, study the programme before accepting or declining the proposal. After that, an individual is chosen to champion the programme and a small group comprising a balance of various backgrounds is formed, care being taken to ensure that the group remains harmonious and free from any interpersonal tensions. Various parameters for the programme such as admissions, fees etc. are then researched by this group, and after they have come up with suitable answers, the Director applies his judgement and the final decisions is made.

THE ONE YEAR POST GRADUATE IN MANAGEMENT FOR EXECUTIVES (PGPX)

The genesis of PGPX can be traced back to January, 1993, when a taskforce was formed to design a Post Graduate Post Experience International Management Programme (IMP). The Faculty Council which discussed the report of the taskforce at its meeting in December, 1993, felt that it was premature for the Institute to start an IMP at that stage and the proposal was shelved. In March, 2001, the idea was revived and a proposal to launch an Executive MBA Programme was presented to the Faculty Council for approval. The Faculty Council discussed the proposal in September, 2001, but no decision could be agreed upon.

In February, 2004, Professor G. Raghuram, Chairman of a six member faculty committee constituted by the Director to examine various operational aspects of starting a programme for executives, submitted the committee's recommendations for starting such a programme to the Faculty Council which, after discussing the same in detail, accepted the proposal with additional inputs from them. A revised proposal incorporating these inputs was presented to the BoG for approval. The BoG cleared it at its meeting in April, 2004, and the One

Year Post Graduate Programme in Management for Executives (PGPX) was launched in April, 2006.

The objective of this Programme is to develop bright, enthusiastic, and aspirational executives to become management leaders and change agents in the global arena. The admission criteria is based on GMAT score, leadership profiling, and interviews. A high intellectual calibre, an entrepreneurial spirit, and a wide range of managerial and cultural exposure are all important attributes. The Programme aims to have an exciting mix of international and Indian participants and considering a large number of applicants come from the western countries, interviews are held not only in India but also in the US and the UK.

The launching of PGP PMP went through similar stages. The idea of starting such a programme arose from the fact that a large percentage of the faculty members were working in areas of public policy. This group would become somewhat isolated within the Institute if there was no such programme. As PGP was expanding, in-company programmes were thriving and PGPX was launched, there was a drive to organize more executive programmes. As a result, the members of faculty in conventional areas were busy and had a lot on their hands but the Public Policy Group did not have any substantial programmes. A PGP PMP type of programme at Bangalore which had been initiated by the GoI in cooperation with IIM Bangalore was not doing well. The Ministry was not happy. A senior official of the Finance Ministry approached the Director and the Director said, 'yes, we can do it'. But he also laid out the terms of admission and fees. He immediately sent out an outline of the programme design. The official came back saying that the admission process needed modifying. IAS officers could not sit for the test. The Director reacted by saying, 'this is a fundamental requirement, we cannot dilute this.' If the officers did not have that humility, then the learning process of the programme would be undermined. Secondly, he said that besides government sponsorship, there would also be open enrollment. His idea was to get as diverse a group as possible working in the public sector and the government. He stuck to this idea. Eventually, the GoI agreed.

PROGRAMME DELIVERY

Three things have helped a great deal with regard to programme delivery. The class of very bright students has ensured that faculty preparation is both hard and deep. Student/participant feedback has ensured that the faculty is fully aware of the students' perception of the effectiveness of the programme delivery. Finally, peer pressure within the Institute has worked indirectly to ensure that everyone consciously strives to teach more and more effectively. As noted earlier, the case method remains the dominant pedagogy. Over the years, the mix of lectures, case discussions, projects etc. has continued to change and evolve. However, I believe that not enough innovation or experimentation has been carried out in order to explore other ways of ensuring more effective delivery. We shall look at this in more detail later.

An important component of programme delivery has always been the mode of assessment. The Institute has followed a policy of leaving the assessment entirely to the faculty who delivers the programme or the course. Assessment can have many components, such as class participation, written tests, projects etc. The relative weightage of each of these components is left to the individual faculty member concerned. However, each faculty member is supposed to announce this to the class at the start of the course and the final assessment has to be turned in within a specified period after the course is finished. By and large, this process has worked well and instances of bias are taken care of through the mechanism of student feedback. Over the years, there have been very few complaints from the student body against any faculty member.

IIMA has followed a very healthy convention of periodically carrying out comprehensive reviews of various programmes. This is based on the observations of the programme faculty, student/participant feedback, client responses, and comments by faculty at large. These have resulted in improvements in programme design, development and incorporation of new content, innovation in pedagogy, and better assessment.

PLACEMENT POLICY

IIMA has long been a pioneer in organizing student placement as an important area of policy. Credit for this goes to Professor S.K. Bhattacharya who was the first Placement Chairman to accord it central importance and to organize placement policy on a sound footing. When no other educational institutions considered themselves responsible for launching and promoting the careers of their students, IIMA resolved to make it a key policy. Professor Bhattacharya systematically prepared a list of prospective companies, established contact with them, sensitized them to the design of programmes and the rigour with which they were delivered and the students assessed. He toured the whole country communicating this. Perhaps for the first time, an Indian educational institution invited companies to come on campus and interview the students. This is being continuously refined to take into account the need for diversity in placement, to analyse what companies are looking for, to loop these findings back into programme design, and to track the career of the students for the next few years. Assistance is also provided for in-career placement. Later, as the companies were vying with each other to recruit students, processes were designed to ensure that on one hand companies were not frustrated and, on the other, the students got a fair chance to decide which individual offer would be the best for them. It involved skilled tightrope walking, and several cases of heartburn. Lately, this has caused some unanticipated consequences in the larger context of student recruitment, fees, and placement activities across other institutions.

Recently, IIMA has revised the placement process by adopting the 'Cohort' system. As the number of students have increased, the day-based placement system creates huge logistics problems and enormous pressure on the students and the employers. Essentially, the new system staggers the process over a two month period and provides more time to students and the employers. The process provides for interactions over weekends, though background preparations are stretched out over two months. However, on balance this system appears to be more practical and less high pressure compared to the old day-based system.

THE FACULTY COUNCIL

As per the MoA, the Director is the Executive Head of the institution. The MoA does not define any other position except that of the Director and the Administrative Officer, who also acts as the Secretary to the BoG. Thus, all executive authority for decision making within the Institute is concentrated with the Director. However, starting from Vikram Sarabhai and Ravi Matthai, these Directors have built a peer culture and a collegial atmosphere. The Faculty Council is the centre piece in this. It was first conceived as the apex body for discussion and resolution of academic issues. The Council, in effect, emerged as the final arbiter on policy and other issues of contention. Although the agenda is set by the Director, any faculty member can bring up any issue relating to academic matters. The culture of faculty freedom has always been nurtured here. The Director's actions could be scrutinized, often vehemently criticized, and his viewpoint assailed. As one senior faculty member and former Director put it, 'it is a great place to learn about democratic habits in the right spirit, it comes up with the best decisions, and it reinforces the collegial structure and culture of the Institute.'

There are two ways in which important decisions can be taken. One way is for a faculty member or a group to raise an issue with the Faculty Council. The other comes about when the Director refers an issue to the Faculty Council for recommendation. The Director, as Chairman of the Faculty Council, will set the agenda, guide the discussion, sometimes manoeuver to block it, and then assess the collective views of the Faculty. The Faculty Council will then vigorously debate various aspects of the issue and often develop a recommendation. If a recommendation emerges, the Director will follow it.

Lately, however, the Faculty Council and its authority are being undermined. The Director tends to form small groups. These groups then make the decisions. The Faculty Council is the symbol of faculty autonomy. It has always been taken very seriously, ever since it was first established, and people have zealously guarded their freedom through the working of the Faculty Council. This is where people mobilize support for their ideas and debate fair practice. This is where the Director submits his authority to the collective wisdom of the faculty. Debates are heated and strong views are expressed. Of course, they are highly time consuming. The Council is often subject to lobbying and group pressures. Still, at the end of the day it acts as the central democratic forum in which the faculty collectively expresses its views, ideas, and recommendations. It is well known that, short of actually coming to blows, faculty members will fight tooth and nail in the Faculty Council but the next day you will see them talking animatedly in a friendly manner in the corridors. In other words, a true democratic culture has been built around the Faculty Council.

In an academic institution, faculty freedom is a basic value which fosters a creative atmosphere and a spirit of enquiry. Long ago, IIMA adopted the model of self regulation in academic matters. This decision was taken when it was not widely practiced in India with its hierarchical university system. The hierarchy consisted of the Vice Chancellor, the Principal of the College, the Head of the Department, Professor, Associate Professor or Reader, Asst. Professor, Senior Lecturer, and Lecturer. Each one in this hierarchy had a superior and a subordinate. At IIMA, Ravi Matthai did not follow this. While all IIMA faculty members had different pay scales, everyone had an equal say in academic matters. This attitude of equality was so ingrained that a newcomer or even many of the existing faculty members would neither know nor care about the grade or designation of their colleagues. Each one was called 'Professor' and each one enjoyed an equal say in academic matters.

Like HBS, IIMA also formed various functional areas such as Finance, Marketing, Economics, Organisational Behaviour, etc. Over the years, some areas were added and some were reorganized. The Area Chairman is appointed by the Director from amongst the area faculty or area members. This position was not hierarchical in character. The Area Chairman has no authority to direct Area members as to which courses to teach, which projects to pursue, which research study to undertake, or whether to appoint research assistants or teaching assistants. His role is simply that of coordinating Area activities, to provide the lead in the allocation of time in the various programmes of the Institute. In the early years, most Area Chairmen were frustrated by their lack of authority. They felt that they had a task to perform but no authority with which to enforce their decisions. The very title implied that they had to provide leadership to the members of the area in the pursuit of an academic task, yet they could not direct them. Initially, this created a great deal of confusion and irritation. Time and again, the issue landed on the desk of the Director. However, he steadfastly refused to give a decision to direct anyone. He insisted that the Area Chairman through interpersonal skills alone should resolve such issues. For any new course to be offered by an Area, the decision was to be taken through a consensus. If the faculty members proposing a new course could not build that consensus, then that course would not go forward. Broadly speaking, this is how the various Areas started and have continued to function ever since.

For overall academic matters whether relating to admissions, new programmes, or rules governing the faculty, there were two forums in which they were discussed. The Programme Committee of the respective programme and the Faculty Council. Programme related matters were resolved in the Programme Committee. Only in the case of serious differences or larger institutional issues, were these brought before the Faculty Council. It was considered to be the highest academic organ where contentious academic management issues could be discussed, debated, and resolved. We may recall how the issue of changing the timetable to accommodate Professor Vijay Vyas was handled by the Chairman of the 3-TP Programme, Uday Pareek.

At the same time, I have heard over the years that the Faculty Council has become a debating forum where issues are debated endlessly and, often, to scuttle any decision. I have also heard that many senior faculty members stopped attending the faculty forum. On contentious issues, faculty members avoided going to the Faculty Council. In Chapter 6, on Issues in Governance, we have seen an issue between a faculty member and a former Director regarding the approval for a foreign visit. Although the issue could have been taken to the Faculty Council, which in my opinion would have been the right forum, it was taken to the BoG and the Chairman. There may have been some special reason for doing so, but I have heard it over and over again that faculty members prefer to avoid taking many such contentious issues to the Faculty Council. This shows that the Faculty Council, as the final decision making or recommendatory authority, has probably lost ground over the years. It is somewhat ironic that a body which represents the ultimate in faculty freedom has lost its functionality even in matters where faculty freedom is concerned. The custodian has given up his prized legacy.

FACULTY RECRUITMENT AND DEVELOPMENT

Faculty Recruitment

The process of faculty recruitment at IIMA has gone through various stages. In the early years, the Director himself took personal initiative to contact potential candidates in US business schools, in business units, government departments, and universities in India and then exercised his discretionary authority to make offers. This was then placed before the BoG or the Personnel Committee for information/formal approval.

Later, the process was formalized and since then the process for recruitment has remained unchanged over the years. The sources for new applicants are varied. The nomination can come from various quarters. A faculty member might make a recommendation, an applicant himself might make an approach, the Director in his external interactions might come across someone, a member of the BoG might suggest someone—there are many sources from where such suggestions or recommendations may originate.

Once a suggestion or recommendation comes, the Director asks the candidate concerned to submit a formal application. After the application is received, it is circulated to the Area without revealing the name of the person or the channel through which the applicant has approached or his name has come. The Area then scrutinizes the application and gives an initial reaction or assessment. After the first filter—such as whether the applicant is a PhD, his research record, publication history etc.—the application moves to the next stage. If the Area for whatever reason turns down a name, then it will not proceed any further.

At the next stage, the Area asks for a seminar from the applicant. Prior to this seminar, there is a process of vetting the application. A Committee is formed. Three members of the Committee are from the Area, including the Area Chairman; Dean and a member of Faculty Development and Evaluation Committee (FDEC), who has some background in the subject in which the applicant has worked, are other members. If this Committee expresses further interest, the applicant moves on to the seminar stage. The seminar is attended by the Doctoral students and the Area members. The Director or the Dean may also suggest to some of faculty members, with experience in the same area or the related area, to attend the seminar. Each member who attends the seminar, completes a feedback sheet. This acts as a perfect check and balance because many people, apart from the sponsor of the applicant who might be the Area Chairman or an Area member, will be providing feedback. The process yields a collective assessment reflecting the views of a diverse group of faculty and not just a few people who may have a personal bias or interest in the applicant. The Dean and the FDEC member provide the feedback on the consensus view to the Director. The Area Chairman then makes a formal recommendation. This recommendation is finally accepted or rejected by the Director. In other words, the process neutralizes personal bias at several stages but it is the tact and sensitivity with which the Director handles this process that finally determines the neutrality of the outcome.

Faculty Development

In the early years, a great deal of investment was made in faculty development. For the first three years, about twenty-five faculty members were sent to HBS for the one year International Teachers Programme. Later, many were encouraged to pursue further studies for MBA or PhD in leading US Universities. Facilities were extended to encourage participation in national and international conferences. Sabbaticals were provided. Faculty members went on deputations in order to set up other institutions. A limited number were encouraged to take up assignments in the public and private sector for periods ranging from six months to a couple of years. Many faculty members were nominated to various GoI committees and taskforces at the request of the GoI. The Institute has followed a conscious policy of distributing consultancy assignments to younger faculty members. Such exposure flowing from a conscious policy has helped to develop the faculty.

PERFORMANCE ASSESSMENT

Some believe that the performance appraisal system in the Institute works very well as far as the confirmation and promotion to the level of Professor is concerned. Before the confirmation stage, the process which is followed is called the 'double referee system'. In other words, the work published or submitted by the faculty member is referred to one internal and one external expert for evaluation. Care is taken to ensure that this reaches the assessors without revealing the identity of the author. Their views are then put together, and the Director also takes the views of the FDEC and the Dean. Based on this, the decision of final confirmation is taken. A similar process is followed for the promotion of Assistant Professor to Associate and full Professor. In the opinion of one of the former Directors with a long association with the Institute, this filtering process has worked well. He states that the Director's job is to very carefully and tactfully convey the outcome to the faculty member concerned and the real test comes whenever there is bad news to be broken. The Director should be able to handle it in such a way that the faculty member about whom a negative decision is taken does not feel unjustly treated, or become disheartened, or feel that his work has not been properly evaluated. In fact, the faculty member should receive constructive suggestions as to how he can improve his performance. This is how the Director should manage the feedback session with his members of faculty.

FACULTY COMPENSATION

Faculty compensation was essentially determined by the GoI. Over the years, this has led to serious problems. The Institute adopted the process of topping up salaries with consultancy, in-company programmes, and incentivized excess teaching loads and research. Other solutions, including contractual appointments, have also been mooted. Many of these devices have brought about unforeseen consequences. Issues relating to this policy have already been discussed at length in the chapter relating to governance.

POLICY AND PROCESSES: SUMMING UP

Two or three important points emerge. One is the collegial culture, or the peer culture, that the Institute has fostered and its value. In part, this is a structural outcome but it is largely built on the processes enunciated and implemented by pioneers such as Ravi Matthai. There are certain basic values at the heart of such a design—all faculty members are equal, they can all participate as equals in the decision making process of the Institute, and the collective wisdom of the faculty must guide all major decisions, whether that be a matter of administration or of faculty evaluation. Merit, and only merit, should be the criteria. Processes must be built in terms of mutual trust and respect. Checks and balances should be designed so as to neutralize personal biases but, at the end of the day, they should not be so rule-bound as to breed a new bureaucracy. Disputes can often arise around interpretation. For every rule which is made, there will be many special cases and these special cases have to be handled on an individual case by case basis. The system cannot be so wooden that it does not recognize such reality and unforeseen situations. Systems and processes cannot be allowed to automate decisions, instead, they should be used only to aid the decision making. Tact and sensitivity are required to make all of these processes and systems work. Processes cannot be designed with potential misuse in mind, on the contrary they should be designed to optimize their use.

8

IIMA Finances

In 2001, Dr I.G. Patel, the Chairman of IIMA, asked the members of the Finance Committee, 'gentlemen, we have to build the new campus. We have selected the architect. The cost of the project is about Rs 38 crore. GoI funds may not be forthcoming. Can we go ahead and undertake the construction of the second campus?' The members of the Finance Committee gave a resounding response—'Yes. We can.'

The GoI initiated the establishment of IIMs as a part of its development strategy. Uniquely, in the case of IIMA, industry was made a partner for partial funding of the institution's infrastructure. This resulted in its association with the management of the institution. Given the commitment and involvement of the early industrial leaders, they were actively associated in the effective management of the Institute. Provision was made for nominating experts and other stakeholders in governance structures. Wise choices made by the GoI and industry brought in public spirited leaders such as Kasturbhai Lalbhai, Vikram Sarabhai, P.L. Tandon, Keshub Mahindra, and others. In turn, they made wise choices in selecting academic leaders like Ravi Matthai. Earlier, we noted the unique pioneering role played by these leaders in establishing IIMA. Funding was, but, a small part of the contribution they made. Far more importantly, the validity of the essence of a PPP model was demonstrated. The issue now is whether the same governance structure that was relevant at the start-up stage, a structure with such a dominant government role and driven largely by development strategy, remains the best arrangement now that times have radically changed. We have already discussed this matter in an earlier chapter.

Now that the original goal of developing such an institution has been achieved, the question of who should fund such education in the future assumes prime relevance. The funding pattern has to be examined from the angle of long term viability as well as growth and development. In this chapter, we examine these changes and what they signify.

HOW WAS THE INITIAL RESOURCE MIX DETERMINED?

As we have seen earlier, the initial resource mix was based on the budget estimates prepared by Dean Robbins. His budget estimates also contained his own views on the resource mix. His estimates and explanations are quoted verbatim on p.26.

BUDGET ESTIMATES

The partners based their contributions on these estimates. This was frozen and recorded in the first meeting of the BoG on February 28, 1962 and is mentioned for quick reference as follows.

1. 'The Government of India will provide 12 lakh of rupees annually for recurring expenses of the Institute;
2. The State Government of Gujarat will provide the land amounting to approximately 64 acres examined at Ahmedabad;
3. The local business community will provide up to Rs. 30 lakh as the need arises for buildings and locally procurable equipment;
4. The FF will provide dollar support for a programme which in its judgment will be adequate for the job to be done.'

   (Note: In that meeting, by way of clarification, it was observed:
   '(a) The term "local" is not appropriate, as the Institute is of an All India character and members of business and industry in the country as a whole are showing interest in promoting the Institute.
   (b) Locally procurable equipment will be the responsibility of State Government and Industry in the ratio of 50:50.)'

Source: IIMA records.

CONTRIBUTION FROM THE FF

The initial contribution from the FF was announced in a letter dated September 24, 1962, to Jivraj Mehta, the Chief Minister of Gujarat and the Chairman of the

IIMA. This contribution has been discussed earlier in Chapter 2. p.38. The detailed break up of the grant under various heads was clearly spelt out. (see Appendix).

SNAPSHOT OF THE FINANCIAL JOURNEY

Starting with this resource mix, IIMA has traversed ground breaking terrain. The changes in the pattern of the resource mix are a reflection of the changes in the environment for management education, the policies of the GoI, internal policy, and the growth of the Institute. These changes also reflect the latent tension between GoI control and institutional policies and aspirations. Since the early days, new, strong stakeholders such as the alumni and faculty have emerged. The roles of all these various stakeholders have changed too.

The balance between external and internal funding has been reversed. Greater self reliance has instilled not only new confidence but also an unexpected assertiveness. The conflict between the 'control' of the GoI, derived from the original MoA, and the aspirations of institutional autonomy has emerged as a central issue in recent years.

When IIMA was first established, education, both traditional and professional, was thought of as a social activity. Predominantly, the government was supposed to fund it. At IIMA, the GoI committed to fund the current deficit. In other words, the underlying idea was that even this form of professional education should be made available at an 'affordable cost'. Hence, the government subsidy.

Right from the beginning, the Institute adopted the principle that financial support would always be made available to those students who had been accepted but needed financial aid to pursue their education. An industry scholarship-cum-loan programme was initiated from the early years, which would even help to finance the modest subsidized fees.

It did not take long for the value of this education to become clear for all to see, as it was soon demonstrated by the success of student placement and their initial salaries. Still, the subsidy policy persisted. This subsidy to students came in the form of a government grant. Having grown used to this government grant, even the BoG did not examine the issue of the 'economic' value of this education or question the need for subsidy. Government grant acted as a sedative.

When the GoI began reviewing their policy of subsidizing professional education, grants became subject to deep scrutiny and basic questions about the cost and benefits were raised. Who benefited? Who should pay for the benefit? By focusing on high value addition, could the governmental grant be substituted by student loans without jeopardizing access to students from less privileged homes? In short, the very basis of policy for funding higher professional education came into sharp focus.

Internal pressure began to mount as the issues of faculty compensation and institute expansion came up. The pinch of GoI control was felt and this led to an examination of the value of IIMA education and the implied proposition of substituting government accountability by market accountability. IIMA was demonstrating its capacity for self reliance.

A few questions about the choice of resource mix still persist.

1. What is a desirable resource mix, given the need for growth and continuous upgrading of the infrastructure?
2. Is it possible to be totally self reliant, i.e., depend solely on internal funding?
3. To what extent, if need be, can it be supplemented from 'quasi internal' funding i.e. alumni contributions, merchandizing, and other product sales?
4. To what extent, if any, can private philanthropy fill the gap? How can this be actively tapped?

FINANCIAL MODEL FOR MANAGEMENT EDUCATION

As we saw earlier in Chapter 2, resource mix fundamentally defines the rights of the initial promoters. Over time, resoruces from different sources have to be raised. A wise balance has to be struck between security, resource head-room, and degrees of freedom. This poses a challenge of accomodating the rights of the new providers with those of the initial promoters.

Institutions require funding for infrastructure, research and renewal, activity expenses, administration and other contingencies. In institutions of management education, there are four categories of beneficiaries— students, knowledge users (often corporate), skilled talent seekers, and general society. If the model is to be self sustaining then there has to be a certain value for each one of the beneficiaries; an enriched career for students, project outcomes for corporate users, ready availability of trained manpower for the economy (all sectors—business, social, and public), and society as a whole by expanding the knowledge pool. A method needs to be developed by which all of these can be reasonably measured. Granted, the precise measurement of value for each beneficiary may not be possible. The vexing question is who should pay, and how much should they pay for these 'benefits'. This issue is debated the world over. For professional education, the beneficiaries have to bear the bulk of, if not the entire, considerable cost. For other programmes, the costs are borne by different beneficiaries or stakeholders. This is especially true in the case of research universities. As education has become increasingly expensive, and as higher education in particular has become more pervasive, the costs have soared. The State is finding it difficult to bear this cost. The debate over who should bear how much has become more and more fierce. However, that is a different debate.

For a professional educational institution, the costs including research costs should be borne by the beneficiaries. One proviso for this is the cost of land. Professional institutions have to be located near the major centres of economic activity. The cost of land in urban or suburban centres is very high. The acquisition of large areas of land is a tortuous process. Many honest initiatives find themselves running aground on this front. Government aid for land is a basic enabler. It is a part of the development strategies of the GoI and of most State Governments.

For management education, the financing model can be developed around the idea that direct beneficiaries should bear the bulk of these costs. In that case, the resource mix would be student fees, 'product' sales, project funding from corporate and beneficiary sectors, infrastructure by philanthropists, and land by government or philanthropists.

Let me explain 'product' sales in the context of management education. Many research universities these days build equity around their research output and convert it into income streams through the creation of businesses. HBS has long been a pioneer in creating such streams of revenue. They have converted their knowledge into valuable products—cases, HBR (Harvard Business Review), and books. Their publication activities generate nearly thirty per cent of their annual revenue. Such a source of revenue remains largely untapped in Indian institutions, due either to a lack of research with real 'product value' or a lack of suitable marketing.

After the institution begins functioning, another stakeholder group develops—alumni. Owing to their past association with the institution and the education and experience they receive, a strong bond develops. In educational institutions around the world, one can notice how these bonds develop into strong support groups which even traverse national boundaries. Take, for example, the case of Anand Mahindra who was moved to donate USD 10,000,000 to the Humanities Centre at Harvard.

So, these possible sources of revenue can be viewed as 'transactional' funding comprising of fees, 'product sales' and project funding, 'emotional' funding by alumni, 'memorial' funding by philanthropists, 'brand' funding by corporates, and 'seed' funding by governments and corporate interests.

Such a balanced approach provides stability and long term viability. It protects against ingress and ensures a degree of freedom to deliver value to each group of beneficiaries. If the institute stumbles or fails in delivering value, its future is doomed. The value surplus then generates the 'goodwill bank', which is essential for long term security. Such an approach needs to be clearly reflected in the structure of governance.

PUBLIC POLICY, FUNDING PATTERN, AND GOVERNANCE STRUCTURE

Fees and Grants

Governments generally consider education as a social responsibility as well as a tool to promote equity. In the past, all education, including professional education was subsidized. Even education that led to creating the capacity for direct and immediate income earning was subsidized. Later in the 1980s, as the cost of higher education began to spiral, governments began to feel the resource crunch. Questions over indiscriminate subsidization as a policy were raised. Should higher education be subsidized? Shouldn't the private sector also be enjoined to share the burden? As the chief beneficiaries will be receiving an education that will increase their lifetime earning potential and better their careers, should they not bear the burden either up front or in the form of student loans against future income?

IIMA students soon began commanding attractive salaries after graduation. In other words, the value addition of the programme was well established and clearly visible for all to see. Still, the proposition that the students, as beneficiaries, should bear the cost of the programme was not accepted. Even I.G. Patel had great difficulty in accepting this proposition. Like many others, he believed that education provides one of the ways by which equity can be promoted in society. Based on this, it was argued that the students and their parents should not be burdened with high fees or by loans. Shrenikbhai and I had strongly argued with him that in view of the fact that our students could command such high salaries on graduation, the Institute could charge higher fees and help them to secure loans from the banks. This proposition would be most valid for terminal professional education where the students enter the job market immediately after completion of their studies. We cited the example of the US experience and the student loan scheme. I mooted the idea with HDFC in 1994, who started extending student loans to five different institutions. Even so, there was still a great resistance to allowing any increase in fees.

But as student placement salaries steadily became heftier, the viewpoint that there was no real justification in subsidizing this form of education began to take root. The GoI then decided to cut back the grant, which put the Institute under severe pressure. Finally, they came up with the idea of the block grant. The block grant meant that the grant became detached from the gap between the recurring expenses and income. It was pegged to a certain figure, irrespective of the changes in recurring expenses or income. This forced the Institute to review the fees structure and the first major fee revision came about in 1993. At that time, Pradip Khandwalla as Director had argued with Arjun Singh, the HRD Minister at the time, that instead of awarding the grant, the Institute should be enabled to build corpus so that they could become financially self reliant. This, then, was the genesis of the matching grant scheme. Surplus was defined in a certain way. Such institutional surplus should be transferred to corpus and the GoI would give an equal amount in the form of a corpus grant. This was called the matching grant and came over and above the recurring grant. The Institute received this matching grant for just a couple of years, although the scheme was originally supposed to remain in force for five years. This sent an important signal. Policy changed and instead of relying on the GoI for an ever increasing subsidy for the PGP programme, it was agreed that the Institute could charge higher fees. The GoI accepted that the costs for the programmes could be recovered by raising the course fees. This also forced the Institute to look into other methods of augmenting income and controlling costs. The Institute tested the pricing assumptions for the EDPs and gradually increased its fees too. It began to charge fees for placement and for admission tests, and a small surplus was also generated by the residential facilities of the Institute.

Discussion on finances is inevitably linked to governance. The question of who should pay for higher professional education lies at the heart of this discussion. This relates to both the recurring or running expenses of the Institute as well as capital expenditure. Those who provide the funds will have a direct or indirect role in governance.

SHIFT IN FUNDING PATTERN: EXTERNAL TO INTERNAL

Often many members of the governing body of education institutions do not seriously engage in discussions about finances. Many people prefer to concentrate on objectives and policies, believing that numbers and figures are too mundane and dull. However, financing patterns reveal the ideology, the objectives, values, and motives, and define the parameters of relationships. While looking at the financing patterns and tracking them over a period of time, one can learn a great deal about governance as well as the basis of decision making and the eventual outcomes of those decisions. Truly, these financial statements are a summary or the epitome of the aggregate decisions made by the authorized persons over a period of time. Careful study of these can reveal strengths and weaknesses, foundations and cracks ahead of time.

The analysis of the decade by decade changes in the resource mix, clearly brings out a major shift in the funding pattern.

INDIAN INSTITUTE OF MANAGEMENT, AHMEDABAD

INCOME & EXPENDITURE ACCOUNT

(in lakhs)

	2010-11	Ratio of Total Income	2009-10	Ratio of Total Income	2003-04	Ratio of Total Income	1999-2000	Ratio of Total Income	1993-94	Ratio of Total Income	1989-90	Ratio of Total Income	1979-80	Ratio of Total Income	1969-70	Ratio of Total Income	1965-66	Ratio of Total Income
Net Income from LDPs	4280	54%	3851	56%	511	18%	330	11%	61	8%	-11	-3%	-5	-5%	0	1%	0	-1%
Net Income from MDPs etc	1038	13%	667	10%	233	8%	163	5%	118	15%	28	7%	7	7%	2	6%	0	3%
Net Income from Consultancy etc	656	8%	470	7%	190	7%	150	5%	30	4%	16	4%	5	4%	1	3%	0	1%
Other income	1552	19%	1448	21%	841	30%	314	10%	148	19%	82	21%	20	18%	6	21%	2	16%
Interest Income	433	5%	425	6%	1031	37%	914	30%	88	11%	0	0%	0	0%	0	0%	0	0%
Internal Income	7959	100%	6861	100%	2806	100%	1871	61%	445	56%	115	29%	26	24%	8	31%	3	20%
Grants	0	0%	0	0%	0	0%	1200	39%	349	44%	275	71%	82	76%	19	69%	12	80%
Total Income	7959	100%	6861	100%	2806	100%	3071	100%	793	100%	389	100%	108	100%	27	100%	15	100%

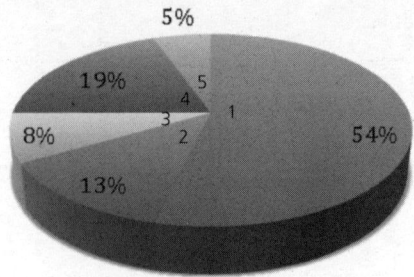

% of Total Income 2010-11

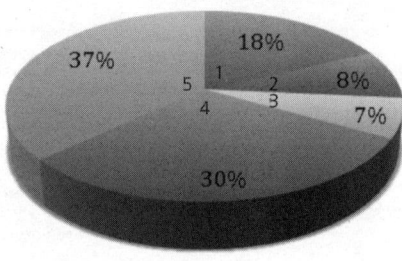

% of Total Income 2003-04

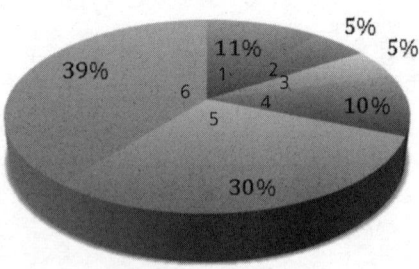

% of Total Income 1999-00

% of Total Income 1993-94

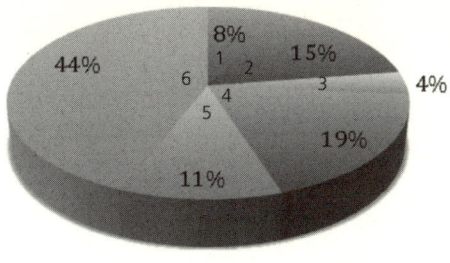

8%
1
2 15%
6
4 3 4%
5
44%
19%
11%

% of Total Income 1989-90

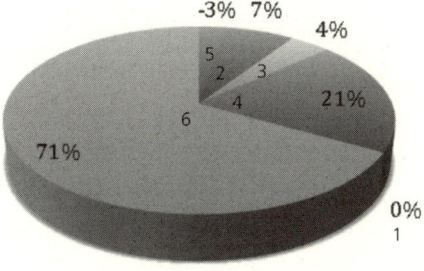

-3% 7%
5 4%
2 3
6 4 21%
71%
0%
1

Legend:

1 Net Income from LDPs

2 Net Income from SDPs(EDPs)

3 Net Income from Research and Consultancy

4 Other Income

5 Interest Income

6 Grants

Note: Net income here is the gross income of the activity minus the related direct expenses. Figures in Chapter 1 refer to the Gross income.

INDIAN INSTITUTE OF MANAGEMENT, AHMEDABAD

Funds & Liabilities	2010-11		2009-10		2003-04		1999-2000	
Trust Fund / Corpus		5549.02		5110.52		9828.68		7264.02
Reserves & Surplus / Income & Expenditure A/c		64.26		59.62		2015.19		0.11
Other Earmarked Funds		25006.48		21744.70		7117.05		5738.47
Current Liabilities & Provisions								
Current Liabilities:								
Statutory Liabilities	41.78		203.15		31.64			
Other Current Liabilities	4365.77		5973.08		1530.45	1562.09		620.37
	4407.55		6176.23					
Provisions:								
Retirement Benefits	3780.96	8188.51	2439.69	8615.92				
Total		38808.27		35530.76		20523.01		13622.97
Assets								
Fixed Assets								
Immovable Properties	10477.01		9440.60		2693.67		1203.45	
Movable Properties	5336.88		5065.01		2508.85		1566.80	
Gross Block	15813.89		14505.61		5202.52		2770.25	
Less: Depreciation Fund	8639.88		7485.75		2676.29			
Net Block		7174.01		7019.86		2526.23		2770.25
Investments		29401.12		25405.40		16633.70		9682.96
Current Assets, Loans & Advances								
Current Assets:								
Stores	7.97		7.17		32.43		2.24	
Cash & bank balances	848.45		959.66		188.90		37.23	
	856.42		966.83		221.33		39.47	
Loans & Advances:								
Employees, Students & Others	366.29		632.19		254.03		500.64	
Income Accrued	765.17		604.32		884.40		623.78	
Deposits & Other Assets	245.26		218.84		3.32		5.87	
	1376.72	2233.14	1455.35	2422.18	1141.75	1363.08	1130.29	1169.76
Debit balance of Income & Expenditure A/c.				683.32				
Total		38808.27		35530.76		20523.01		13622.97

1993-94		1989-90		1979-80		1969-70		1965-66	
	319.63								
	0.02		0.12		0.50		0.02		0.98
	3223.64		1970.35		775.84		172.52		74.54
	421.87		225.54		77.12		11.40		8.53
	3965.16		**2196.01**		**853.46**		**183.94**		**84.05**
1020.96		791.67		412.48		112.73		48.67	
701.95		438.30		142.86		27.46		11.63	
1722.91		1229.97		555.34		140.19		60.30	
	1722.91		**1229.97**		**555.34**		**140.19**		**60.30**
	1934.71		**778.19**		**249.44**		**0.01**		
2.82		1.70		0.96		0.08		0.22	
25.84		53.04		20.28		32.41		20.89	
28.66		**54.74**		**21.24**		**32.49**		**21.11**	
83.55		62.56		22.19		10.37		2.10	
194.15		68.91		4.01		0.67		0.38	
1.18		1.64		1.24		0.21		0.16	
278.88	307.54	133.11	187.85	27.44	48.68	11.25	43.74	2.64	23.75
	3965.16		**2196.01**		**853.46**		**183.94**		**84.05**

As we look at IIMA's financial statements, three distinct phases become clearly apparent. The first phase—where GoI support in the form of grants was dominant; this lasted until the year 1993-94. The second phase—where continuing GoI support came under review and the Government grant was frozen; this lasted until 2003-04. In the third phase, a self-reliant financial model emerged from 2003–04 onwards.

The first phase takes us from the inception of the Institute right up to 1993. During this period, the GoI grant was the main source of IIMA finances for recurring expenses. Generating revenue took a back seat. The issue of whether there was any scope or justification in raising fees never came under scrutiny. After the first campus was more or less complete, capital expenditure was incremental and mainly confined to the creation of the IT infrastructure.

The second phase covers the ten years from 1993 to 2003. These ten years mark a significant shift from government grants to greater self reliance for both recurring expenses and capital expenditure. This was done through a combination of factors. Tuition fees were increased, other income was boosted, costs were controlled, and income from investment soared. By 2003, the Institute had become more or less completely self reliant.

The third phase begins in 2003. From that date onwards, the Institute neither sought, nor received any grant for recurring expenses. IIMA became completely self reliant as far as recurring expenses were concerned. When it came to capital expenditure, the Institute relied on its own internal resources. The building of the new campus was paid for by the Institute's own internal resources. Work on the new campus began when I.G. Patel was the Chairman. The Institute had approached the GoI for a grant in order to build the new campus, but apart from a small grant of Rs. 2 crore, for an international business centre, no other funds were forthcoming. I.G. Patel asked the Finance Committee members whether the Institute could go ahead with building the campus and whether it had sufficient resources. The Committee reckoned that this was possible and gave a green signal. The idea of raising money through donations from alumni and industry was mooted but it never came to fruition. A high power Alumni Committee was formed. In short, except for the expansion necessitated by the GoI decision to increase seats for the students belonging to 'other backward castes'(OBC) in 2008, the Institute financed the capital expenditure wholly from its own internal sources. Even for the capital expenditure for accommodating these additional seats, the funds which came by way of a government grant for capital expenses were inadequate and had to be supplemented by the Institute's own internal resources. So it was that the period from 1993 onwards saw a major transformation of IIMA's finances.

Fees were brought into alignment with the rising costs of the Institute. This led to a huge hike in fees, which was buttressed by an expanded programme of financial aid. Fees for the executive programmes also increased and income from student placement, CAT, and the hostel facilities grew. Costs were tightly controlled, but major ad-hoc expenses continued to rise; pensions needed to be provided for, and the Sixth Pay Commission report placed a huge burden on the Institute. The Institute managed to cope with all these expenses, and fully provided the entire liability for the pension scheme, all from internal resources. IIMA is one of just a handful institutions, which have provided pensions entirely from their own internal resources. As a result of all these concerted efforts on revenues and costs, the Institute now has an investment portfolio worth nearly Rs 300 crore.

In the first phase, accountability came through the budget approval and grant negotiation process. In the second, it began shifting towards market accountability as the fees began to be looked at from the angle of value addition. Even so, the budget and grant process was still active. In the third, market accountability predominated as the grants came to an end; both for recurring and capital expenditure (Capex). Market accountability came in the form of fees based on value addition, need assessment, the design of new programmes, and the exploration of endowment funding for future stability and growth. The form of governance remained unchanged but the underlying power had shifted. A new accountability framework was needed and IIMA proposed this to the GoI in 2005 as part of the plan to modify the structure of governance.

In other words, as the public policy on the funding of higher professional education began to change, the financial management of the Institute also changed. The financial records clearly show this to be the case.

Over the last twelve years, IIMA has spent Rs 133 crore on Capex. Its investment portfolio has grown by nearly Rs 300 crore. It provided Rs 37.8 crore for retirement benefits. In this period, the total grant received from the GoI was Rs 43.65 crore towards the block grant and matching grant, and Rs 10.68 crore towards capacity expansion for meeting the obligation under the OBC reservation. Other external funding in the form of donations was only about Rs 15 crore. In order to achieve this, IIMA tapped the 'value reservoir' of its programmes. IIMA is now not only operationally self reliant, it has also started to secure its future growth and development.

FUNDING FOR OPERATING COSTS

We can divide our analysis of IIMA's finances into two parts—how the capex was financed and how the Institute's recurring expenses were financed. Initially, this pattern strictly reflected the constitution. As we have seen, the land was provided by the GoG, the initial building expenditure was provided by industry, the cost of equipment was to be shared between the GoG and industry. The foreign exchange component of recurring expenses such as visits of HBS faculty to India, faculty development visits by Indian faculty to Harvard, and library books were provided by the FF. The GoI had agreed to provide the grant to bridge the gap between recurring expenses and actual and eventual income. In the first year, this was pegged at Rs 12 lakh. This pattern is captured in the balance sheet of the first full operational year of IIMA.

The GoI provided a grant for recurring expenses. This worked on a simple formula; recurring expenses minus income equal to the grant. The Institute was supposed to prepare a budget and project the gap between recurring expenses and income, and submit the same for authorization of the grant. In view of the grant provided by the GoI, it was stipulated that the accounts of the Institute would be subject to a CAG audit. This is how the GoI exercised its check on expenses.

INDIAN INSTITUTE OF MANAGEMENT, AHMEDABAD
INCOME & EXPENDITURE ACCOUNT

	2010-11	% of Total Net Income	2009-10	% of Total Net Income	2003-04	% of Total Net Income	1999-2000
Contribution from LDPs	4280.23	56.9%	3851.04	59.8%	510.95	28.8%	330.28
Contribution from MDPs etc	1037.70	13.8%	667.12	10.4%	233.12	13.1%	162.52
Contribution from Consultancy etc	656.17	8.7%	469.72	7.3%	189.92	10.7%	150.45
Other Income	1117.47	14.8%	855.49	13.3%	291.92	16.4%	208.44
Transfer from Funds	434.34	5.8%	592.70	9.2%	549.25	30.9%	105.40
TOTAL NET INCOME (A)	7525.91	100.0%	6436.07	100.0%	1775.16	100.0%	957.09
EXPENDITURE							
Establishment Expenses	4593.01		4840.96		1197.27		1026.82
Other Administrative Expenses	1086.27		923.87		514.5		237.72
TOTAL EXPENSES	5679.28		5764.83		1711.77		1264.54
Operating Surplus before Depreciation	1846.63		671.24		63.39		-307.45
Depreciation	1157.44		1146.39		284.97		
Net Operating Surplus (deficit)	689.19		-475.15		-221.58		-307.45
Interest Income	432.99		424.66		1030.52		913.58
Net Internal Accruals	1122.18		-50.49		808.94		606.13
Grants	0.00		0.00		0.00		1200.00
Excess of I over E - Total	1122.18		-50.49		808.94		1806.13
Cash Flow w/o Grant	2279.62		1095.90		1093.91		606.13
Cash Flow with Grant	2279.62		1095.90		1093.91		1806.13

The table brings out the percent-wise contribution of different activities.

The Institute found this stipulation of the CAG audit both irksome and somewhat unnecessary. The Institute functioned as a not-for-profit service organization. Costs were incurred on activities, which brought in revenue. In operating such an organization, flexibility and judgment were necessary and the GoI audit would constrict this. The Institute had appointed its own auditor, a reputed firm of Chartered Accountants, and felt that CAG audit was not required over and above the audit by the Institute's own auditors. The way this issue of the CAG audit was handled reveals an important difference in the approach by the GoG at IIMA when compared to other similar institutions. Vikram Sarabhai argued that in the case of TIFR and PRL, the GoI had accepted an audit by a reputed private firm of auditors with the stipulation that CAG could test check the accounts, to certify that the GoI grant had been spent on the purpose for which it had been originally disbursed. The same ruling should therefore apply to IIMA too, it was only fair. This argument was accepted by the GoI in November, 1963. Later, when the issue came up again, Ravi Matthai argued that IIMA should be exempt from the CAG audit under the rule that the same was applicable to institutions receiving more than fifty per cent of its expenses in the form of a grant. IIMA generated over fifty per cent income from sources other than the GoI grant. So it was that since the very beginning, IIMA's auditor was appointed by the BoG.

(`in lakhs)

% of Total Net Income	1993-94	% of Total Net Income	1989-90	% of Total Net Income	1979-80	% of Total Net Income	1969-70	% of Total Net Income	1965-66
34.5%	60.58	17.0%	-10.89	-9.5%	-5.19	-19.6%	0.24	2.8%	-0.09
17.0%	118.46	33.2%	27.75	24.2%	7.06	26.7%	1.70	20.1%	0.41
15.7%	30.29	8.5%	16.21	14.1%	4.64	17.6%	0.91	10.8%	0.14
21.8%	101.39	28.4%	48.23	42.1%	5.43	20.6%	1.57	18.6%	0.05
11.0%	46.19	12.9%	33.34	29.1%	14.48	54.8%	4.02	47.6%	2.35
100.0%	356.91	100.0%	114.64	100.0%	26.42	100.0%	8.44	100.0%	2.86
	404.79		290.4		73.13		18.81		9.58
	134.47		98.64		33.00		8.37		4.6
	539.26		389.04		106.13		27.18		14.18
	-182.35		-274.40		-79.71		-18.74		-11.32
	-182.35		-274.40		-79.71		-18.74		-11.32
	87.83		0.01		0.05		0.04		0.01
	-94.52		-274.39		-79.66		-18.70		-11.31
	348.74		274.51		81.96		18.70		11.80
	254.22		0.12		2.30		0.00		0.49
	-94.52		-274.39		-79.66		-18.70		-11.31
	254.22		0.12		2.30		0.00		0.49

The share of LDP to total contribution and grants has climbed from a negative figure (in %) up until 1989–90 to a positive figure of more than 55 percent in the last few years. This is down due to the impact of the PGP fee increase and the introduction of new LDPs like PGPX and PGP–PMP. On the other hand, the share of executive education i.e. MDPs had been high in the 25–30 percent range up until the early 1990s. Since 1993–94, it has consistently gone down to touch about 12 percent over the last two years. Consultancy and research projects follow a more or less similar pattern. In other words, the Institute has relied increasingly on LDP fees in order to consolidate its finances.

In terms of the contribution of various programme categories, PGP has made the highest contribution since the introduction of the block grant scheme and it has continued to do so even after the grants stopped. Other LDPs have contributed less. However, LDPs taken as a whole have consistently maintained a far higher contribution when compared to MDPs. This reflects the relative pricing power of IIMA for PGP compared to executive education. It reveals a serious weakness in the Institute's strategy and capability. Most research driven business schools have been able to garner a larger share of the total revenue and also higher contributions from their executive education programmes. Institutions like IMD (Lausanne) survive and thrive on it and so does HBS, whose income from executive education programmes is nearly 25 percent compared to less than 20 percent for MBA.

Grants reached a high of Rs 12 crore in 1999–2000. The final grant of Rs 8 crore was received in 2002–03.

The GoI had asked IIMA not to provide for depreciation, arguing that as the GoI funded deficits there was no need to provide for it. This policy changed in 2001–02 when the GoI asked the Institute to provide for depreciation. In the first four years of the new century, there was an operating deficit before depreciation, interest earned, and grants received.

Interest was the mainstay that helped to keep IIMA afloat and gradually build cash reserves. In terms of cash flow when interest earned is accounted, it has been positive for the last ten to twelve years ranging from Rs 6 crore per year in 1999–2000 to Rs 17 crore in 2007–08. Even after financing the new campus, and the consequent drop in interest income, the cash surplus still remained positive in the range of Rs 10–17 crore. It dropped to Rs 5 crore in 2008–09 owing to the first impact of the tremors of the Sixth Pay Commission. It has recovered over the last two years with a surge in PGP income from increased numbers and higher fees.

INTEREST INCOME AND THE MANAGEMENT OF INVESTMENTS

As we can see from an examination of the accounts, interest income has been substantial over the last twenty years.

INVESTMENTS AND AVERAGE RATE OF INTEREST
(1999–00 TO 2010–11)

Year	Invest-ment	Total Interest	Average Rate of Interest (%)	10 Yr G-Sec yield	Difference
	Average				
2010-11	27403	2207	8.05%	7.99%	0.06%
2009-10	22733	1878	8.26%	7.83%	0.43%
2008-09	18823	1698	9.02%	7.01%	2.01%
2007-08	17231	1435	8.33%	7.96%	0.37%
2006-07	16957	1423	8.39%	7.98%	0.41%
2005-06	16638	1527	9.18%	7.55%	1.63%
2004-05	16436	1662	10.11%	6.69%	3.42%
2003-04	15693	1710	10.90%	5.16%	5.74%
2002-03	14313	1716	11.99%	6.15%	5.84%
2001-02	12868	1587	12.33%	7.43%	4.90%
2000-01	10773	1384	12.84%	10.17%	2.67%
1999-00	8496	1188	13.98%	10.79%	3.19%

All investments were handled by the Finance Committee. The Finance Committee was predominantly made up of local members of the BoG from the Society constituency. The Chairman has always been a senior member of the BoG. These members served long terms, providing a sense of much needed continuity. The Finance Committee has always been very active and has provided advice on policy as well as execution. The yield on the investments of IIMA, as has been noted elsewhere, has been far greater than the G-Sec (GoI Securities) yield and far more than any other IIMs. This has happened because of the close watch that the local members representing the Society have always kept on the investment policy and its execution. No doubt they have taken a few calls which, though safe, were not as secure as G-Sec. For example, in the 1980s and 1990s, many public sector undertakings—both State and Central— had come out with deposit programmes and issued bonds which gave a higher yield. The Finance Committee decided that wherever a State Government or the Central Government guarantee was available, it could invest in the bonds or deposit in order to maximize the yield. Later, some members of the BoG felt that even these guarantees might go into default and therefore we should get out of these investments. The Institute had followed a policy of holding these investments to maturity thereby protecting the capital against the risk of fluctuating interest rates and the bond price. It needs to be noted that there had been no default in these investments including the investment in the Industrial Finance Corporation, which had to be rescheduled but was honoured fully. As a result, the yield on Institute investments had been consistently higher by a substantial margin over the G-Sec yield. This is an example of the commitment and involvement of the local members of the BoG representing the Society and the kind of benefits this brings to the functioning of the Institute.

The financial advisors of the GoI on the IIMA BoG were amazed at the returns that the Institute was generating. Initially, there was disbelief and they felt that something must be wrong; that we might be violating the norms. But once this fear was allayed, they began to ask other institutions to look at how the IIMA managed its investments.

ADMINISTRATIVE EXPENSES

Administrative expenses as a percentage of total expenses fell steadily until the end of the grant regime. After which, it has fallen precipitously as PGP and other fees were jacked up in order to tap surplus value. Its Compound Annual Growth Rate (CAGR) over the last ten to twelve years is around 15 percent, in spite of inflation, the launch of the second campus, and a substantial expansion in student intake.

Establishment expenses, which predominantly comprise of faculty salaries, also display a similar CAGR signifying higher faculty productivity in teaching. Whether this has adversely affected research, is a moot point. But as reflected in lower realizations in MDPs, there is perhaps some substance to it.

Two important developments need to be noted while looking at this financial journey.

Due to the matching grant scheme, there was a great incentive to generate a surplus as defined under the scheme. Pradip Khandwalla saw this and took the lead, cutting down on many expenses. In later years, people criticized the IIMA for allowing our buildings to fall into disrepair. In part, the observation was correct. In the years of the matching grant, the Institute did cut back on maintenance expenditure. It tried to increase income from other sources, and thereby tried to generate a higher surplus as was defined under the scheme. Pradip Khandwalla, being a chartered accountant, vigorously drove this control on expenses and the exploration of income sources with great zeal. All this was done in order to make IIMA more self reliant and to build the corpus fund. Remember, when he took over, there was no corpus. When he left, there was a corpus fund of more than Rs. 30 crore. More importantly, he brought about the change in the basic economics of management education. For the first time, a serious attempt was made to work out the cost of the PGP programme per student. Probably for the first time, the assumptions about executive education fees were questioned and tested. The value proposition was carefully evaluated. This brought about significant changes in the design and marketing of programmes. Internally, a new market consciousness, cost control, and cost–revenue relationship began taking hold. This was a significant turning point in the way in which IIMA began looking at its finances. The journey towards financial self reliance had begun.

A MAJOR JOLT: THE SIXTH PAY COMMISSION

In the year 2007–08, the recommendations of the Sixth Pay Commission became a major issue. The salary structure had to be revised upwards by a very hefty margin. Not only that, the recommendations came in 2009 but it was applied retrospectively by two years. This created a huge burden on the Institute's resources. The average salary increase was about 55 percent. The Institute had been making provisions for this since the first report came in 2009, and did not wait until another committee; the Govardhan Committee gave the final decision about its applicability to the Institute. Having accepted the position that the Institute would follow the GoI scales of pay as per the original MoA it had no option but to follow the sixth Pay Commission fully in all its details. However, this is an example as to how being linked to GoI pay scales can bring huge jolts and shocks which many institutions can find difficult to deal with. IIMA was probably one of the few institutions which managed to absorb the huge rise without recourse either to the GoI or to other sources of funding. Had it not been linked to the GoI pay scale, the whole adjustment and transition to a higher scale would have been much smoother as it would have been spread over a period of time.

IIMA is probably the only institution among the 'public' institutions to have made full provision for pensions even after the impact of the sixth pay commission.

FUNDING FOR CAPEX

For capital expenditure, contributions from various sources have undergone several major changes. Initially, industry was supposed to raise funds for building, and the FF was to provide money and library books. Two things happened. The earlier estimate of the infrastructure made by Dean Robbins at Rs 30 lakh was found to be inadequate; later estimates were coming in at over Rs 80 lakh. Industry had committed up to Rs 30 lakh. There was a huge shortfall. Secondly, in 1962, there was the war with China. This had a severe effect on the profitability of the companies involved. Kasturbhai Lalbhai faced considerable difficulties in raising funds from industry. This put severe pressure on the Institute to raise money for the building programme.

The question as to why the initial estimate by Dean Robbins fell so short of the actual need is difficult to answer. Partly it may be because of the inflationary environment during that period whereby building costs rose considerably. But even that cannot fully explain the huge difference between Rs 30 lakh and Rs 80 lakh. The only possible explanation is that Dean Robbins' estimate was based on different assumptions over space and cost—most likely in estimating the area required for the buildings. It is quite possible, though, that the scope of the buildings might also have changed. There was no provision, for example, for faculty housing. He estimated 25,000 sq.ft. for offices, classrooms, auditorium, library, etc. and 75,000 sq.ft. for student residences; all in all, that was 100,000 sq.ft. at a cost of Rs 30 per sq.ft. A combination of all these factors can account for the discrepancy.

All of this put severe pressure on the management to raise funds. The matter came before the BoG on several occasions. It was discussed and finally the major initiative in raising the resources fell on the shoulders of the management, i.e. the Director. Vikram Sarabhai explored many possibilities. He considered taking loans from the bank, PL480 funds from the GoI were also considered with the consent of the US government. The FF was also tapped. The construction programme was delayed because of this crunch. Then in 1965-66, the FF provided about Rs 15 lakh for construction. Later, Ravi pursued the GoI and received a special grant towards the construction of the Institute buildings.

APPLICATION OF FUNDS (BUILDING)

Year	Govt of India	Others*	Total	Share of GoI	Share of Others
1962			0.00		
Sub-Total 1st Decade (1963-72)	66.16	82.12	148.28	44.6%	55.4%
Sub-Total 2nd Decade (1973-82)	210.50	157.63	368.13	57.2%	42.8%
Sub-Total 3rd Decade (1983-92)	255.23	124.58	379.81	67.2%	32.8%
Sub-Total 4th Decade (1993-02)	130.35	411.59	541.94	24.1%	75.9%
Sub-Total 5th Decade 9 yrs (2003-11)	1337.88	7733.90	9071.78	14.7%	85.3%
TOTAL	2000.12	8509.82	10509.94	19.0%	81.0%

Although funding for the building programme started with industry funding, it was then supplemented by the FF and after about five years (from 1966-67), GoI began to supplement it. Part funding by the GoI continued until 1995-96. As can be seen from the table, the share of funds for building, progressively shifted from the GoI to the Institute's own internal sources. The decline becomes steep from 1993, the year in which the block grant scheme first signalled the tapering off of grants from the GoI. After 1995-96, no grant was received from the GoI except just once, in 2002-03, for an international centre and in the last three years to help accommodate the OBC quota.

It is a significant point that no funds for building came through major donations. The BoG discussed the matter several times, but no effective mobilization ever took place. In part, this was due to the policy on the naming of buildings and facilities. The BoG had decided at an earlier meeting that buildings or facilities would not necessarily be named after anyone who provided a suitable donation. Instead, the names of companies or individuals who were either seen as being deeply committed to the cause of education, or who had contributed towards institution building, would be attached. In short, the naming of the institution's facilities would not be 'sold'. A dorm or a group of dorms could perhaps have been named, let's say, after Tata, State Bank of India, Larsen & Toubro, or the Lalbhai Group, but it appears that no serious effort was ever made to raise money this way. The pioneers were commemorated though. In 1972, the library was named after Vikram Sarabhai, the MDC was named after Kasturbhai Lalbhai, and the auditorium after Ravi Matthai. The only other facility to be named was a small conference room in the name of Sunil Mehta, who was a PGP 1988 alumnus. A donation of Rs 70 lakh (69,97,500) was received in 2009, from his family and classmates.

EXPENSE CONTROL

The financial outcomes described above had cultural underpinnings. Even from the early days, costs at the Institute were internally controlled through various rules and processes. The Institute was never profligate. Ravi worked on trust and conscientiousness; and the funds crunch, GoI scrutiny, and the ever watchful Finance Committee served to reinforce this. This fostered a culture of frugality; a concern which comes from the feeling of being owners of the Institute. This value system was reflected in all areas, whether it was in the use of stationery, the use of air conditioning, or a question of furnishing the offices—these simple, frugal habits were visible everywhere. It became one of the Institute's core values and any extravagance was viewed as vulgar. One might even be tempted to say that the monastic image of the architecture was reflected in the values of the people.

There is an interesting example of this culture of frugality. One of the newly appointed Chairmen directed the MDC manager to keep a room permanently at his disposal and to improve its furniture, furnishings, and facilities. When the Director was approached about this, he wrote to the Chairman informing him that a permanent room at his disposal would entail a substantial loss of revenue for the Institute. Instead, he suggested that a room would be furnished to his satisfaction, and he could stay in it whenever he was in town, but that when not needed by him, it would be used for institutional purposes. If he so preferred, he could stay in a hotel of his choice whenever he came for BoG meetings. When the Chairman persisted with his demand, the Director told him that he would put the matter before the MDP Committee. The Director also informally talked to some of the BoG members who unequivocally agreed that keeping a room exclusively for the use of the Chairman was contrary to the IIMA culture. That did the trick and the request was quietly dropped.

During one of the Finance Committee meetings, the Director mentioned that the students had been asking why it was that a world class institution like IIMA did not have air conditioned classrooms? The first reaction of the members of the Finance Committee was that air conditioning was unnecessary, it was an extravagance that did not fit in with either the Institute's culture, or its core value system. The Director had to ask the Finance Committee Chairman to accompany him to a classroom on one April afternoon, in order to feel the heat for himself. The exercise was enough to convince the Chairman to change his mind.

THE DEVELOPMENT OF THE IT INFRASTRUCTURE

One finds the echo of the same culture in the capex decisions. Apart from land and building, the main capex was on IT infrastructure.

The development of the IT infrastructure at IIMA is characterized by varied degrees of success, an insufficient degree of funding in the early days, a lack of strong commitment across management levels to harness the potential of IT for the automation of administrative processes, and a lack of well qualified professionals to take the lead and implement MIS systems. IIMA had been a leader when it came to computer networking, end user computing, the use of Information and Communication Technologies (ICT) for communication, and Internet connectivity. As early as 1992-93, the Institute had adopted the use of email and electronic notice boards for internal and external communication, well ahead of most other institutions in India. However, when it came to deploying IT infrastructure for enhancing productivity in administrative processes and the use of ICT for the delivery of education, it lagged significantly behind other international benchmark institutions. Given its culture of frugality and accountability, it built its campus wide LAN piece-by-piece and by the year 2000 it had a campus wide, robust LAN infrastructure, providing Internet connectivity to every room in the dormitories. Unlike engineering or science colleges, its needs were relatively limited and varied a great deal between various areas—e.g. a faculty in the finance area might need greater processing power, number crunching, the capability to build financial models but the rest of the faculty might need lesser computing power.

IT is a classic case in which the cost of technology drops precipitously after its first emergence. As technology improves, it is debugged and its cost falls.

Given the culture of frugality and accountability present at IIMA, the early adoption of IT was never going to happen. Not only would early adoption be more expensive, but the technology bought would also be somewhat immature.

As the leadership had not yet grasped the true power of technology, and remained unconvinced with regard to its need, the budget allocation for building IT infrastructure was limited. Generally, the Institute's investment in the IT infrastructure came from whatever was left over from the budget. No real attempt was made to raise resources for the development of IT capabilities. Under the circumstances, what was actually built was optimal. This happened because of the true ownership attitude of the faculty members behind the development of the IT infrastructure. Prof. B. H. Jajoo played a crucial role. He acted more or less an internal consultant for developing this. Going beyond that role, he supervised the implementation at every stage. Optimal design was developed, tight specs were derived, hard bargaining was conducted with the vendors, and resources were rationally distributed among faculty and supporting staff. This led to a lot of friction and heartburn, and sometimes one wonders whether all these efforts were truly worth it or whether the Institute should have proactively tried to overcome the funding constraints.

Another factor lay behind these developments. Right from the beginning, when the only technology we had was the typewriter, we had provided for relatively generous secretarial support. In many cases, one secretary was attached to a faculty member but usually one secretary was shared between two faculty members. Such secretarial support covered up for our basic lack of technology. Secretaries used to take down memos, dictation about articles, procure stationery, keep accounts, contact other secretaries or faculty members, maintain the faculty member's diary and much more. These secretaries were good and efficient. As a result, the faculty never felt the pressing need to adopt technology to do many of these tasks. This meant that while IIMA had some of the best secretaries, it also had some of the most outdated technology.

Another feature of the Institute's approach to technology is to use it as an enabler, not as an important driver in designing and delivering education, and achieving improved administrative capability and efficiency. When one looks at alumni records and our early documents, one realizes that the Institute still has not developed an important data base, an efficient filing system, or the modern document archives. Recently, I was looking for the original version of Robbins Report. This report has been quoted at various places, throughout this book and I needed either the original document or an authentic copy. The library did not have it. The CAO's office did not have it. Eventually, after a long search, it was finally located in the papers kept by the successive secretaries in the Director's office. This is just one example, but it is indicative of the lack of application of technology in the Institute's record keeping. When it comes to the delivery of education, the story is somewhat similar. How much coursework is online? How much student feedback is online? How much faculty feedback to students is online? How much work is done in real time with collaborators scattered all over the country or abroad? Has the Institute thought of creating virtual classrooms? Does it not need to think in terms of creating interactive classrooms across locations? Many possibilities exist that have not been tapped yet. The Institute has yet to create a solid IT infrastructure which will facilitate their delivery. True, it will require substantial funding, but many business schools these days have budgets of nearly a million dollars per year for both creation and maintenance of new infrastructure. IIMA is late in realizing this need and in providing adequate funding. I believe the funding can be found, but the first step is to realize the need and then to build a case. Take for example, the development of multimedia cases. Again, the Institute is lagging behind its competitors. One of the first cases was the Philips Matsushita case of HBS. This goes back to nearly fifteen years. The proposal to develop multimedia cases was discussed but no real effective steps came through. The Institute should have read the signal. It was in a better position to develop such cases at a lower cost than American universities. Now HBS has come to India and started developing multimedia cases. Going forward, this is one shortcoming which needs addressing as soon as possible.

As mentioned earlier, when the block grant scheme was introduced and grants were more or less frozen, the signals were clear that the Institute would have to rely on its own capacity to generate resources for growth and development and even for its existing operations. Pradip read the signals correctly and began working hard to save costs. His prime motive was to generate the surplus by which he could qualify for matching the grant and then build the corpus. In the process, he often postponed some discretionary but essential expenses. Building maintenance was one of these. At the same time, it was recognized that financial self reliance consistent with our core values was the only thing that could assure the future of the Institute. This brought about a very heightened sense of cost consciousness. Take for example, energy costs. When we look at the energy costs, either in terms of ratio per 1000 sq.ft. of built up space or in terms of the number of people on the campus, and then track it over a period of time; it is clear that our energy costs have been carefully controlled. The same could also be seen in cost heads such as printing, stationery, travel, and so on.

The main capital expenditure of the Institute has been on creation of infrastructure and creation of a solid IT backbone. In these cases, the approach has been different. For creation of building and infrastructure, the primary focus was on architecture, functionality, and durability. The cost per sq.ft. was seen or interpreted in this context. As far as IT infrastructure is concerned, this was built incrementally. Instead of going for a turnkey project incurring heavy costs, Prof. Jajoo spent a great deal of his own time building an efficient IT backbone. For example, when it came to purchase of computers, the guiding principle was not to simply buy the latest and the best but rather the most appropriate ones. As new computers came, the older ones were handed down to people for whose use the older computers were appropriate. Secretaries generally only used them for word processing. This did not require high speed. Neither did it require any other software. So the older computers were often transferred to the secretaries for whose use this was sufficient. A similar approach was adopted across the board. In terms of software also, composite deals were concluded. Often some of the faculty lamented the fact that the Institute was using outdated or slower IT processing. However, the needs were all adequately served.

FINANCING FOR THE FUTURE

Over the last few years, the Institute's finances have been subject of much debate. Are the fees too high? Is the Insitute making its education unaffordable? Is it guilty of profiteering? Does it have enough resources to ensure its future? Does it have the financial reserves to ensure growth and development? Can it find funds for new initiatives which may be risky or may have a longer gestation period? Does it have the latest IT infrastructure and other technologies? These are all questions around which the debate is centered. Serious views and reservations have been expressed about the adequacy of the Institute's finances. In some cases, a scare has been created. Comparisons have been made with leading business schools in the US, especially with HBS. A strong view has been expressed that the Institute needs to have a large corpus fund built primarily through endowments, which will provide substantial income for all of the contingencies mentioned above.

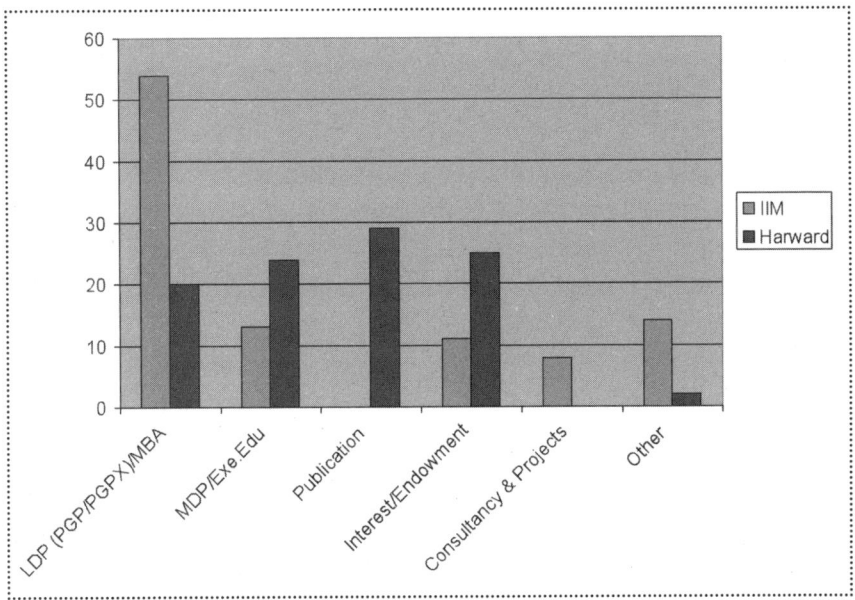

When one compares the financing patterns of HBS and IIMA, two things stand out. This is represented in the chart above. HBS earns a substantial income from publications amounting to nearly 30 percent of its total revenue. This includes the sale of cases too. HBS also has income from endowments to the tune of about 25 percent of the total revenue. IIMA earns next to nothing from publication activities. Income from endowments in IIMA's case is 11 percent. If we take the gross income, including both tied and untied funds, it works out to almost 22 percent. In other words, while there is scope for improving the income from endowment by building a larger corpus, the main difference comes in the shape of income from publications.

A few observations can be made. Possibly research and cases are not yielding enough marketable products or the Institute is not able to market its research, i.e. new knowledge. Furthermore, it has not focused on publication as a major centre of revenue. Structurally, it has not designed an organizational place by which it receives the kind of attention a profit centre should. A concerted effort is required along with a person whose job it is to continuously generate new ideas by which more income can be generated from publications. This is a business activity and a different mindset is needed. This won't happen overnight, but a beginning must be broached. Over a period of time, publishing has the potential to generate large income. This must be recognized because if it isn't, it could be interpreted as if the Institute does not create enough marketable new knowledge. When Dr Mashelkar took over as Director General of CSIR (Council of Scientific & Industrial Research) he argued that the National Labs should become self reliant through the marketing of IPR from their research activities. True, research feeds teaching and consultancy; but its potential to generate revenue directly through publication also needs to be seriously explored.

As far as corpus is concerned, we need to ask a question. How does the Institute build corpus? From operating surplus? From donations? These are two main sources—for generating operating surplus, tuition fees could be one; executive education could be a second, and as we have seen; publications could be the third. As far as tuition fee for the PGP programme is concerned, the Institute has ramped this up considerably over the last two years. One could argue that maybe the price rise was too fast, but by all analysis, the costs have been covered. It would be unwise to place a further burden on this source for generating further operating surplus. It also raises the question of the inter-generational transfer of funds. We need to look at other factors. Has the Institute got the right product for executive education? Does it market these products properly? It is clear that the Institute is still not up there with the best products attracting the best companies or executives to enable it to charge higher fees. Many foreign business schools come to India, offering such programmes and are able to charge far higher fees. Many executives from larger companies go to European and American schools and pay nearly three to four times higher fees. Is there any scope for the Institute to charge more? If so, how does it do it? Should it improve the programme design? Make it more relevant? Differentiate it from other offerings? Reinforce the programme with new research and then market it well? Whichever way one looks at it, either a straight comparison between per day charge for the executive education fees or the percentage of executive education in the total income, it is clear that there is significant scope for augmenting resources through this avenue.

The second source is from direct donations for augmenting the corpus. Here also the record is poor. Over the last twenty or thirty years, this source has not generated any significant amount. All that has come, is by way of endowments for Chairs. Even that has not been satisfactorily executed and the donors have expressed their dissatisfaction time and again. There is a huge 'Goodwill Bank' which still remains untapped. This 'Goodwill Bank' is comprised of alumni, participants of the executive programme, the corporate sector, and the philanthropy foundations. The Institute's image is high. Its capacity to manage funds has been lauded. Its integrity is beyond question. Its ability to put resources to good use has been firmly established. Yet, it has been unable to raise funds from this source. It needs to ask why? Look at its alumni body. Where are they placed? How highly are they placed? What do they think about the education they received? What kind of bonds do they feel for their old alma mater? And, yet, this is not reflected in their contribution to the corpus fund. A few initiatives have been taken but these have more or less amounted to very little. The Institute needs to look at the whole thing very seriously. In my conversations with some leading alumni, what emerges is not very satisfactory. Many alumni feel that the Institute takes the position that alumni should feel 'obliged' to contribute to the Institute. The Institute does not try to reach out to them. The Institute does not make an active effort to develop connections with them. In many cases, they are not asking for special recognition. But there are many ways of developing positive feelings, a sense of bond, and a continuing relationship. This is missing. Is it because the Institute needs an imaginative executive in charge of this task? Is it because its attitude is more passive than active? The matter really does require some serious attention if the Institute is to raise and tap this particular source for augmenting its corpus. Getting donations from corporates, foundations, and alumni requires three or four basic elements: good performance, credibility of the Institute, good communication, imaginative 'products', follow up and reporting. We have to analyse where the Institute has missed out. It requires a different skill set and passionate commitment.

By and large, the Institute has managed its finances well over the years. Compared to other institutions, it is much better placed. Operational self reliance has been more or less fully achieved, a reasonable corpus exists, all contingent liabilities have been provided for, and the yield record on our investments has been outstanding. We have consistently controlled costs and we have been free from any financial scandal. What IIMA has achieved in the academic field is matched by what it has achieved in managing its own finances. Values like simplicity, frugality, functionality, and accountability have all been reflected in the management of its finances. The culture of 'value for money' is reflected in all its financial transactions. A large and modern infrastructure has been created, substantially, from its own resources and dependency on the government has been reduced to nil. This is a record to be proud of.

Moving ahead, however, the Institute needs to address a few issues. There is emerging competition; new institutions mushrooming with modern infrastructure, especially when it comes to technology. Classroom design is undergoing major changes and the use of technology is accelerating. All of this will require substantial investments. The Institute's spending on technology is still minimal. Funds will be required for growth in terms of new infrastructure, the upgrading or renovation of existing facilities, new research, the collection and updating of teaching materials, etc. All of this will require funding. There are three ways in which the Institute can hope to raise funds—executive education, publication activity, and donations. This will require some structural change and it will involve the tapping of new and different talent. Above all it will require a deeper involvement and commitment at BoG, Director, and Dean level. It is not beyond IIMA's capabilities to rise to this challenge.

9

On Challenges

'Time present and time past
Are both perhaps present in time future
And time future contained in time past.'

T.S Eliot

FACING THE CHALLENGES AHEAD

The values, the processes, and the selection of early faculty and staff were the pillars on which IIMA was built. The early pioneers had ensured that IIMA's foundations were strong and deep, and the subsequent leaders contributed to its development and growth. That culture of basic values and processes was so strong that it survives to this day. The leaders who followed have shown foresight, determination, skill and tact, whilst navigating the various trials, tribulations, and tests that IIMA has found itself facing. Of all the many things that the later leadership have achieved, financial self reliance, the essential continuity of core values, and consolidation all stand out. This provides a unique launching pad for the future course for the IIMA.

Many new and different challenges are emerging. Take for example, the major trend towards the globalization of education. For centuries education was a local activity, students and scholars were all home grown. These scholars rarely travelled further than their home towns, let alone to other countries. The enrollment of foreign students in institutions of education is a phenomenon of the late twentieth century and now, every year it is gathering momentum.

THE CHANGING BUSINESS SCENARIO: REFORMS

1991 was a watershed year in the history of the country. It was a major departure point. The central change was liberalization. After some forty years of an insulated, inward looking, centrally controlled economy, the so-called Nehruvian model was finally replaced. One often wonders why it took so long for the Indian policy makers to see the destructive impact of these insular policies. Many international economists sneered at the growth of the Indian economy, especially when comparing it with the so-called Asian dragons. South Korea, Taiwan, and Singapore were cited as the success stories of the seventies and eighties. Indian policy makers tended to explain this away by saying that South Korea was a client state of the United States and that Taiwan and Singapore were city states or small states, and that our problems were completely different. This self delusion persisted for too long, but finally, when the Chinese story began unfolding, after 1983, the lesson began to sink in. The foreign exchange crisis of the late eighties and early nineties drove the final nail in the coffin. Rajiv Gandhi had begun the process in the second half of the eighties and by the nineties, Rao and Singh had irreversibly committed India to the path of liberalization. Politicians who clung to Nehruvian economics as an election currency were finally silenced. Competition substituted controls and the result was a reluctant embrace of the market forces.

Starting with industrial licensing and import controls, the programme of reforms gradually moved forward. The great fear that the OGL regime would lead to the mass importation of luxury goods and drive the Indian balance of payments situation into bankruptcy was belied. The opening up of the economy led to neither wastage nor mass closures. Indian industry adapted as globally competitive, agile, and sure footed enterprises. The confidence of the policy makers grew and fiscal reforms followed. Excise duties were cut along with custom duties and direct tax rates were brought down. The East India Company syndrome was finally purged. Indian industry quickly adjusted itself to the new situation and proudly marched forward. It became cost competitive, new products were introduced, technology was imported, developed, and adapted. We saw an end of the import substitution model of growth and began to embrace the export driven model adopted by countries like South Korea, Taiwan, and Singapore.

Indian industry has witnessed far reaching trends, especially over the last twenty years. Obviously the size of our industry has grown considerably. In the past, the Fortune 500 was a starry goal for Indian companies, but today many of them now figure there. They have grown not only in size, but also in complexity and in geography. The process is accelerating day by day. Indian companies have followed a similar path as the global leaders. For example, more than 50 percent of the Tata Group turnover comes from foreign operations. At the same time, these leaders are rooted in our environment with all its special challenges.

Post liberalization in 1991, Indian industry had to quickly adapt to global competition after being insulated for more than fifty years. This was not a question of choice, it was a question of survival. Global competition was at the doorstep. Industrial licensing was a thing of the past, as was import licensing, but many other niggling controls still remained. There were artificially regulated prices, constricting labour laws, and the infrastructure of industries such as power and transport lagged severely behind the times. The transaction cost in India persisted at high levels. Even today it is so—whether it is starting a new company or completing a shipment to a foreign location—India is not the best place to do business. Our rank in ease of doing business, as rated by the World Economic Forum, is still very low; in 2011, we rank fifty third in the world for start-up procedures and forty ninth for start-up days. It is in this mixed environment that Indian professional managers have to operate.

After a while, the government also realized that public sector undertakings were a drag on the economy. Their poor performance contrasted with the shining examples of the private sector. Opinion leaders, the media, and policy makers began to see the negative impact of the PSUs. Disinvestment policies gradually began gaining momentum. After a long struggle, steps were taken along the road to privatization, albeit partial privatization. This had a salutary effect. The earlier model of holding companies detaching the undertaking from the mother ministries had not been successful. Various other management changes failed to bring any positive results. But the market accountability to the shareholders had a clear and positive impact on the working of the PSUs. This was reinforced by the abandonment of the monopoly status of the PSUs. Private telecom companies emerged as strong competitors of BSNL. The same happened in steel, banking, oil exploration etc. All of these transformed Indian industry and the economy.

GLOBALIZATION

Along with this came globalization. All over the world there was a strong movement towards liberalizing trade between nations. Many countries took advantage of liberal trade and their growth only supported the demand for more globalization. It was demonstrated that liberal trade benefitted the developed world as well as the developing world. It led to an efficient allocation of resources across the countries and rearranged the relative competitiveness of industries across countries. This resulted in lower costs and the opening of new markets. Once global markets became accessible, even smaller companies could think in terms of growth. The Indian pharma industry, for example, was very small compared to the pharma industry of the developed world; yet with the opening up of the market, the Indian pharma industry made a huge impact on the generic drug industry of the developed countries. They emerged as champions, dominating these markets. Gradually, they became feared by the large pharma industries of the world. It was not just the free flow of trade but gradually the free flow of technology and management ideas that improved the competitiveness of Indian industry.

The rise of the IT industry in India has been another example of what liberalization and globalization have done. The bright young people of India, whose plans and ambitions for growth were smothered by the constricting atmosphere of the pre-liberalization economic environment, found that this was one industry where the government had not yet placed any restrictions. They found a natural outlet, worked hard and saw the opportunities. They went to the world leaders. Starting with the body shopping, they moved up the value chain, provided services, provided solutions, and then moved towards innovative products. All of this has happened in a period of about thirty to thirty five years. It is a shining example of what an unshackled Indian industry can do. The world was amazed and they were forced to take note. All those long hard years of struggling with the balance of payment had been reversed. The OGL regime did not bleed the Indian foreign exchange dry; on the contrary, the Indian foreign exchange reserves grew by leaps and bounds. This gave new confidence to Indian entrepreneurs as well as the Indian intelligentsia. Bright young students from various academic backgrounds were attracted to this sector and many companies became globally known. Most of the IT companies received more than 70 percent of their revenues from international operations. This exposure to large multinational companies, industrial conglomerates, and leading companies of various industries rubbed off on Indian industry in many ways. The 'can do' spirit had been ignited.

Other Changes
Back home, two or three things started changing. A communications revolution was initiated with the introduction of mobile services. We leapfrogged into the

modern communications industry. People who had never had a landline before, adopted the mobile phone immediately. Instead of being a status symbol of the elite of Indian society, mobile phones became ubiquitous and a handy business tool. The speed of transactions increased, the cost of transactions came down, and the productivity of mobile workers increased greatly. This included not just high flying business executives but basic service providers such as carpenters and plumbers.

With this global orientation and the rise of the IT industry, educational aspirations were also on the rise. Every parent wanted his or her child to go to an English-medium school, to be computer savvy, and to get a university degree. It became their first priority. The family tightened their belts when it came to food, travel, and other expenses so as to be able to provide higher education to their children. For an institution like IIMA, it meant that the applicant pool rose up from tens of thousands to hundreds of thousands. The same was true for every other recognized institution of higher education.

As all this was unleashed, the media—both print and electronic—became more active. Literacy was higher and so were aspirations. As the population became more educated, the media business became very profitable. It also began to change. New talent was attracted to the media—both for entertainment as well as for news, information, and discussion. Opinion leaders emerged in this process and debate became sharpened. The debating forum overflowed from the legislatures and parliament into the pages of newspapers, magazines, and TV shows. Entertainment had also changed and the increased percentage of the middleclass reinforced the emergence of news, information, and commentary media. The competition between them, and the attitudes of an enlightened leadership, improved the level of debate as well as helped unearth many hidden issues. Scandals were highlighted and corruption was underlined. There was competition among newspapers and other media to lead this enlightenment in order to build their circulation. Wider and freer availability of news and information also sparked greater judicial engagement. The judiciary became active, reassessed its role, and attracted favourable attention.

In all of these changes, technology played a stellar role—whether it was communication, manufacturing technology, or services such as banking. Technology became an important driver for cost competitiveness, for product improvement, for developing new models of business, for a greater exchange of ideas, for improving access, and for a more democratic sharing of resources. The genie was well and truly out of the bottle!

Another dimension for Indian companies and businesses has been the regulatory and political framework. Sometimes the regulatory framework can be over zealous. Sometimes it is waived completely in favour of those who can cut corners and the political approach is often short sighted, sometimes irrational, and always biased against business albeit outwardly.

Two or three other phenomena have emerged. Business media has become very active. Business management, practices, and the conduct of professional managers have come under the lens of the business media. Their actions are scrutinized as their movements are tracked and their views analysed. All in the blinding public glare. The recent controversy over the Radia tapes is a case in point.

A recent phenomenon to emerge in the Indian environment is the emerging market for companies and businesses. Mergers and acquisitions have become an important activity. In the modern world, entering and exiting businesses are no longer cataclysmic events forced by extraneous factors but a matter of strategic choice. Gone are the days when entering and building a business required years of persistence. Gone also are the days when leaving a business was painful, tainted with social disgrace, and happened only through attrition. People and companies come with different value propositions. Raiders can see value and often succeed in adding value where the incumbents may fail to see it or may not add it. With the financial market becoming more sophisticated, the mobilization of funds for such takeovers has become easier and the market for businesses has really taken off in India.

The growth of the NGO—both for profit and not for profit—is another major development. This has spawned new business models. The delivery of social goods such as health, education, and so on has seen lots of different approaches. Many of these organizations work on the borderline of economic and social enterprises. They have a mixed set of goals. Examples abound. SEWA, Arvind Eye Care, etc. have been in the vanguard of this response to our economic and social problems. Apart from these more visible initiatives, there are a large number of NGOs working in every part of the country. They have risen up in response to the extremely complex transition from a society that was economically and socially backward and conventional into a truly modern society.

All these changes have thrown up some very major outcomes. The inequality between the extremely poor and the extremely rich has widened a great deal. The difference in their lifestyle is extreme and because they often live more or less cheek by jowl, tensions arise. To operate business and economic enterprises in a competitive global environment requires skills, and skills are in short supply. High rewards have to be paid for these skills and this serves to exacerbate the existing inequality created by wealth and privilege. As material success becomes the central mantra, many temptations have led to political and economic scandals. There is still a huge amount of money to be made by policy favours from the government. Recently, a spate of scandals such as the 2G spectrum, CWG etc, have been hitting us every day. Industry has to operate in this environment and management schools have to protect the professional integrity of its cadre.

To these challenges, one should also add the challenge of sensitizing the students about the various ethical and political issues encountered in everyday business life. What we have done, in terms of aligning our teaching with practice, in such an environment assumes still greater importance. The loop between classroom and practice now becomes still more complex because it has wider ramifications. Faculty compensation is another area impacted by these national and global changes. These issues will have to be handled very carefully.

EMERGENCE OF THE NEW EXECUTIVE

Simultaneously with liberalized rules for international trade, Indian business executives got the opportunity to see first hand the working of leading companies all over the world. With the new tie-ups, there was an exchange of technical and managerial personnel. They learnt new technologies as well as new management practices. Many Indian students travelled to the developed countries for their Master's and Doctoral studies. Some of them came back and some were recruited and posted by multinational companies in India. Some settled down there. But what effectively happened was that these people became models for aspiring Indian students, executives and technologists; and with their home links, became a magnet for friends, relations, and associates for either migration or global exposure. Initially, this was lamented as brain drain. But slowly and surely, the brain started circulating.

All this is reflected in the movement of the alumni of the IIMs and IITs. These alumni have now formed a global network and a global diaspora. They have acquired positions in academic and business cadres in developed countries and they are getting noticed. This leadership, with their connections and roots in India, reinforced by a natural feeling of empathy and obligation has helped the brain circulation mentioned earlier. Its impact is felt in business as well as academics. Today, when one visits the academic campuses of the leading universities around the world, especially in the English speaking world, we find that between 10–20 percent of the faculty members are of Indian origin. Nitin Nohria has become the Dean of HBS. Finally, the Indian brain has begun to find its place in the world.

As a result of all the forces described subsequent to the liberalization process of 1991, a new profile of business executive has emerged. The modern executive requires high skills for dealing with increasingly complex management problems arising out of the international competition at our doorstep. Due to global integration, he has to be culturally adaptable—at home in India, the USA, Europe, or Japan. He will be highly mobile between companies and between locations—both nationally and globally. He will be both tech and media savvy. He needs to be innovative in terms of management practice and in tune with the latest technology and management trends. He will be research oriented and research driven for both products and processes. He will command far greater dignity. He will be a leader of men and he will build teams that can deliver. His salary will be linked to performance and as the stakes are higher than ever, so too will be his salary. He will be supremely confident and in the mould of such iconic global executives as Indra Nooyi or Vikram Pandit.

A few things stand out in this profile. One is global orientation; second is being tech savvy and research driven; third is cultural adaptation and mobility; fourth is the importance of leadership qualities and soft skills; and the fifth is cutting edge analytical skills. This is the executive of the future. This is the executive that IIMA has to prepare. The challenge is to design programmes and courses which meet these needs.

The issues raised by these changes can be summarized in a few central points. Indian businesses, and even social organizations, have to shift their thinking from focusing on maximizing the present to visualizing and maximizing the future.

More than merely training managers, IIMA has to concentrate on developing transformative leaders. Managers focus on optimizing current outcomes within the constraints of the environment, available resources, and the objectives of the stakeholders. The leader or an entrepreneur works on loosening the constraints, extending the boundaries of operation, visualizing a new future, and then selling it to the stakeholders. This requires a different mindset and the imparting of different skills. The role of the management institutes has changed.

IMPACT ON MANAGEMENT EDUCATION

There are a large number of management training institutes in the country as compared to when the IIMs first started. The mission to professionalize management was very relevant and important at that time. These days, training managers who can handle problems relating to optimization e.g. increasing the market share of an existing product, reducing the logistic costs by applying operation research techniques, evaluating capital budgeting decisions through the discounted cash flow method etc., can be done by many institutions. An institution like IIMA faces the more relevant and the more difficult task of training leaders who can think about the products of tomorrow, who understand how technology and disruptive technology will render existing products obsolete, who understand how the cost competitiveness can suddenly alter with a change in leadership and policies of new and emerging countries, who can understand what talented young people aspire to today and how to harness their aspirations and energies in order to develop new and exciting strategies. These leaders also have to work under the intense public glare of the hyper active business media. It is a challenge for them to strike a balance between too much exposure or too little, between quarterly results and the long term future, between maximizing share holder values and the wider stake holder concerns. This is not easy. In order to distinguish itself from the crowd, an institution like IIMA has to focus on all of these issues; study them, research them, innovate pedagogy by which the students or the participants can be sensitized to this, to change their mind set, to be adaptive, to constantly renew themselves, to look at technology trends, social trends, economic policies all around the world, and distill that complexity into simple understandable propositions for business strategies and policies.

It should also be remembered that as a result of the rapidly shifting competitive advantages arising out of globalization, the margin for error has shrunk considerably. In the sixties and seventies, you could get away with flogging old products or being late in spotting changes in consumer trends. Today, it would lead to an irretrievable loss of the market share.

All of this means that a complex challenge has emerged for institutes like IIMA. How can we sensitize young students to the complexity and dynamics of these major changes? How do we train them into a habit of mind by which even after leaving IIMA they can think about these trends on their own? How to bring such experiences into the classroom and then reflect on them? How can we integrate all of these complexities and ambiguities into a workable vision for the organization and derive strategies and policies from the same? What are the implications for admission policy to move towards implementing such a mission? What kind of target class composition should IIMA be working for? What will be the new courseware? How will the course be taught and how will the students be assessed? How do we cultivate habits of mind when the students are on the campus for just a limited period of time? How do we relate the classroom experience and learning to make greater sense out of life lessons later? In short, out there, in the big wide world—there is great complexity; there are major political, social, economic, and technological trends. They impact fundamentally on the organizations. These students have to be prepared so that they can steer such organizations. How do we organize the classroom activity in order to enable these students to deal with the complex ever changing reality? It is a huge challenge.

EXAMPLE OF DISRUPTIVE TECHNOLOGY

What has happened to the music and entertainment industry in the last fifty years provides an example of how technology can completely disrupt the basics of an industry. In the past, consuming music meant going to a place where a performance was scheduled to take place. Concert houses, opera houses, and the like provided the venue and facilities for the performers to present music to their audience. Then came the recording industry. Initially it was analog recording. So besides consuming music in a concert house, it was now possible to consume music at home or at a different location. In other words, consuming music became independent of the time and space at which it was being created. Vinyl records and cassettes came. The competition was based on developing recording and playback technology with ever more fidelity. The recording industry made it possible to consume music at limited fixed places. Then came the walkman. Now, the consumer could take music anywhere and listen to whatever he fancied. This was a major breakthrough and the walkman was a huge success. Sony became a household name worldwide. Digital technology changed all that. Fidelity was not an issue. Compression became possible. MP3 players became ubiquitous. At the same time, development in communication technology made it possible to transmit music wirelessly over long distances via the internet. Copying and transmission without loss of quality became possible. The very basis of selling recorded music had been undermined. First the vinyl records disappeared, then cassettes, and now even the CDs. A completely new business model emerged. iTunes was born.

EMERGENCE OF GLOBAL MARKET FOR EDUCATION

The globalization of education has happened on both the supply and demand side. Educational institutions began actively looking at the global recruitment of students who were passively attracted over the last fifty or sixty years. They enriched the programmes offered by such institutions. A diversity of students with different nationalities clearly added to the value of the programmes. As the economy became more sophisticated, the size of businesses expanded and the great multinationals emerged. This had an impact on the business schools—in terms of the curriculum, the student body, the faculty body, and the size and complexity of the institution. In response to these changes, the early pioneers expanded. New innovative programmes were introduced. A new balance between money and mission had to be developed. From the demand side, since the industries developed and became global, the need for professionally trained managerial manpower was urgent. The multinationals set an example. They trained professional managers. They also took professional managers from business schools. And this body of professional executives demonstrated that a formal business education can prove invaluable for the success of the enterprises. This success brought rewards for the people in business. Executives' salaries soared. This was the magnet which really attracted students to the business schools. This increase in demand began in the developed countries before spreading and stimulating similar demands in the emerging countries. Overall, a huge demand surge has arisen.

The business schools came up with different programmes. The faculty began pursuing research in various aspects of running businesses of all kinds. They developed insights into business processes. Technology enabled wider classroom activity. With an increase in general mobility, enabled by the development of air transport, the participants could be drawn from any part of the world. The multinational had to operate in different parts of the world with widely varying local conditions and cultures. The time of the global manager had come.

OTHER CHANGES IMPACTING NEW PROGRAMMES

With the proliferation of basic management education, businesses have become more sophisticated in their management practices and as a result they have become more demanding. They expect executives or students entering their business to become effective immediately. They expect the students or executives entering their businesses to understand the complexity of business. They expect a deeper knowledge of all the various functions. In the past, an MBA entering a finance sector company could do well with his basic finance knowledge, nowadays, the financial companies have become much more sophisticated, their operations more complex, and their models much more intricate. The risks are higher and so are the rewards. This means that the managers and executives entering the sector have to be well prepared to not only understand the complexity and risks but to handle them effectively. The task for an institute like IIMA is to design management programmes which prepare fresh students or experienced executives to handle these more complex jobs and situations.

The second related change comes from another angle. Management or business schools around the world have begun to realize and recognize that all expertise either about market or cultural differences or about various sectors cannot be gathered in one single institution. Some institutions because of their location understand certain businesses well. It may be textile, it may be pharma, or it may be financial institutions. Some schools understand the emerging markets better. Some understand the developed markets better. In a globalized world, industries have to operate in multi cultural locations. This requires understanding and adaptation to local cultures. These changes are crucial. As a result, many business schools and other institutions have now begun recognizing the limits of their internal competence and have initiated collaborative models. There are many examples of this. Collaboration is across institutions, universities, and geographies. They take the form of joint programmes, dual degree programmes, assisted programmes etc. Columbia University and London Business School offer joint Programmes. Sectoral collaboration examples are the Medical MBA offered by Harvard or the dual degree programmes of Columbia University. Even in India, Pharma MBA Programmes are being offered by a few institutions. This is just the beginning. Many more such collaborative programmes are in the offing and will come in the next few years.

The third major change impacting the programmes is technology. Information and communication technology has opened up new pedagogies as well as provided various possibilities in the design of programmes. Blends of online–offline, contact–distant, and different variations of them have now become possible. It has added another complication which is to build a technology platform specific to the design of the programmes. This platform has to be very adaptive, as technology changes so rapidly. In August, 2011, Prof. Sebastian

Thrun and Peter Norvig, two of the world's best known artificial intelligence experts of Stanford University offered a free online course on Artificial Intelligence. Global registrations exceeded 800,000 in just three week's time. Technology is not just an enabler but it is also an integral part of the design of the programme.

The delivery of a programme can now be far more sophisticated than in the past. Paper, pencil, and printed material are increasingly being replaced by computer, iPads, and clickers. This can have an enormous impact on the length of the programme and the faculty time required to deliver the programme. The faculty participant ratio can also change considerably as can infrastructure design. The various innovations such as the new interactive classrooms design at MIT are pointers. Another dimension is a mash up of learning and doing. Simulated learning labs are gradually being introduced into the business schools. This also requires collaboration across the faculties. Take, for example, the innovation and entrepreneurship labs at Stanford, MIT, and other institutions. Here technology, design, marketing, and finance are all integrated. These changes would have a profound impact on business education going forward.

The effects of all this change will be felt strongly at IIMA. It affects how IIMA should react and what it should do over the coming decades. It has an impact on all of its programmes and on its governance, both internal and external, it has impact on its values and processes, and, of course, on its finances. The response to this exploding reality will determine the future of IIMA. In the following paragraphs we will examine the contours of response required by the faculty, the BoG, and other stakeholders.

IMPACT ON IIMA: MODIFYING THE MISSION

As the size and complexity of business increased in India, the earlier model of the entrepreneur running his business hands-on became unworkable. The professionalization of management was the mission. Entrepreneurs and managers had to be trained to use analytical techniques in all the various functions of the business. This improvement greatly enhanced the efficiency of business. Nowadays, it is impossible for the top management to handle all parts of the business and run them effectively with a hands-on approach. Complex structures have to be designed in order to run multiple businesses at multiple locations. This requires a corporate group to guide the overall strategies and policies, an executive group to run businesses, and managers to handle the various functions. As this happened, one of the most important jobs of the top management became spotting, recruiting, motivating, and retaining top management talent. But how can we monitor this talent? How can we motivate managers working at various layers? This has become a huge challenge and the Institute has begun to recognize and develop programmes, courseware, and pedagogies in order to address this need of Indian businesses. The mission has to be redefined; from professionalizing management to developing transformative leaders.

A REVIEW OF PROGRAMME INITIATIVES

When one looks back over the last fifty years, two or three major programme initiatives stand out. The first of these is PGP. The design was initially modeled on the HBS MBA Programme and gradually adapted to the changing Indian situation. Second is the 3-TP Programme. This was an innovative programme with which the Institute began. It was based on a reading of the need for professionalizing management in Indian business. It proved to be very accurate in its judgement and execution. Research agenda built by CMA, whereby management tools were brought to bear on issues in the agricultural sector was also a pioneering breakthrough. The third is the Executive MBA Programme. This programme also addressed an emerging need. However, it must also be noted that IIMA was not a pioneer in this field. It did not read this need ahead of time and ahead of others. In fact it followed a few other institutions who stole the march over IIMA. Another initiative was the Programme for the Management of Public Enterprises or the PMP. This initiative stumbled. This needs a careful and critical study. What lesson does IIMA draw from this failure? Was there a misreading of the need? Was a lack of marketing to blame? Was there a flaw in the design? Was the financial model not properly conceived? All of these issues need to be analyzed carefully. My own feeling is that there was a failure on almost all of these aspects. The need is there, the client system wants it; design and marketing issues need to be addressed along with the issue of proper and adequate preparation.

There has been a sea change in the needs of the nation's corporate sector over the last several decades. In the first thirty or forty years of IIM's existence, Indian industry operated in a highly regulated environment. This was marked by the lack of global and internal competition. It was subject to detailed regulation which led to built-in inefficiency, high friction losses, and a perversion of motives. It was easier to be successful by managing the government relations rather than focusing on strategic thinking and operational efficiency. Both markets and competition could be managed through this route. There was no need to adapt, let alone bother with developing new technology. From 1991 onwards, when the call for liberalization gathered momentum, competition both internal and global became much more intense. The initial response was for a sharper focus on operational efficiency.

Progressive Indian companies responded well to the management programmes offered by IIMA and other leading institutions. This improved their operational efficiency substantially and made them leaders in their respective industries. Their success amply demonstrated that modern management techniques can greatly help improve company performance. IIMA's reading of the market proved correct.

Today, the game has changed. Many emerging countries have also liberalized. Take for example Vietnam, Bangladesh, Singapore, and others. Operating efficiency has become an enabling factor but not a differentiating factor. In the next few decades, innovation will provide that competitive advantage— innovation in product design, innovation in processes, and innovation in business models. The question is, has IIMA read this emerging need adequately? Has IIMA begun to take new initiatives and design the new programmes required to meet this need? I sit on a few Boards and I am struck by the number of proposals for sponsoring executives to programmes offered by foreign business schools. They cost a fortune but managements seem to find them worthwhile. Each such proposal represents a loss of market share for IIMA.

To design new programmes or initiatives requires considerable preparation. The lead time for such programmes or design changes, can easily be three to five years. My sense is that IIMA has not yet fully woken up to the changing needs and initiated the design of new programmes to meet them. That, in itself, requires innovation on its part. To offer programmes of an established model is one thing but to design an extensive package or a completely different programme is another.

Indian industry has started allocating more resources for research and development. If we look at the balance sheets of pharma companies, this becomes very clear. This is happening across industries too. Indian industry is also becoming aware of the need for investment in design. Many leading units have even begun to establish global resources for supplementing their development efforts in India. Managing these R&D and design initiatives, and making them productive is going to be a crucial management challenge for Indian businesses in the coming decades.

Has IIMA recognized this need? Has IIMA understood this need? Does IIMA have a programme to meet this need? Has IIMA started preparing a detailed design for such a programme? Has IIMA entered into a dialogue with industry to refine our understanding of the need? Has IIMA even set the parameters of the design for such a programme? A host of questions are staring us in the face. It is not just a question of responding to the need, it is also a question of anticipating that need. It is a question of the timely development of a programme that can meet this need. In the past, IIMA's programmes, as we saw earlier, became successful because of a timely reading of the need and the delivery of the programme ahead of many others. The same is true for programmes of this kind. In my view, these are very important questions to which IIMA has yet to find viable answers.

THE DIRECTION FOR NEW PROGRAMMES

Executive Development Programmes (EDP/MDP)

The development of new programmes and courses that will focus on harnessing the latest innovations presents great opportunities and even greater challenges. Take for example, the challenge of working out how to set up productive, efficient and effective R&D units within an organization for the development of new products and processes? Alternatively, how to build relationships with other R&D units and labs using a model of cooperative R&D? Then, figuring out how to outsource or license them from national labs? Could this be done by supporting academic groups in universities? Is it a better option? There are various ways by which innovative products, services, and models can be developed. Indian businesses are becoming more and more aware of the need to do this. A research based programme designed to meet this need would be truly ground breaking.

The other major challenge in organizing programmes for executives is that of sensitizing them towards cultural diversity. This means that the programmes will have to bridge geographical barriers, be multi-locational, and the subject expertise will have to be drawn from other institutions.

Rather than concentrating solely on training, our executive development programmes have to stretch the mind, expanding the horizons of the students' thinking rather than merely optimizing current operations.

There is a large gap between the EDP fees IIMA charges and the fees that global business schools are charging even for the programmes organized in India. In the chapter on Finances, we saw the huge difference between the income earned by EDPs at HBS and IIMA. The main reason for this is the per day fee differential and not the number of such programmes. This is a major challenge. How can IIMA increase the fees? Why are they low? Are IIMA's programmes not relevant? Are they not properly designed? Do they not enhance the insights of the executives? Are they not able to attract the attention of the top management? Why do Indian managements sponsor their executives to programmes offered by HBS, IMD, LBS, and Warwick even though they are about four or five times more expensive? Is this a problem of perception or communication? IIMA needs to form a strategy for improving the pricing and overall net revenue from the EDPs.

LONG DURATION PROGRAMMES (LDP)

For the LDPs there are two other directions IIMA has to explore. Up until now, the focus of these programmes has been on general management. This has worked well, but as businesses expand and they become more complex, we notice that a new category is emerging, i.e. specialists with general management orientation. These specialists could be either functional or they could be domain experts. One can tackle this in two ways. A post PGP module for specific domains or specific functions could be created, or dual degree programmes could be initiated. IIMA could produce a PGP programme with multiple components, which would be interspersed with experience over an extended period of time. In other words, after the two year PGP programme, the students could begin work and then at a suitable time in their careers they could return and pursue a specialized domain, or a sector or function specialized programme. Retail management, pharma sector management, finance sector management— these are just a few examples. The first institution to launch a programme such as this which fills the need in such a creative manner will have a huge first mover advantage over the competition.

PEDAGOGY

IIMA's early collaboration with HBS brought a strong pedagogical bias towards the case method. The case method was originally created with a view to connecting classroom learning with actual practice and real life problems. We have a similar parallel with the medical profession. In medicine, internship is an important component of formal education. Clinical analysis is learned as a student examines the patient along with the teacher. In business education, students need to be sensitized to real life problems. Through the case method, classrooms became a simulated clinic. The real life case of a business situation is brought into the classroom. Often some of the real life players are also present in the classrooms. The teacher develops various perspectives of the case. Students analyse and then discuss a range of various possibilities in order to resolve the issues. This is the essence of the case method. Over the years, other business schools have also begun to realize the value of case method and have introduced cases into the design of their courses. However, for the practice of the case method to be successful, a number of conditions have to be fulfilled. Case writing is an art. How do we capture a real life business situation without revealing the outcome? At the same time, framing the issues also requires a great deal of practice and understanding. Even among the HBS cases, there are great cases and ordinary cases. This also presupposes the case writer's familiarity with the business domain, the context of the situation, and an understanding of the state of mind of the players concerned. Capturing all these in a short case requires both writing skills and experience. At HBS, case writing is almost at par with research.

As we have already seen, the case method became a corner stone of pedagogy at IIMA. Adherence to the case method became diluted when other sectors of the economy were added into the scope of management education at IIMA. It led Ravi Matthai to make the observation, 'let's not equate case method to the Roman Catholic Church'. In the area of public policy and the management of other sectors, the case method has a limited role and environmental analysis assumes a greater significance. So the debate between the protagonists and the sceptics of the case method had its root in the scope of management education, as it gradually evolved at IIMA. However, it should be noted that many generations of IIM graduates brought up largely on the case method have found that it has accelerated their ability to understand business situations and deal with them.

Another important skill that is required when practicing the case method is the ability to handle the class. One has to enable the students to see the various key points, formulate alternative solutions, debate the pros and cons, assess the rewards and penalties for each option, and then reach a conclusion. Often there is no one solution to the issue at hand. This creates ambiguity in the minds of the students. The teacher's skill can help the student come to terms with this ambiguity. To help the students understand that real life is complex and that this complexity is not reducible to simple propositions. It is only through reflection and experience that one can make sense of this complexity and ambiguity.

LONG TERM VIABILITY: SIZE, SCOPE, AND SCALE

Self reliance and long term viability have been identified as two important goals for IIMA. The CFD of 2008–10 debated how to achieve these goals. Some felt that IIMA could tackle this challenge by expanding in size, scope, and scale. This was debated at length in the recently concluded CFD. A number of faculty members made out a strong case for having a minimum faculty strength of about two hundred. The case was based on economies of scale. It was argued that this alone would help in improving the viability of our programmes. I have taken a different view, which I expressed at the CFD as well. But before I state my conclusion, let us examine the considerations involved in approaching this issue.

The first question is, how do we define size? Is it the number of students? Is it the number of faculty? Or is it the number of throughput? Obviously, the number of students or throughput can vary depending on the number of programmes, the size of programme, the duration of each programme, and so on. In any case, for various reasons—which we will analyse soon—the best indicator for size is faculty. What then are the considerations in determining appropriate size?

We must remember that an institute like IIMA is based on a collegial culture which is participative and democratic. It is not hierarchical in nature. In an organization of this type, the binding force for effective functioning is shared goals, values, and processes. The larger the group, the harder it is to reach agreement on these crucial parameters. Therefore, one finds that the flatter the organization, the smaller the size. We need to bear this in mind when approaching the issue of size and determining the faculty number required for optimal functioning. I believe that a size of between 100 to 125 would be optimal. Beyond this it becomes very difficult to operate within the collegial culture.

However, I believe that it is possible to stretch the size in a different way, and that is to maximize the reach and impact of the faculty. This can be done in several ways. If IIMA provides Teaching Asssitants (TAs) and Research Assistants (RAs) to faculty members, thereby freeing their time from some of the common chores, their effectiveness and the time that they can spend on research and developmental activities becomes far greater. This is one way. The other way is the use of technology. Many of the jobs that a faculty member is supposed to undertake could probably be done much faster with the adoption of technology. True, it would require more training for the faculty members, but the rewards are obvious. A third way to stretch the faculty size is to extend their reach. This reach can be considerably extended by using video recording, audio recording, and the transmission of the same across classrooms and across campuses. In my view, the scope for improvement in effective use of the faculty time through these methods is considerable and I would not be surprised if IIMA could achieve at least 50 percent more reach out of this slack.

There is another consideration which has been argued with great force. Faculty strength has to be determined with reference to the number of areas and the minimum number of faculty in each of those areas. This is a valid point. If IIMA has a newly emerging area like IT or International Business and if it has only one or two faculty members, this could be very suboptimal from various angles. IIMA cannot offer many electives. The lively interaction which is required among the faculty members of the same Area would be missing. This would hurt both the quality of teaching and the quality of research. Any depletion at all could be disastrous. Each Area has a number of specializations and if it has a very limited number of faculty in that area, then the number of specialists or super specialists in that area would also be very limited. In short, a minimum critical size of around four to five is necessary for any Area to be effective and to maintain high quality standards.

When we look at the size of faculty in this context, there is an important distinction between two organizational situations. In the case of a standalone institution this poses a very huge challenge. As part of the university, the smaller size can be supplemented by drawing on the faculty resources from other departments or other faculty of the university. Take for example, Psychology. If the area of organizational behaviour has fewer numbers, the same can be supplemented by Industrial Psychologists or Social Psychologists drawn from the department of Psychology of the University. If it is a standalone institution this can be much more difficult and therefore the argument goes that IIMA needs to have a larger number of faculty.

Yet I believe another approach can be taken. In Ahmedabad, which offers several advantages, there are a number of good institutions clustered in a small area. If IIMA works effectively with some of these institutions whose quality, either at the individual or institutional level or at both, is high, then it can supplement its resources through a network relationship. This happens in various business schools all around the world. Of course, the difference is that many of them draw the faculty members from other departments of the University rather than from other institutions which are under a different organization altogether. HBS draws some of the services of social psychologists, economists and the like from across the Charles River from other Harvard institutions. But let us not forget that although many of these schools or faculties are part of the same university they are also fiercely independent in their working. So, having to work with network partners who are drawn from different organizational entities and partners who are drawn from different institutions of the same organization is really a matter of degree and not of category. I think IIMA has not explored this option enough or tried to make it work. It certainly has potential and IIMA needs to work for it. Ahmedabad is mentioned because of the locational factor but these days collaborative academic activity takes place over far greater distances. I have some more comments on the issue of augmenting the size of the faculty in a subsequent section.

There is an important perspective we need to examine in this regard. IIMA has always striven hard to be an institution of excellence. In the first few decades, this excellence was understood with reference to the Indian institutional scenario but over the last twenty years our reference point has become global. Huge efforts have gone into building this excellence. Every one associated with IIMA (myself included) would be greatly pained and indeed indicted by future generations, if this value were to be bartered away or even diluted in pursuit of scale and scope.

Of course, there is a need for expansion. But this expansion should be viewed in terms of impact and not necessarily numbers as implied in scale. From the very beginning, IIMA was the 'first call for help' for the corporate, social, and public sector. Today, at least as far as the corporate sector is concerned, that is no longer the case. Choosing important areas of national and corporate concerns and using research and training programmes to effectively address them is of great importance and this, in my view, also counts as expansion.

There is one more dimension which has been identified by all the members of the CFD, and that is the use of technology to extend our reach—be it students, executives, or the public at large—and to develop innovative design and delivery. A great deal is possible and it needs to be done soon.

All over the world, it has been recognized that a multi disciplinary approach to learning is more effective in dealing with real life problems. The CFD has also expressed its affirmation of this position. Some have termed it as expanding the scope. The debate is about how to achieve it. There has been a suggestion that the Institute should deepen and widen the areas which in some way impact management practice. Some have gone to the extent of saying that IIMA should evolve into a full-fledged University. My belief is that Ahmedabad has a unique education cluster. This has not yet been properly recognized and exploited. A more productive and effective way to ensure delivery of multi disciplinary education is to develop this cluster and to effectively work out networking arrangements within it. Such a model would pose great challenges to ensure its effective implementation. Faculty members all have different affiliations and each institution has different programme concepts. To harness them for a common objective would be no simple task. A deeper collaborative effort would be required between faculty members working together as well as inter-institutional understanding. For example, a professor of Psychology in an arts college working with a faculty colleague in the OB area in IIMA might have to spend considerable time understanding the objectives of the courses at IIMA, the pedagogy used, and its linkage with other courses. Despite such extensive co-engagement, such efforts could have a huge academic pay off. In other words, IIMA should address the issue of scale and scope through impact and cluster, without risking its position as an 'Institute of Excellence'. Interpreted in this way, the size issue becomes well and truly downsized!

ECONOMIES OF SCALE AND COST EFFECTIVENESS

The argument for size and scale was made for achieving self reliance without depending heavily on teaching for generating resources. Many faculty members felt this would help to save time which could then be devoted to research. Others based their position mainly on cutting costs and break-even analysis.

As I expressed at the CFD, I find this point unsound. Although many faculty members believe that the key to financial viability is economies of scale, this claim is not supported by any data. Before accepting this proposition one needs to satisfy oneself on two or three points. First, is there a scope for reducing the fixed cost in any case? IIMA has been saddled with a large number of employees in the support category, especially those relating to security and the maintenance of the infrastructure. This is a legacy from the past and the possibility of outsourcing needs to be explored. This could happen over a period of time either by attrition or by voluntary retirement.

Secondly, many of the institution's administrative positions could be made more efficient in two ways. Either IIMA could recruit people with broader skills and therefore utilize their time more effectively or find other ways of sharing the services. When one looks at the support staff, we often find that the time utilization of the staff is low. It is my belief that if a rational sharing pattern is evolved and the support staff are trained in multiple skills, it should be possible to work with less people. This is with regard to cutting the fixed costs of the institution.

Now let us approach this problem from another side. Over a period of time, in institutions, the nature of fixed costs becomes similar to variable costs. In other words, these so-called fixed costs do not remain 'fixed' over a long period of time. Obviously, all the fixed costs move in steps, except, for example, depreciation, which moves in very, very large steps. But all other costs move in steps and as far as a teaching institution like IIMA is concerned, these steps are not relatively small. When one increases the faculty size, let us say from 100 to 125, the so-called fixed costs would also rise up at almost the same proportion. The only fixed cost which may remain the same, one might argue is the salary of the CAO or the CFO. This proposition can be verified by looking at the cost structures of industries and institutions from various fields and various countries. Today, it might appear that size can provide better viability by spreading the fixed costs over a larger number; but once innovative ways are pursued to reduce these costs, the scale solution will no longer make that much sense.

What we have discussed so far are general issues of scale. While I am convinced, based on my experience and an analysis of various industries and institutions, regarding the nature of fixed costs and their behaviour over different capacity levels; I think a more detailed exercise might help us to resolve the issue once and for all.

The third point about the future direction of IIMA relates to the scope. I dealt with this in part when I discussed the matter of network relationship. There are two factors to be considered here. One relates to size. The number of faculty beyond a certain point creates various problems which all lead towards sub-optimal operation. The world over, there is now a perceived need to draw upon different disciplines and domains to develop specialized innovative programmes. In search of solutions to real life problems; a wider multi-disciplinary approach has emerged. There are domain specific or multi-disciplinary programmes offered by business schools in collaboration with institutions from the same university or other universities. Apart from this, institutions have also realized that the cultural diversity of business operations in this globalized world calls for culture specific specializations.

It is impossible for any single institution, based in just one country, to develop and offer this in an effective manner. The last ten years have seen several global collaborations emerging in order to offer this kind of programme. Some programmes are so designed that parts of the programme are even delivered in different continents by collaborating institutions. This is just the beginning; I strongly believe that many more such collaborative innovations are now in the offing.

The business world has seen many new innovative organizational structures come into being in order to deal with the changing environment. This will happen to business schools as well. Business schools will have to create new ways of working to be able to offer differentiated innovative programmes that meet the specific needs of various groups of executives and students.

In short, it is my strong belief that IIMA needs to start understanding, learning, and effectively implementing network relationships as a basis for future growth and expansion and future quality offerings. If it remains insular in this regard, its reach will be limited as will its quality and effectiveness. In most institutions, the ratio of full time faculty to visiting/adjunct is falling.

While IIMA needs to expand in scale and scope, that should not be detrimental to the pursuit of excellence. IIMA needs to be aware of the possible conflict between the two. In other words, IIMA should address the issue of scale and scope through impact and cluster, without risking the position as an 'Institute of Excellence'.

FACULTY RECRUITMENT

Supplementing faculty resources is a huge challenge. Over the years, the overall strength of faculty has fluctuated between seventy-five and ninety-five. IIMA has not been able to increase the strength on a permanent basis. This is difficult, and more innovative ways of recruiting faculty will have to be put in place. But there are other avenues besides recruiting permanent faculty which need to be recognized and explored. In the modern world, collaboration across institutions and across geographies has become a reality. IIMA needs to review the ratio of permanent to temporary faculty. Can IIMA get temporary faculty from any part of the world? Can it get temporary faculty from the practicing world? Can we build up faculty collaboration within the region? These avenues are all possible. As we look to the future, with great improvements in communication technology facilitating an improved audio/video presence, near virtual classrooms can be created. The possibilities of faculty being available from any part of the world can become a reality. New issues of motivation, of salaries, of logistics, and scheduling will crop up. Handled well, this could provide a huge advantage in designing better programmes and delivering them more effectively without having to expand a permanent faculty pool which would bring its own limitations and problems.

Many of the faculty members in various global institutions are connected with IIMA—either as alumni or former faculty members; some others through joint research projects or visiting faculty. These people understand IIMA, its values and culture, and they have an affinity to the Institute. This presents an opportunity to attract and engage them in our new activities. This could be based on a loose network relationship. Such a relationship is based on collaborative interest rather than material gain or the offer of a stable permanent job. Managing such loose relationships and still keeping focus on a programme or activity, requires high levels of interpersonal and inter-institutional skills. Meeting this challenge would not only improve the scale of operations at IIMA but also take it to the cutting edge.

Due to the pressure of numbers and economies of scale, a case is being made out for a larger faculty pool to handle a greater number of students. As mentioned earlier, development in technology can help improve the reach without necessarily expanding the permanent faculty pool. Management education covers some basic disciplines as well as many applied ones. Many of these basic disciplines require developing and communicating analytical frame works. The applied disciplines require more interaction between the students and the teachers. The former can expand the class size by creating virtual classrooms. For the latter, experiments with different virtual classroom designs may be possible. We should explore whether an interactive session in a physical location can be transmitted in real time or offline related to another group located in a different location. This can be further facilitated by a TA to help the students learn nearly as effectively as the physical classroom. Such possibilities need exploring. There may be a little 'transmission loss' in the process but by imaginative handling, this could be kept to a minimal level. If done well, this provides a huge opportunity for scaling up and leveraging the small faculty resources.

We have discussed the issue of size, scale, and scope. Faculty is the main resource for an academic institution. There has been an acute shortage of high quality trained managers in the country and this has created tremendous pressure over the years on IIMA to expand. Apart from external pressures, there have been internal aspirations for growth and development. Yet IIMA has not been able to substantially expand its faculty resources. There are various reasons for this. One of the reasons often advanced has been the poor pay scale. The market for high quality talent in the field of management is global. Professors move from one country to another, from one institution to another, and often straddle many institutions across the globe in various continents. Today, you can find many faculty members lecturing in a US Business School one week, and the following week they will be doing the same thing in Singapore. Even in a profession where people like to strike roots and not like to move, the rate of mobility has gone up substantially. With the use of technology, the academic collaboration between faculty members of different institutions has become simple, easy, and seamless.

This phenomenon has considerably loosened the bond between the faculty and the institution. Institutions have also begun to realize this and to make adjustments in their policies. Business schools allow, and in many cases encourage, their faculty members to associate with other business schools in other parts of the world and even within the same geographical region. This has been done for positive as well as negative reasons. The positive reason is that whatever leads to the personal development of the faculty member is eventually beneficial to the institution where he works. It also means that the research output of the institution can increase substantially through inter-institutional and inter-faculty collaboration. It leads to a greater diversity in the experience of the faculty member, the subjects or the issue of research that they pursue, and the context in which such research is carried out. The mother institution benefits. The main negative reason is that given the current shortage of good faculty around the world, the institution has little choice but to accommodate the needs of the faculty member if it wishes to keep him. This is the global reality of business schools today.

Given this situation, the faculty at IIMA has also begun to develop contacts and working relationships with other institutions and the faculty of other institutions. There is an underlying competition between institutions to attract faculty by way of either compensation or facilities granted or the degree of freedom provided in pursuing their work. While it is possible for IIMA to gradually begin to loosen its rules relating to full time commitment to IIMA, compensation has been a big bottleneck. I have discussed elsewhere the deleterious effects of the GoI regulations on compensation.

In recent years, through various top-up mechanisms, the problem of compensation has been handled to deal reasonably well with the reality. A greater flexibility of attachment is also gradually being provided. But all of this serves to bring into focus the issues relating to faculty recruitment and development processes.

When one looks at the recruits of the last few years, one is struck by the paucity of the number recruited and sometimes by the qualifications, experience, and research output of the prospective faculty members. Recently, a study was conducted of the background of the recruits in IIMA and IIM Bangalore. It was found that nearly seventy per cent of IIM Bangalore's recruits received their PhDs from foreign universities, whereas in the case of IIMA it was the other way round. It is not that PhDs from Indian institutions are of poor quality, indeed there have been many real stars that have come through that system. At the same time, it is generally recognized in academic circles that the rigour through which PhD students pass in foreign universities is of a much higher order. As a result, on an average, foreign PhDs have proved to be of significantly higher quality, especially in the area of research. What then do these statistics reveal? Does it mean that for some reason, the IIMA recruitment process is working against foreign PhDs and in favour of Indian PhDs? It cannot be argued that IIMA is inferior or pays poorly compared to Bangalore. In fact, IIMA has always been the institution of first choice as far as faculty members are concerned. Then how do we explain this anomaly? Is the process of filtering the nominations through the Area working against the nomination of good PhDs from foreign universities? Is there a bias against foreign PhDs? Whether it is down to a sense of pride or a sense of insecurity is a moot question. The point is, the process needs reviewing and counter checking.

The recruitment of fresh faculty is one of the ways to supplement our faculty resources. But it has been the tradition at IIMA to also invest a great deal in faculty development. In the early years, potential faculty was recruited and the Institute facilitated their enrollment for Master's and PhD programmes at HBS and other leading business schools. Many of them were recruited as research associates before they went on to complete their PhDs in foreign universities. Balakrishnan, Prahlad, Jahar Saha—these are just a few of the names which come to mind. In some cases, the Institute provided some support. They also gave a lien on the job. The FF grant supported some initial inductions. Institutional recommendations also helped some faculty members. This was a semi-active policy. In some cases, the Institute encouraged and sponsored candidates. In other cases, the research associates and the faculty members approached the Institute for facilitation. The process worked well and the yield has been reasonably good. Lately, however, it would appear that this process has fallen into disuse just when the Institute most needs an active policy to do this. IIMA has used FPM programme as one of the devices to develop faculty. For quite some time, it followed the policy of not recruiting its own FPMs. The reason behind this was that it would lead to inbreeding. That policy has become somewhat loosened in the present day.

In my view, the entire gamut of policies relating to faculty development requires a serious review. The problem of faculty shortage is real and acute. It requires innovative ways to deal with it and means a complete redesign of the compensation package. IIMA needs to nurture potential faculty resources. A more flexible approach to faculty attachments to the Institute is also required. All the talk about scale and size will become sterile unless we tackle the issue of faculty resource development.

INTERNAL RECRUITMENT

In the early years, there was a policy to not offer faculty positions to our doctoral students. The idea was that this might lead to inbreeding. Later on, as faculty recruitment became more and more difficult, this policy was relaxed. The same happened when it came to the selection of directors. There was a strong belief that IIMA was a unique institution with a unique culture. In the successive selection of directors, the faculty strongly influenced the Search Committee to look for internal candidates. As I have mentioned, even I was initially a votary of this convention. However, there is something to be said about periodic challenges to the established institutional ways of doing things. This happened when I.G. Patel was inducted. IIMA has not had an 'external' Director since. The inbreeding has probably closed the Institute off from the benefits of experimentation and innovation arising out of a fresh look from an outsider. It is time for IIMA to shed this bias.

BALANCE IN FACULTY ACTIVITY: ROLE OF RESEARCH

Right from the beginning, the faculty was expected to do teaching, case writing, research, and consulting. This was done with a view that the faculty remains continuously in touch with the practicing reality and that the teaching in the classroom was not purely theoretical with little connection to everyday business reality. It was felt that these four activities reinforce each other and help achieve the basic objective of connecting the classroom to the complexity of the real world.

It is recognized that IIM has done an excellent job of teaching over the years. The students who have come out of the Institute vouch for this and global ranking on this parameter has been consistently high. However, lately, people have started questioning even this. They argue that the ability to attract the best students in itself ensures that the quality of our graduates is very high. We need to attempt the difficult task of measuring value addition.

Research on the other hand, has been an area of weakness as far as the IIMA faculty is concerned. Every Committee has noted this. There clearly is a huge gap in this area. The number of articles in peer reviewed journals has been miniscule. In one of the BoG Meetings, which was held at the Infosys Campus in the year 2003, the BoG raised a pertinent question while discussing faculty compensation. How many articles have been published by IIMA faculty in peer reviewed journals over the last five years? The Director was hard put to come up with the number. Later, it transpired that hardly any such papers were published. In recognition of this fact, in the review of the compensation, the BoG decided to incentivize research. Even so, research remains a weak area. It needs to be strengthened and no one now questions this conclusion.

Once we are clear about our positioning, a research agenda has to be derived. Positioning leads to redefining the mission. Developing transformative leaders for Indian organizations should be our central mission. Once we adopt that mission, programmes—both short term and long term—have to be designed and developed in order to fulfill that mission. For effective delivery of these programmes, research in these areas becomes absolutely essential. Unless we undertake an extensive programme of research into how complex trends in economic, social, political, and technology fields impact different businesses, delivery of the programmes will not be effective. The faculty will have to be motivated to engage in this kind of research. The Institute's fund allocation, processes and performance system, need to be integrated with this thrust.

In the early days of the Institute, case writing had a high priority. Initially, IIMA was using HBS cases. On a crash basis, the Institute developed nearly sixty to seventy per cent of Indian cases to replace the Harvard cases in the first five to seven years. However, after that initial burst of creativity, case writing has slowed down.

IIMA also needed to support the placement of our graduates in positions within Indian industry. Unlike the conventional universities, IIMA wanted to fully connect with the real world. Executive education was in great demand. This led to a closer relationship with industry executives and companies. IIMA's contribution to their problem solving built positive relationships and rewards.

Extensive work, for example, was done for companies such as L&T, State Bank of India, Hindustan Lever, and so on. This also led to an indirect accreditation of the Institute. A bias was built for corporate industrial relationships and individual problem solving. This helped consultancy as well. But research was always much more than that. Research meant looking at broad trends. It meant looking at new knowledge that would be applicable not just to one unit but to an entire industry or even the country as a whole. It required a different mental discipline, a more rigorous approach, and evaluation by a different constituency. Problem solving was addressed to a particular business. Research would be addressed to and evaluated by faculty members and researchers in the same or similar field all around the world, a different constituency altogether. Early recognition of case writing and consultancy became embedded in the culture of the institution. To strike a different balance between the problem solving approach for individual units and research orientation, I believe, is a task that still needs to be addressed.

The other reason also has cultural roots. Ravi Matthai was a great believer in research leading to improved practices. He considered organization at work was a management lab. He believed that by studying current practices and the reactions to interventions, observing and collecting data and processes as they unfolded in real life held many lessons and provided insights. He called this 'action research'. This was the counterpart to learning by doing. However, it must be noted that this idea of research took a deeper meaning for Ravi after he stepped down from the Directorship and began his project of The Rural University. This approach also probably contributed to conventional research not really taking off at IIMA.

Some also believe that the culture of faculty freedom that IIMA espoused so deeply, no doubt had a great impact on the balance between teaching and research. Faculty freedom helped build good delivery practices as far as the PGP programme was concerned. The freedom to design the course, the pedagogy used, and the assessment made helped a great deal in developing the best teaching practices. One would have expected faculty freedom to do the same or probably more for pursuing research agenda. However, in practice, this did not happen. Teaching students and executives was the central focus in those early days. Individual faculty as well as the Institute reaped substantial benefits by doing this well. The faculty became known in business circles, landed consultancy projects and became inducted into the corporate world through directorships and other engagements. For the Institute this helped consultancy and placement activities. Initially, this did not require original research backup to maintain high teaching standards. A strong integration of research in the performance measurement system was lacking and as a result, faculty freedom worked in a counterproductive manner as far as research was concerned.

These days research has become a widely collaborative effort. It has grown more feasible because of mobility as well as technology. Globalization has given great impetus to such studies. In fact, western business schools have focused on globalization and its impact as a major part of the research agenda. Markets have shifted. Competitive advantage has also shifted from the western world to the Asian countries. This has posed a great challenge to business schools in advanced countries. It has become the centerpiece of their research focus. Research in this phenomenon requires collaboration because of cultural differences and contextual factors. It is here that IIMA has been too slow to rise to the challenge. HBS has established a centre to support research in India. Many other leading institutions are planning similar ventures. What steps have our faculty members taken to exploit this major trend? What institutional policies have been formulated to deal with this? These questions need to be tackled immediately. IIMA has lost too much ground and at this rate, if it does not take action straight away, the situation will become irredeemable.

ISSUE OF FACULTY COMPENSATION AND PERFORMANCE MANAGEMENT

In 2003, a committee was formed by the BoG to go into the issue of faculty compensation. Given the GoI regulation on the grade/scale revision the only option was to design an add-on or top-up package. This was designed as additional compensation for extra teaching, special research output, or special admin responsibilities. The Institute was expanding and there was a need to ensure that the programmes were properly taught. The faculty stretched themselves to do their best for the programmes. Many, but not all, were taking large teaching loads. The programmes were expanding, but the faculty wasn't. To tackle this, the Director introduced as a first step, a greater reliance on the visiting faculty and as a result he increased their compensation. This set a shadow price for faculty teaching. After that, a norm was set up for teaching by the faculty. Whoever taught more was rewarded at the increased rate of compensation. In this way, teaching became incentivized.

It also meant that people came up with more electives, to earn more money. This also involved case writing, putting together research studies, thereby extending their own work in the area. In other words, this helped to stimulate some research activity. Measuring the performance often involved subjective factors in evaluation and judgement. Measuring output on the other hand was more straightforward. The implication was that if the outcome was higher it meant that either the demand was higher or the person concerned was able to deliver it well so that the demand became sustained. So using output as a benchmark of performance, and rewarding it, can be said to be part of the performance management system.

One of the recent Directors cited one incident. The norm was that if there were a minimum of five enrolments, the elective could be offered and it would count in teaching load. The PGP Chairman expressed his fears that some people could manipulate the students ensuring that at least five people registered for the elective and thereby earn lakhs of rupees. He responded by saying, 'okay, the idea is not wrong. You can change the norm from five to ten or 5 percent of the total student strength.' In other words, he argued that just because there is a likelihood of misuse, one should not give up on an idea or complicate it to such an extent that it becomes totally bureaucratic and ineffective. This applies to any system and any situation.

FACULTY MOTIVATION

Why have the challenges of faculty recruitment and the development of research failed to produce the required institutional response? Is it because IIMA has not been able to see the emerging challenges? Is it because the Institute has not been able to find good answers to these problems? Is it because of the culture and rigidity of the processes? We need to look at these questions very carefully. It could be a question of the leadership being unable to spot these challenges in time. It could even be termed as a failure of leadership to adapt the processes in order to meet these emerging challenges. Lately, Directors have lamented the fact that the culture of faculty freedom has become highly dysfunctional as far as the welfare of the Institute is concerned. This has been taken to extremes.

In one such debate, I had to formulate my question somewhat sharply. My poser was, what does the faculty want as a model for the management of the Institute? Is the Institute a polyclinic where the faculties park themselves and do their own work? The Institute provides the infrastructure within which they operate. But there is no integration between what the faculty does and what the Institute requires. Or is it a faculty cooperative whereby the faculty themselves decide what the agenda is and how it should be executed? Their accountability is to themselves. Or is it more like an orchestra, perhaps? In other words, there are institutional goals and objectives towards which everyone contributes and a Director, like a conductor, ensures that the faculty works in harmony to achieve these goals and objectives.

This issue is very, very central. It epitomizes a basic clash between the concept of faculty freedom that the Institute has espoused all these years and the need to harness them towards institutional needs. There is an apparent conflict between the two. In the past, the binding force was shared values and shared objectives. Faculty freedom was viewed in this context. The conflicts were minimal because of these shared values and culture. In some ways, the leadership was more contextual. The other crucial factor was the pioneering spirit of adventure for building our very own world class institution right here in India. The pride one felt, the satisfaction it gave, and the recognition it brought were great motivators and unifiers. After the first twenty or so years, this gradually began to diminish. IIMA had arrived, it was recognized, and it was put on a pedestal. Then came the liberalization of industry. Industry began looking at the global market and tapping global resources. Industry discovered that it could learn from international practices. Collaboration came, foreign businesses came, and the horizon became much wider. The easy pickings were gone, exploited and exhausted, and more complex managerial practices were required. Now, it was possible to import these practices. It was possible to understand them, companies could even send their executives abroad to study them, to learn from them. They could even get some of the foreign executives to come to India and train their people and show them; how to get things done. The environment had changed and IIMA found itself late in realizing the situation. Even now, I think it is still lagging behind. Why is it that the leading companies in each sector go to international consulting firms to study their problems and to give advice? Why don't they come to IIMA? In the past L&T, Hindustan Lever, the State Bank of India and many multinationals came to us, but not now. Not anymore. Why is it that so few members of the upper levels of management bother to enroll in the executive education programmes? Why do they flock instead to programmes offered by the likes of HBS, IMD, Stanford, and so on? I fear we are becoming disconnected and this is an area of major concern.

It is easy to blame all of this on a lack of compensation flexibility, but to my mind that is over simplifying the facts. It is also quite tempting to say that the Director should have more authority to direct faculty resources to centrally defined priorities, to frame more rules for the faculty, for allocating their time, or for linking benefits to such allocations. This will be intensely debated; freedom on the one hand and rules on the other; autonomy and accountability. The culture and processes were certainly relevant in the past, but in a dynamic world, culture and processes have to be adaptable. While a major shift has taken place in the last fifteen years, a radical look at these processes is called for. Care has to be exercised to identify the core and to preserve it as we develop adaptive responses. Let us never forget the need for checks and balances.

The faculty as a collective body has been a source of great strength in times of crises. It has also acted as a self correcting mechanism because of the debate and introspection that it generates. IIMA should not give up that. The solution therefore lies in striking a balance between rules and values, regulations and autonomous actions. Putting this into practice is an art in itself. It requires leadership qualities, refined judgement, and sensitive support from the other organs of the governance structure. It also requires deep introspection by the faculty themselves.

The performance management system is often mentioned, but in an academic institution it is difficult to design and operate. Even more so in an institution like IIMA, with its deep culture of faculty freedom. In a collegial system there are no bosses or subordinates. Who reviews whose performance— now that is the question. In other words, colleagues have to play the role of assessors and that is never easy. The Institute needs to come up with an innovative way to handle this. What is the metrix of performance for teaching, research and 'consultancy', i.e. what is the impact on practice? What about the balance between these activities? What is the appropriate time horizon over which it should be measured? Performance can be viewed from the perspective of an individual faculty member—the kind of work he does, the research he carries out, the publications record, the teaching he does in the classroom, his standing with industry and so on. But there is also another perspective. Does all of this add up to what the Institute wants to achieve? Is it aligned to the goals and objectives of the Institute? Both these perspectives have to be considered in evaluating or assessing performance. Of course, this is difficult to put into operation. But to leave it unattended, not to recognize, nor even to attempt it would greatly harm the Institute. Unless this issue is recognized at BoG and Director level, IIMA will face problems in recruiting and retaining the type and number of faculty we need. Yes, mistakes will be made, things won't always run smooth and there will be conflicts, but without such a system it will be impossible to develop a faculty group deeply committed to the goals and objectives of the Institute. This is the huge challenge facing the leaders of IIMA today.

Two or three important points emerge here. One is the collegial or peer culture that the Institute has built and its value. This is in part a structural outcome but largely it is built on the processes implemented by Ravi Matthai and the other early pioneers. There are certain basic values at the heart of this design, that all faculty members are equal, that they can participate as equals in the decision making process of the Institute, that the collective wisdom of the faculty must guide the major decisions—whether it is administration or faculty evaluation. Merit, and only merit, should be the criteria. Processes must be built on mutual trust and respect. Ravi followed the model of participative democratic leadership. Faculty freedom and self regulation were the essence of this culture. What it meant was that faculty had to ensure acceptance of any institutional activity proposed by them. They had to get others to 'purchase' their point of view on academic and institutional matters. Ravi wanted to avoid the creation of a hierarchy and the use of authority. As a consequence, in many activities, acceptability became a major criteria overshadowing capability. I believe that the balance between acceptability and capability was heavily tilted towards the former. It is time now to redress the balance. Unless this is done, the quality of any decision making is sure to suffer. However, this should be done carefully, after all IIMA does not want to throw away the baby with the bath water.

A system of checks and balances should be designed so as to neutralize personal biases but at the same time they should not be so rule bound as to breed a new bureaucracy. Disputes often arise around interpretation. For every rule which is made, there will be many special cases and these special cases will need to be handled on a case by case basis. The system cannot be so rigid that it becomes blind to any unforeseen situations. Systems and processes cannot automate decisions, they can only aid them. Tact and sensitivity are required to make these processes and systems work. They can't be designed with potential misuse in mind, but should be designed to optimize their use.

INTERNAL GOVERNANCE

There is the issue of governance at both the level of internal academic management and at BoG level. I have stated my views about board level governance extensively in an earlier chapter. Here I will deal with the issue of internal governance. I have separately commented on this in the section dealing with faculty and the role of the director. Here is a brief summary.

Internal governance has come under severe pressure because of several factors. There has been a large expansion in the number of programmes and enrolment over the last five or seven years and we have not been able to increase the number of faculty significantly. A few years back, there was severe pressure to improve the compensation package of the faculty within the framework of the existing government rules. These factors led to the modification of the compensation package which was designed to serve both the overall improvement in the package as well as to incentivize certain activities. In the chapter on governance, I have dealt at length with the details of the changes in the compensation package proposed by the committee of the Board and subsequently adopted by the BoG and the faculty in 2003. I understand there have been some unexpected consequences flowing from these incentives, such as a strong bias towards teaching in-company training programmes at the expense of allocating time for research. This can be reviewed and corrected.

At the same time, there is a constant need for ensuring that IIMA aligns the faculty interest with the institutional goals. Faculty freedom is an extremely important value, but obviously it has to be aligned to the institutional mission and goals. The BoG, represented by the stakeholders, defines the mission and goals of the institution. The academic management needs to chalk out a way to achieve them and they should have full freedom to decide how this is to be done. The BoG would have the responsibility of monitoring the same periodically through various processes. I have spelt out in details my position on accountability in a note which forms the appendix to the chapter on governance.

Internal governance requires academic decisions to be aligned with the goals of the Institute. The process of debate and discussions should illuminate decision making but in a timely manner. These should be carried out swiftly and efficiently, and accountability for the outcomes should be clearly defined and monitored. The key process in regard to this is a well designed performance management system. Here one has to strike a balance between judgement, discretion, and flexibility on the one hand and the rule bound process on the other. It is a delicate balance but a leadership embodying transparency and integrity of purpose can make it work effectively.

ROLE OF THE DIRECTOR

There are three important dimensions to this role. One is to interface with the outside world, whether it is government, business or other academic institutions. The second is the management of the Institute, which is basically the internal management of the institute. This is also often described as internal governance. The third is to play the role of a faculty member for teaching, research and in some cases consultancy as long as it does not result in any conflict of interest.

The GoI is still the main promoter of the Institute and it plays that role quite actively. Many crucial decisions are still taken by the GoI, often unilaterally, and sometimes in a consultative manner. We have looked at the appointment of the Chairman, the appointment of the Director, the compensation of faculty, the acquisition of physical assets, and the preparation and submission of budgets and accounts. These are all very powerful levers in the hands of the GoI. Expansion, faculty compensation, and financial matters are the primary issues that a Director, once appointed, must deal with the GoI over.

The Director also needs to maintain live contacts with industry leaders and business organizations at various levels. This is important when it comes to understanding the needs of the corporate sector in terms of the executive skills they are looking for and therefore the design of the course programmes. It is necessary for the development of case material and research projects. IIMA graduates need to be placed within industries as well. The stronger and more active the bond with industry, the greater the chances of financial and academic support. IIMA has always distinguished itself from other institutions by maintaining and developing such contacts. As we noted earlier, nearly all the Chairmen came from industry and it was the pioneering leaders with their industry background and connections who helped to build these bridges. HBS had underlined this and the early leaders at IIMA accepted this and assiduously built this relationship. This is not confined only to business organizations but also with various levels of government—Central, State, local, other NGOs, and academic institutions within and outside the country. It is the Director who has to play this role actively if he is to develop and promote these relationships.

There is another side to the role of Director, and that is the regulatory side. The government wants the Institute to follow certain directions. Often this is a matter of negotiation and active engagement in the formulation of the same. This is a time consuming and stressful exercise. It is the leadership quality of the Director, the support that he garners from the Chairman, Board members, other IIMs and well wishers of the Institute, the contacts within the government system, the respect that he commands—all these factors play an important role in managing the external relationship.

The external relationship has yet another facet and this is more of a social nature. Often, being located in a particular area, the Director has to maintain relationships with the local leaders in various fields. He has to make appearances at social or other semi-formal events. All of this takes a toll on his time. It also means that he has to be extremely selective when it comes to allocating his time between all of these various competing demands.

Every Director has had a unique style and priority. But increasingly, the demands of the external environment have grown. Apart from dealing with the government and the local community, the maintenance of global relationships has become more urgent and takes up a heavier demand on his time. I believe that in the discharge of these important functions, some structural changes might have to be introduced. A Dean of International Relations, a Senior Compliance Officer, a Community Relations Manager—these are various possibilities which need to be explored.

While implementing structural changes at the academic management level it is important to remember the role of the Director as the gatekeeper. He has to guard against the ingress of external influences and the BoG on internal academic management and also the other way around. Managing these boundary relationships is the real test of a successful director. While reviewing this structure to help reduce the load of the Director, IIMA must be careful not to lose sight of this crucial aspect of the role of the head of the institution.

IIMA is at a crossroads. The challenges ahead are huge and complex. IIMA has to devise ways of doing things differently. The job of the Director is far more complicated. To carve out a new mission, to raise resources and to guide the faculty pool towards that mission while preserving faculty freedom requires leadership of a different kind. A recognized academic specialist may not be able to play this role. The role can best be described as an academic entrepreneur with a high level of leadership skills. This also means that he will have to create a support structure for other functions such as programme planning, research and publication, innovative pedagogies, alumni relationships, and placements. This means that while the culture of faculty freedom and faculty autonomy will be retained, policies and processes will be developed to harmonize their personal objectives with the institutional mission and goals. The central change will be developing a performance management system which is not only well designed but seriously implemented. This is the major change in internal governance that is required to meet the challenges of tomorrow.

FINANCE MANAGEMENT AND FUND RAISING

Promoters are a group of initial stakeholders who provide funds and other support. As we saw earlier, new stakeholders have emerged in the form of alumni and faculty. The environment has also changed completely. Self reliance has to be viewed in the context of larger resource needs for growth, development, and long term security. There are various ways by which resources can be mobilized. The scope and limits of using the different sources of funds have to be clearly understood and balanced. Carving out a model of self reliance for current and future operations, balancing the various pulls and pressures, possibilities and constraints is going to be difficult. One single mistake or mishap could prove disastrous to our future. Given the enormous goodwill and brand equity, however, our degrees of freedom in this area are extensive.

Perceptions about the Institute's financial position have created a great deal of confusion. I think IIMA needs to look at its finances in a proper perspective. In the earlier chapter on IIMA Finances, I have dealt with this issue at length. Often there is a sense of panic in its approach to finance. I find this totally misplaced. IIMA has to mobilize resources if it hopes to strengthen the infrastructure and give support to future innovative programmes. On the issue of resource mobilization, I would like to state that every source of funding has its pros and cons; limitations and stretchability; freedom and shackles. The resource mix must be chosen very carefully to ensure that our vulnerability is manageable. I believe, given its 'Goodwill Bank', the demand supply scenario and its tangible and intangible assets, finance really is the least of the problems facing the Institute.

Most financial issues relate to fund raising. This is an important activity which has not received enough attention at IIMA. Time and again, I have heard many Directors and other senior faculty members lamenting the fact that IIMA does not have enough depth in financial resources. This is required for development and future security. While the need is obvious, the efforts made to secure this remain sketchy. In the past, many initiatives were taken, especially mobilizing resources from alumni, but these have not borne substantial fruits. IIMA has a huge 'Goodwill Bank' with their alumni, with business organizations and other associates, and past faculty and staff. These people all have strong emotional ties to IIMA. Many of them have been great beneficiaries of IIMA and for most of them, their association with the Institute has been a life changing experience. These bonds are strong and they provide latent support possibilities. I say 'latent' because this has not been systematically analyzed, imaginatively formulated, creatively designed or vigorously tapped. Many alumni have expressed the feeling that they have greatly benefitted from IIMA. They would like to do something for IIMA, but they don't know what to do. Nor have they been approached in a systematic manner or with a well formulated scheme, detailing ways in which they can support IIMA. Even the alumni group events have not been engaging enough. Many alumni when visiting IIMA have not felt especially welcome. Many of them are important alumni who have done very well in their professional lives. A continuing relationship has to be built and not just an occasional fund raising forum. This effort has received neither the importance it deserves nor the organizational focus or the special kind of skills required to develop this. As a result this 'Goodwill Bank' of alumni has remained largely untapped. Other institutions both at home and abroad have successfully managed to raise funds, so why not IIMA? I should note that the realization is beginning to be felt and lately efforts towards this have developed a much sharper focus.

Fund raising requires the integration of three or four things. A solid performance in terms of delivering programmes to the beneficiaries. Second, a clear well defined articulation of the needs of the organization. Why it is needed? What will the Institute do to develop this and where it will lead to? Third, in order to gain credibility, the Institute needs to show a proven track record of using the funds effectively. Fourth, an ability to package and to communicate these needs in an appealing manner to the alumni and private foundations. IIMA has not gone beyond expressing in a general sort of way its need for funds. Neither have they gone beyond sending out general appeals to the alumni asking for support. As a result, these initiatives have remained more or less barren. Sometimes it has been suggested that we need to induct professionals to handle this function. Professionals can help but I think the Director will have to guide such professionals and maintain a certain supportive role as far as such professionals are concerned. This is how it is done in other successful institutions. There are lessons to be learnt. IIMA is great. But to put it on a pedestal and bow down to it won't help anyone.

DEVELOPING INFRASTRUCTURE AND NEW BUILDINGS

That the Building Committee has existed for all fifty years is a unique phenomenon. It has acquired the status of a standing committee. One often one wonders why IIMA has kept this more or less permanent Building

Committee. IIMA does not have many other committees. In fact there are only two Board Committees— the Finance Committee and the Building Committee. Why the Building Committee has been given this importance is a question to ponder upon. Initially, when the new campus had to be designed and built one could understand the need for a Project or Building Committee. Also, in the case of IIMA, local industry had provided funds for the construction of buildings. Kasturbhai Lalbhai had a great sense of design and architecture for new buildings. Local industry having provided the funds for the building had the right to have its say in the selection of the architect, the design of the buildings and its construction. This was the origination of the Building Committee. Construction activity has been more or less continuous for many years except for a brief lull of about ten years in the mid eighties to mid nineties. The maintenance of the buildings is also an important function. The Building Committee looks after the construction of new buildings as well as their maintenance.

The early leaders paid great attention to the design and architecture of the Institute. IIMA has become a symbol of institutional architecture. The image it has created is deeply engraved in the minds of all those who came into contact with it and lately among the general public as well. Today, when anyone talks about management education, the image of the Louis Kahn Plaza or the entrance steps spring to one's mind.

This is how the Building Committee and its role have acquired an important place at IIMA.

As IIMA expands, more building space is required. The original architect is no longer with him. The people who worked with him are also ageing. New buildings have to be built which cater to different needs. The pedagogy and technology have changed. Programme designs have introduced new requirements. Expectations about convenience and comfort have also changed. The norms and standards and even the values represented by the buildings have all changed. In the earlier years, air conditioning the building would have been considered profligate and unthinkable. Today, it is considered to be a norm. As a result of all these changes, the new generation expects the buildings to be designed differently and with much greater amenities.

At the same time these new buildings must maintain a certain harmony and architectural vocabulary with the old buildings. This often represents a clash of values. The old buildings represent a certain asceticism. They represent grandeur through simplicity. They create an image of a monument which is far greater than any individual. On the other hand, the new buildings require greater comfort, a design which recognizes the change in the availability of material. The quality of bricks which were available earlier is no longer so. Maintenance of a brick structure over long periods is more difficult than concrete but its aesthetics also have to be balanced.

Grandeur, even if simple, usually results in some kind of inefficiency when it comes to building space. This presents an important trade-off. The early leaders balanced them. Today, the Institute management thinks differently. They think far more in terms of efficiency. The image and symbolism and the values which they represent have probably taken a lower priority. All these link to a different sense of accountability and perhaps an overriding sense of a more mundane and short term view of efficiency. Buildings last centuries, they leave an everlasting image in the minds of those who live there or even those who are just passing through. Is IIMA losing sight of this aspect of design of building? Is it fully understood or is it even appreciated? The worry is that it will probably come up with a series of nondescript buildings. The feelings and thoughts and emotions that the grand buildings evoke would be lost. When one visits global campuses like Harvard, Yale, Stanford etc. one comes back with the feeling as to how these institutions have maintained a certain consistency and harmony and held up the need for consistent image and values. I truly hope we are not abandoning our architectural image.

This difference in philosophy about the buildings has been the source of tension between the Building Committee on the one hand and the Director and some of the faculty members on the other. I believe that the importance of the design of architecture and building has not been fully understood or communicated. I feel that perhaps the Institute has taken a very short term view on this matter. It has constrained itself unwisely over the issues of the costs of building and funding. In my view, the Institute should have worked on eliminating or loosening that constraint rather than accepting it. This position needs to be re-evaluated at the earliest opportunity. Henceforth, while designing buildings priority should be given to the image and the values that they represent. The trade-off between image and values, and cost is not as stark as it is made out to be.

GOVERNANCE STRUCTURE

In an earlier chapter we examined at length the issues relating to governance structure at the BoG level and in the context of the overriding nature of the GoI's authority. Specifically this related to the following.

a. The selection of Director
b. The composition of the BoG
c. The selection of Chairman
d. Faculty compensation
e. The acquisition of assets and the opening of new campus.

We also saw how the clauses in the original MoA are heavily tilted in favour of GoI authority. We also looked at how on many occasions this had a dysfunctional impact. The potential for damage still exists. The time for modifying the original MoA has come. Happily, the IIMA Society has already modified these clauses through appropriate resolutions at its recent meeting in March, 2011. The government hopefully will accept these changes. That would remove the debris accumulated over years of operation and lead to a structural coherence paving the way for the onward march of the Institute. IIMA richly deserves it!

.... WHERE FROM AND WHERE TO...

The Institute started with a unique PPP structure based on faith and confidence. There were no models to follow nor experience to guide, only frontiers to explore. Truly, it was not a venture but an adventure. While there were many towering leaders, it is the collective leadership which navigated the Institute to where it is today. They created the ethos, built the culture, embedded the values, and established the processes. The hidden genes have revealed their attributes and their capacity to mutate and adapt to the dynamic environment.

The journey is on, we have barely begun!

Epilogue

In institution building, purpose and design have a huge role to play. But sometimes some larger forces come into play which defy analysis. Reasoning reaches its limits. Design is overtaken by happenstance. As Ravi famously observed, 'the building of an institution is often an *act of faith* and the expression of that faith is in a philosophy on the basis of which those who build these institutions act.' (*The Underlying basis of IIMA Organisation*, by Ravi J. Matthai, June 1973)

As we saw, IIMA came into being in unique and extraordinary circumstances. In my view that has defined its character and culture.

Let me recap some unique factors in its formation and its early years.

These days PPP is in vogue as a form of organization where public purpose and private enterprise and efficiency have to be melded together. Economic literature abounds with critical analysis of relevance and application of this form and sing paens of its curing power for ailing public sector organizations. However, not many realize that in the wake of nationalist fervour, IIMA was one of the first and most successful examples of implementing such a form; an apt example of practice leading theory.

It is amazing that IIMA was not hurt despite the fact that for nearly four years of its establishment it did not have a full time Director. Robbins Report as well as the context of management education and establishment of such an institution—an innovative and complex one without any previous model—clearly underlines the absolute necessity of a full time Director. It is either a miracle or the genius of Vikram and others that a certain disaster was averted.

Organizing EDPs for middle and senior management was recommended by Robbins and Harvard. All the same, 3-TP was a real innovation. The concept was based on Dr Kamla Chaudhary's insight. It exemplified the academic philosophy pioneered by Vikram and Ravi. Both of them never allowed themselves to be shackled by earlier precedents or established models for programmes. Their mantra was: *Think creatively, design functionally, assess practically and empower boldly.* Outcome: Risks were taken and results delivered. There is a lurking fear that this has waned as the institute has 'settled down'. Ageing? What a pity!

Another major departure from the US model and Robbins' recommendation was in respect of administrative duties handled by faculty. Vikram pioneered it and Ravi took it forward. This along with faculty self regulation culture conceptualized and built by Ravi is another innovative risky structural idea successfully adopted at IIMA. Thus, huge risks were taken probably without fully realizing the damage that could happen in case things went wrong. Maybe some 'escape hatch' was planned although not apparent from records. At the same time, the success achieved cannot be attributed to chance.

IIMA practiced some very basic values like simplicity, frugality, excellence, meritocracy, openness, integrity, and trust. It conducted itself with rare self belief and dignity despite the pressure on resources. There have been vehement arguments and heated debates on issues but no rancour or alienation.

IIMA departed from received wisdom in several fundamental respects.

1. A complex governance structure—four parties
2. Location—instead of a varied and diversified industrial base like Mumbai, one championed by local business leaders.
3. Initial full time director not appointed for four years
4. First full time director for at least ten to fifteen years. Instead Ravi stepped down in seven years.
5. Faculty not to get involved in administration
6. Culture of self regulation versus authority structure
7. 3-TP as the first EDP
8. Confine to 'enterprise management'—IIMA took a broader view—for example, agriculture
9. IIMA grew far more rapidly than initially estimated by Robbins.
10. Faculty compensation far below the recommended—twice the UGC level—still good faculty group raised
11. Allowing faculty to do consulting.

These have helped chart the Institute's journey so far. Armed only with these values and culture IIMA achieved iconic success consistently over fifty years. What now? The world has changed. India has changed. Have these factors still relevance? Do they still contain the basic elements to generate capacity to perpetually re-invent itself in its pursuit of excellence? Despite formidable challenges the habit of looking within, reflect, introspect and free open debate should lead IIMA to a path of what works best rather than the smug feeling of 'We have arrived'.

As Ravi had noted the Shakespearean dictum is as much applicable to an institution as to a human being.

'This above all—to thine self be true,
And it must follow, as the night the day,
Thou canst not then be false to any man.'

Abbreviations

AES	Ahmedabad Education Society
AICTE	All India Council of Technical Education
AMA	Ahmedabad Management Association
ASCI	Administrative Staff College of India
ATIRA	Ahmedabad Textile Industry's Research Association
BSNL	Bharat Sanchar Nigam Limited
CAG	Comptroller & Auditor General of India
CAGR	Compound Annual Growth Rate
CAO	Chief Administrative Officer
CFO	Chief Finance Officer
CIDCO	City and Industrial Development Corporation of Maharashtra Limited
CM	Chief Minister
CS	Chief Secretary
CSIR	Council of Scientific & Industrial Research
CWG	Commonwealth Games
DNA	Deoxyribonucleic Acid
EDP/MDP/SDP	Executive Development Programmes/Management Development Programmes/Short Duration Programmes
FDEC	Faculty Development and Evaluation Committee
FF	Ford Foundation
FICCI	Federation of Indian Chamber of Commerce & Industry
GD	Gannon Dunkerly

GoG	Government of Gujarat
GoI	Government of India
HBS	Harvard Business School
ICT	Information and Communication Technologies
IIMA	Indian Institute of Management Ahmedabad
IIMC	Indian Institute of Management Calcutta
IISc	Indian Institute of Science
IIT	Indian Institute of Technology
IMD	IMD, Laussanne
IPR	Independent Project Report
IT	Information Technology
L&T	Larsen & Toubro
LAN	Local Area Network
LDP	Long Duration Programmes
LMAs	Local Management Associations
LSE	London School of Economics
MD	Managing Director
MIS	Management Information System
MIT	Massachusetts Institute of Technology
MNCs	Multi National Companies
MoA	Memorandum of Agreement
NID	National Institute of Design
NGO	Non Governmental Organization
OGL	Open General Licence
PGP	Two Year Post Graduate Programme in Management
PGP-PMP	One Year Post Graduate Programme in Public Management and Policy
PGPX	One Year Post Graduate Programme in Management for Executives
PPP	Public Private Partnership
PRL	Physical Research Laboratory
PSUs	Public Sector Undertakings

R&D	Research and Development
RAs	Research Assistants / Research Associates
SBI	State Bank of India
SEWA	Self Employed Women's Association
TAs	Technical Assistants
TIFR	Tata Institute of Fundamental Research
TTK	T T Krishnamachari
UCLA	University of California at Los Angeles
USSR	United Soviet Socialist Republic

Appendix

INTRODUCTION

APPENDIX 1

List of the first signatories of the MOA	Name, Address, and Occupation	
1. The Chairman (appointed by the Central Government in consultation with the State Government)	Dr Jivraj Mehta Chief Minister, Gujarat, Ahmedabad	Chairman
2. Nominee of the Central Government to represent its Ministry of Scientific Research and Cultural Affairs	Prof. M.S.Thacker, Secretary, Ministry of Scientific Research & Cultural Affairs, New Delhi	Member
3. Nominee of the Central Government to represent its Ministry of Finance	Mr. A.Venkateswaran, Joint Secretary, Ministry of Finance, New Delhi	Member
4. Nominee of the Central Government to represent its Ministry of Commerce and Industry	Nomination awaited (As of the date of signing the name had not been sent.)	

5. & 6. Nominees of the Government of Gujarat	Shri V. Isvaran, Chief Secretary, Government of Gujarat, Ahmedabad	Member
	Shri V.L. Gidwani, Secretary, Finance Department Government of Gujarat, Ahmedabad	Member
7. Representative of the All India Council for Technical Education	Shri N. Dandekar, I.C.S. (Retd.) Southlands 177 Upper Colaba, Bomaby 5	Member
8. to 11. Four persons to be nominated by the Central Government in consultation with the State Government to represent Commerce, Industry, Labour and other interests	Dr Vikram Sarabhai Shahibaug, Ahmedabad	Member
	Shri Kasturbhai Lalbhai Pankore Naka, Ahmedabad	Member
	Shri D.S. Choksi, Director Tata Sons Pvt Ltd, Mumbai House Bruce Street, Fort, Mumbai 1	Member
	Shri Shanta Ram S. Tawde, Secretary, Engineering Mazdoor Sabha Nawab Tank Road Mazagaon, Mumbai 10	Member
12. A representative of the All India Management Association	Name awaited (When the MoA was signed)	
13. A representative of the National Productivity Council of India	Shri H.D. Shourie, Executive Director National Productivity Council 38, Golf Links, New Delhi	
14. Director of the Institute Secretary	Ex-officio	Member

APPENDIX 2

LIST OF CHAIRMEN OF IIMA BOARD SINCE THE INCEPTION OF THE INSTITUTE AND THEIR TENURE

Sr. No.	Name	Duration
1.	Dr Jivraj N. Mehta	From the inception of the Institute to 22 January 1964
2.	Shri Prakash Tandon	24-04-1964 to 23-04-1969
3.	Shri S.L. Kirloskar	24-07-1969 to 23-07-1974
4.	Shri Keshub Mahindra	24-07-1974 to 23-07-1979
5.	-do-	27-07-1979 to 24-07-1984
6.	Mr V. Krishnamurthy	29-07-1985 to 28-07-1990
7.	Mr A.P. Venkateswaran	09-10-1990 to 02-05-1991
8.	Prof. S.K. Khanna	03-05-1991 to 08-08-1996
9.	Dr I.G. Patel	08-08-1996 to 07-08-2001
10.	Mr N.R. Narayana Murthy	11-03- 2002 to 10-03- 2007
11.	Dr Vijaypat Singhania	March 23, 2007 onwards

APPENDIX 3

LIST OF DIRECTORS SINCE THE INCEPTION OF THE INSTITUTE AND THEIR TENURE

Sr.No.	Name	Duration
1	Vikram A. Sarabhai (Hon. Director)	30-06-1962 to 28-08-1965
2	Ravi J. Matthai	29-08-1965 to 06-09-1972
3	Samuel Paul	08-09-1972 to 30-06-1978
4	V.S. Vyas	07-07-1978 to 30-09-1982
5	I.G. Patel	01-10-1982 to 12-07-1984
6	N.R. Sheth	13-07-1984 to 03-05-1991
7	P.N. Khandwala	04-05-1991 to 31-08-1996
8	P.M. Shingi (Acting Director)	01-09-1996 to 08-04-1997
9	Jahar Saha	09-04-1997 to 07-07-2002
10	J.S. Chhokar (Acting Director)	08-07-2002 to 28-09-2002
11	Bakul H. Dholakia (Acting Director)	28-09-2002 to 09-10-2002
12	Bakul H. Dholakia	10-10-2002 to 09-10-2007
13	Jayant R. Varma (Acting Director)	07-10-2007 to 07-11-2007
14	Samir K. Barua	08-11-2007 onwards

APPENDIX 4

NUMBER OF APPLICANTS AND STUDENTS

IIMA: GRADUATING STUDENTS 1966-2010					
Year	No. of Applicants	PGP	SPA/ ABM*	Total	Admission Success rate (one out of __)
1966	747	48	-	48	16
1970	2,321	106	-	106	22
1980	5,419	135	16	151	40
1990	10,089	165	23	188	61
2000	37,097	169	13	182	220
2010	2,02,166	283	19	302	714
2011	2,38,765	316	37	353	676

APPENDIX 5

FACULTY STRENGTH

Year	Faculty	Foreign Faculty
1963-64	13	21
1970-71	46	
1980-81	87	
1990-91	83	
2010-11	90	

(Foreign faculty is the total number of such faculty with varying duration during that period and not all on full time basis).

APPENDIX 6

NUMBER OF BUILDINGS AND AREA

Period	Buildings	Area (Sq.ft.)
By 1970	95	21,920
Before New Campus	317	7,08,970
After New Campus - 2010	378	14,95,777
After New Campus - 2011	386	16,52,982

APPENDIX 7

SYNOPSIS OF IIMA FINANCES

(Rs in Lakhs)

	65-66	2010-11
PGP & LDP fees	3.13	6159
SDP	2.89	2025
Consultancy	0.14	2664
GoI Grant	11.81	Nil
PGP expenses	2.80	1879
SDP exp.	2.48	1018
Establishment Expenses	12.52	4707
Immovable Property	48.66	10477
Investments	Nil	29401.12

APPENDIX 8

GENERAL DATA

Description	UNIT	1969-70	
PGP	Student	106	
SPA	,,	–	
ABM	,,	–	
PGP-X	,,	–	
PGP-PMP	,,	–	
MDP (EDP)	Participants	338	
Faculty Strenght	Number	48	
Cases and Papers Cumulative	,,	1,192	
PGP Fees	In Rs. '000	1.58	
Avg. PGP Placement Salary	,,	11.4	
3-TP Fees			
Tier I	,,	3	
Tier II	,,	1.7	
Tier II	,,	0.75	
Building area	In sq. ft.	2,44990	

Note: The figures of Cases and Papers—Cumulative here are decade-wise while in Appendix 7 it is for 10 year periods from the beginning and hence some differences.

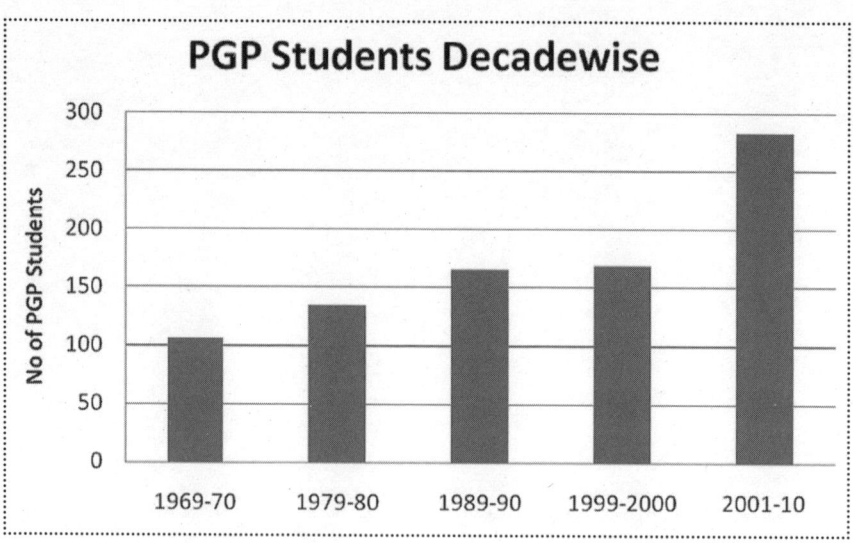

PGP Students Decadewise

Note: There is an error in the last column. The year should be 2009–10 and not 2001–10.

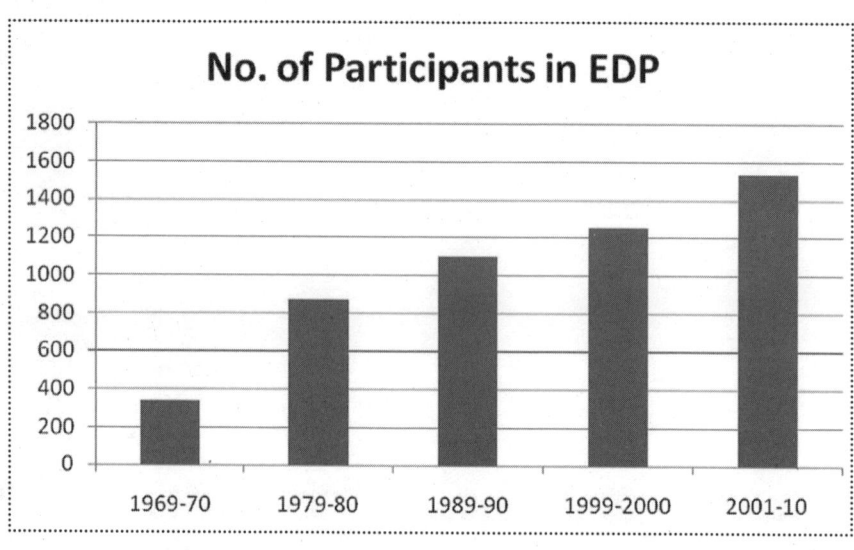

No. of Participants in EDP

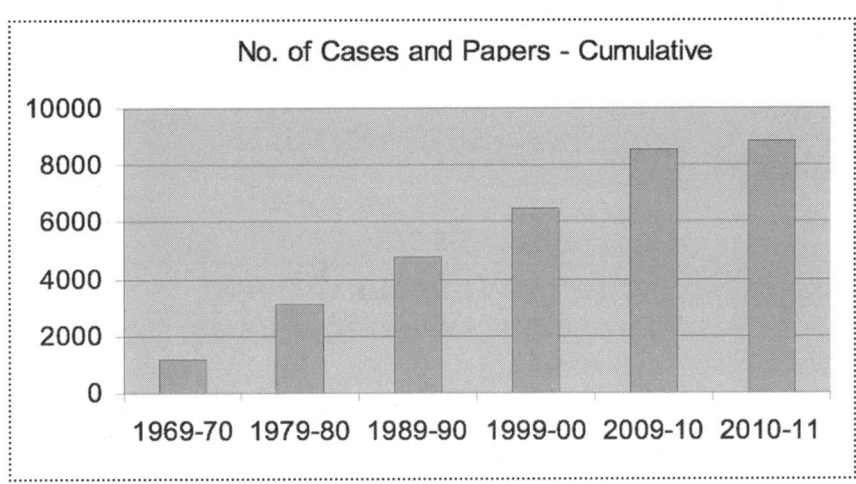

No. of Cases and Papers - Cumulative

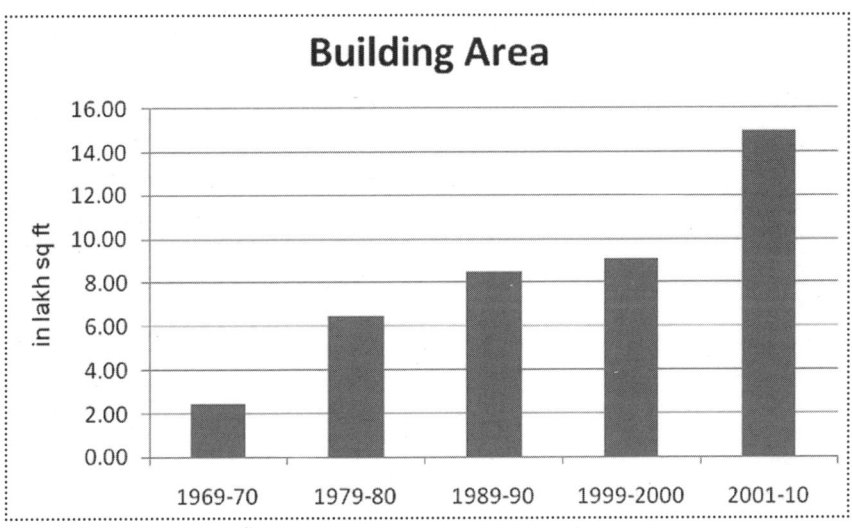

Building Area

CHAPTER-1

APPENDIX 1

LETTER FROM VIKRAM TO V.T. KRISHNAMACHARI, VICE-CHAIRMAN OF THE PLANNING COMMISSION, GOVERNMENT OF INDIA

April 16, 1960

My dear Sir Krishnamachari,

I am grateful for the time you could spare on the 3rd of April to discuss the location of the proposed All India Institute of Management to be established in collaboration with the FF. I write this to convey a keen interest in Ahmedabad for the location of the Institute in this city.

Some of the significant factors important for the success of the Institute are:

a. local initiative and leadership

b. capacity to organize and develop institutions along new patterns to meet contemporary needs and to sustain them with the accent on quality;

c. a ready climate in which the need for management training at all levels is recognized;

d. existence of professional research groups active in the field of management and training which could provide close collaborative and sustaining relationships.

The interaction of all these factors provide the overall climate which makes it possible for a new institution to find roots for healthy development. I believe that an appropriate climate exists in Ahmedabad perhaps to a wider degree than in any other city. Evidence of this climate can be seen from the growth, during the last ten years, of several new and forward looking institutions. Moreover, there is, in this city, a background of almost ten years of active research pertaining to industrial problems.

In the enclosure I give some details of the factors indicated above in relation to Ahmedabad.

I have read the report submitted by Dean Robbins, Consultant to the FF, and I believe the general principles and the programme outlined in the report would find ready acceptance and support in this city.

I shall therefore be grateful if our proposal for locating the Institute at Ahmedabad receives serious consideration and at the appropriate time an opportunity is provided to discuss specific issues connected with the project.

With kind regards,

Yours sincerely,

Sd/-

Vikram A Sarabahi

Sir V.T. Krishnamachari
Vice-Chairman
Planning Commission
New Delhi

Enclosure to the above letter from Vikram to V T Krishnamachari

Some Factors of Significance to the Proposed Establishment of an All-India Institute of Management in Ahmedabad

LETTER FROM GOVERNMENT OF INDIA TO THE CHIEF MINISTER OF GUJARAT ABOUT ESTABLISHMENT OF IIMA

D.O.No.F.10-6/60-T.2

GOVERNMENT OF INDIA

Ministry of Scientific Research & Cultural Affairs

New Delhi, the 15th November 1960

My Dear Dr Mehta,

Reference our discussions on the question of establishment of an All India Institute of Management, I am setting out below the obligations which will devolve on the State Government and the Industry in Gujarat, as also the assistance that will be given by the Central Government:

a. The Institution will be autonomous and though it may have close relations with Universities, the institution should at least at the outset give its own certificates;

b. the cost of land and buildings for this institution should be found by local industrialists and the State Government; and

c. the Central Government should assist the institution by providing for recurring expenses.

The FF have offered that they would be willing to help in the following three ways:

a. Finding for at least the first five years top ranking experts from abroad who would come as whole time teachers in this institution;

b. providing Fellowships to enable Indian teachers of this institution to go abroad for further studies and observation tours; and

c. finding the necessary funds for building up the Libraries of this institution. Since almost all books will have to be from abroad, this amount will be entirely in foreign exchange.

In order to ensure that trainees who obtain the certificates of this institution are profitably absorbed after training, we would like to make it a condition that industrialists who participate in the scheme should send their employees on deputation and account the period of their study at the institution as a duty period with all normal allowances and any additional amount that may be required at the institute. For industrialists who participate in this way, the institution will accept their employees for the first five years without charging any premium. For other industrialists, a premium would be prescribed.

The institution might have a Council of about 25 or 30 with representatives of industrialists, businessmen, the State and the Central Governments. There may be a smaller Board of Management to administer the affairs of the Institution from day to day.

2. I heard from my Minister that you told him that the State Government is agreeable to the above arrangements. Kindly send us an official letter so that we can move further in the matter. A copy of the report of Dean Robbins which will generally form the basis for the establishment of the Institute is enclosed.
With my kind regards,

Yours sincerely,
Sd/- M S Thacker

Dr Jivraj Mehta
Chief Minister
Gujarat
Ahmedabad

APPENDIX-3

LETTER OF ACCEPTANCE TO ESTABLISH IIMA BY GOVERNMENT OF GUJARAT TO GOVERNMENT OF INDIA

V Isvaran, ICS
Chief Secretary

D.O. No.
Sachivalaya, Ahmedabad 15
3rd December, 1960

Please refer to your D.O. letter No.F.10-6/60-T.2 dated 15th November, 1960 addressed to the Chief Minister, Gujarat on the subject of establishment of an All India Institute of Management. We agree to the terms and conditions mentioned in your above letter and would request you to take necessary action in the matter. With regards,

Yours sincerely,
Sd/- V Isvaran

Dr M.S. Thacker
Secretary
Ministry of Scientific Research and Cultural Affairs
Government of India
New Delhi

CHAPTER-6

APPENDIX 1

INDIAN INSTITUTE OF MANAGEMENT
Vastrapur, Ahmedabad–15

Gram: INDINMAN ★ Telex: 012–351 ★ Phone: 83–411/2/3/4/6/8

[handwritten note: Amended by Chairman SLK on 19/1/72 at 1430 hrs — He requested that this be kept on my file at IIMA.]

17 January, 1972

Mr. S.L. Kirloskar
Chairman, Board of Governors
Indian Institute of Management
Ahmedabad.15

Dear Mr. Kirloskar:

I have decided to resign from the Directorship of the Institute.
I write this formal letter to request that I be relieved from my
directorial responsibilities from the 1st June, 1972. You will
recall that I had raised the question of my being replaced at the
31st meeting of the Board of Governors held on the 18th July, 1970.
I regard the fact that no action was taken as a gentle compliment
from the Board, which I value. But I also do realise that it could
have been embarrassing if too great an eagerness were shown to
"follow through" on my suggestion! However, the Board has trusted
me so far and has supported my judgement. I hope it will do so
again. I consider that a change is desirable and that my resignation is the appropriate initiative which will bring it about.

May I explain why I have decided to take this step?

While each of our educational institutions needs a vision to which
it may aspire, the vision must not become a sacrosanct ideology,
nor should the individual in charge of the institution become the
ideologically vested focal point of no change. I have appointed a
committee which will, within a few months, recommend to the Faculty
a re-organisation of the Institute in form and substance. Important
and necessary though it is, I doubt that it is enough to review the
working of the Institute. Changes will be suggested and the community might even accept some part of those changes. I earnestly hope
that the change will be substantial, but, on the other hand, the
"status quo" might prevail. An acceptance of change for change's
sake is not suggested. But even if this change were to be so regarded, it could be a healthy precursor of worthwhile and appropriate
changes in the long run. A new person is required with whom the
"vision" is not a "vested interest" and we will have a fresh point
of view from which to determine how the Institute can move.

An applied institution such as ours, must relate itself to national
needs. The tasks can be enormous and numerous. The temptation, to
which I certainly have yielded, is to move fast in new fields of
academic endeavour. With this in view, at the IIMA, I have empha-
sised "academic entrepreneurship" which constantly demands new
activities, uncertain structures and, often, conflicting values.

At each major stage of the Institute's growth a change of style might be desirable. I think we have arrived at the end of the first phase of the Institute's growth, nine years after it started. This Institute might need to consolidate and stabilise for a period, or it might need to change the direction of development. For this there will be others whose styles are more suited and whose capabilities are more appropriate than mine.

Many institutions in India have suffered either from instability due to the too frequent changes of the "chief executive" as decided by "the powers that be" irrespective of institutional needs, or, have suffered from stagnation as a result of the perpetuation of an individual who becomes the institutionalised image of a no-change continuity, once again, irrespective of institutional needs. I hope that, after a reasonable period, the next Director will step down if he feels there may be more appropriate persons to determine a new direction for the Institute.

In requesting a change of Directors, I am conscious of the possibility that I may be asked to take part in the choice of my successor. I think it would be self-defeating if I were to influence the perpetuation, even inadvertantly, of my own preferences. I therefore feel that I should not take part in this selection and that it should be done by the Board and the faculty.

My emotional involvement with the Institute is considerable. While I am resigning as Director, if my successor and the Board allow me to work here, I would like to continue as a member of the faculty.

When Dr. Vikram Sarabhai and Mr. Prakash Tandon first invited me to accept the Directorship of the IIMA, I was reluctant to assume an administrative role having but recently left Industry. However, this period of over six years has been most exciting and I am grateful to the Society, Board, Faculty, Staff and Alumni of the Institute for their trust and support. Theirs is the credit for whatever has been achieved.

With very best wishes,

Yours sincerely,

Ravi J. Matthai
DIRECTOR

CHAPTER-9

APPENDIX 1

FF INITIAL GRANT AND ITS USAGE UP TO AUGUST 1963.

Financial Statement of Funds Paid to Harvard University in Connection with the Indian Institute of Management, Ahmedabad

	Budget	Actual to Aug. 13, 1963	Projected to Aug. 31, 1964	Total	(Over) Under Budget
Long term foreign advisers	$215,000	$67,727	$97,415	$165,142*	$49,858
Short term consultants	60,000	18,664	33,252	51,916	8,084
Fellowships	65,000	46,640	36,160	82,800	(17,800)
Books and equipment	75,000	28,919	46,081	75,000	--
Project adminis- tration costs	29,000	13,201	20,596	33,797	(4,797)
Overhead	21,700	8,739	11,184	19,923	1,777
	$465,700	$183,890	$244,688	$428,578	$37,122

*Current plans call for some increase in the projected expense of long term foreign advisers.)

Bibliography

Bhargava, R C and Others. 2008, *Report of IIM Review Committee*

Datar Srikant M, David A Garvin, and Patrick G Cullen.2010, *Rethinking the MBA: Business Education at Crossroads*

Doshi, Balakrishna. 2000, *Architectural Legacies of Ahmedabad: Canvas of Modern Masters*
_____. 2007, Louis Kahn

Ford Foundation, New York, Papers from Archives

Hansen, Harry. 1962, *Memorandum Concerning the Institute of Management, Ahmedabad*, 7 February

_____. 1963, *Report to Ford Foundation on the Progress of IIMA*, 31 December

_____. 1964, *Report to Ford Foundation on the Progress of IIMA*, 31 December

_____. 1965, *Report to Ford Foundation on the Progress of IIMA*, 31 December

HARBUS. 1963, 'HBS Helps Launch Indian B School', 1 February

Harvard Business School, Boston, Papers from Archives

Hill, Thomas, Warren Haynes, and Howard Baumgartel.1973, *Institution Building in India – A Study of International Collaboration in Management Education*

Indian Institute of Management Ahmedabad, *Memorandum of Association and Rules*

_____. *Minutes of the Meetings of the BoG and Committees of the BoG*

_____.1993, *Institution Building: The IIMA Experience – Vol I: The Early Years*

_____.1994, *Institution Building: The IIMA Experience – Vol II: Subsequent Years*

_____.1977, *Report of the Committee on Future Directions* (Chairman: Rangarajan, C)

_____. 1983, *Report of the Committee on Future Directions* (Chairman: Khandwalla, P N)

_____. 1997, *Report of the Committee on Future Directions* (Chairman: Kalro, Amarlal H), 1997)

_____. 2010, *Report of the Committee on Future Directions* (Chairman: Morris, Sebastian)

_____. *Files of Vikram Sarabhai*

Kurien, V and Others. 1992, *Report and Recommendations of the Committee to Review the Functioning of IIM Ahmedabad, Bangalore, Calcutta, Lucknow*

Lalbhai, Kasturbhai, Papers from National Archives, New Delhi

Matthai, Ravi J, Udai Pareek, and T V Rao (eds). 1977, *Institution Building in Education and Research – From Stagnation to Self Renewal*

Nanda, H P and Others. 1981, *Report and Recommendations of the Review Committee for IIM Calcutta, Ahmedabad, Bangalore and Promotion and Development of Management Education*

New York Times Art & Design. 2010, Nicolai Ouroussoff, 26 May

Pareek, Udai.1981, *Beyond Management: Essays on the Process of Institution Building*

Pareek, Udai.1994, *Beyond Management: Essays on the Process of Institution Building and Related Topics*

Robbins, George W. 1959, *Recommendations for an All-India Institute of Management,* A Report

Sherry Chand, Vijaya and T V Rao.2011, *Nurturing Institutional Excellence – Indian Institute of Management Ahmedabad*

Tandon, Prakash. 1980, *Return to Punjab 1961-1975,* p.112

A Note on the Author

Prafull Anubhai has been associated with the Indian Institute of Management Ahmedabad (IIMA) for over forty-five years as visiting faculty and as a Board member. He did his BSc (Economics) from the London School of Economics and attended the Programme for Management Development (PMD) at Harvard Business School. He has thirty years of experience as chief executive of textile manufacturing operations and has been a corporate advisor associated with educational institutions like IIMA, Ahmedabad Education Society (AES), Ahmedabad University, and Centre for Science Technology and Policy (CSTEP).

Prafull is the Chairman of the Board of Management of the Ahmedabad University, a member of the Governing Board of AES and the Honorary Director of Saptak Archives—an institution dedicated towards the preservation and dissemination of Indian classical music. Presently, he is a Director in companies like Unichem Laboratories Ltd., Vardhman Textiles Ltd., Birla Sun Life Trustee Co. Pvt. Ltd, GRUH Finance Ltd. (a subsidiary of HDFC Ltd), and The Emerging Markets South Asian Fund (EMSAF), Mauritius, among others. He lives in Ahmedabad.

A Note on the Type

Cronos is a sans serif typeface family, designed by Robert Slimbach in 2001, that embodies the warmth and flow of Oldstyle Roman typefaces.

It gets much of its appearance from the calligraphically inspired type of the Italian Renaissance. Its nearly handwritten appearance sets it apart from most other sans serif designs. The Italic design was inspired by early Chancery style Italics and is both exquisite and distinguished.

Douglas Ensminger, Kamla Chaudhari, P.L. Tandon, K.L. Varshneya, a member of the faculty, and students

P.L. Tandon, Kasturbhai, Charat Ram, Vikram Sarabhai, Kamala Chaudhary at a Board of Governors (BoG) meeting

Campus under construction

Jivraj Mehta, Chief Minister of Gujarat
and the first Chairman of the BoG

Warren Hayes of Harvard Business School (HBS) in a meeting with faculty

Vikram Sarabhai, P.L. Tandon, M.C. Chagla, the Chief Guest, Ravi Matthai, and Douglas Ensminger at the first convocation

Houses within the campus under construction

The launch of the first batch of PGP in 1964

Shahibaug Bungalow—from where we started

Harry Hansen at the first convocation

A view of the old campus

The dorms at the old campus

The new campus

Kahn and Doshi in conversation

The Louis Kahn Plaza

Another view of the Louis Kahn Plaza

Louis Kahn with Ravi at the campus

The dorms of the new campus

The arches at the old campus

The famous steps at IIMA

Students stepping up

Samuel Paul, Director; V.M. Dandekar, Chief Guest; and Keshub Mahindra, Chairman; at the 1976 convocation

Narayana Murthy, Chairman BoG, addressing the convocation

I.G. Patel, Chairman; and Jahar Saha, Director, during the Bhoomi Pujan at the new campus

Kamla Chaudhary

Kasturbhai, Vikram, and Ravi at the 1967 convocation

Shriman Narayan, Governor of Gujarat; P.L. Tandon, Chairman; Indira Gandhi, Chief Guest; Ravi Matthai, Director, at the 1968 convocation

Author with other IIMA members at the Golden Jubilee Inaugural Function

Another view of the Golden Jubilee Inaugural Function

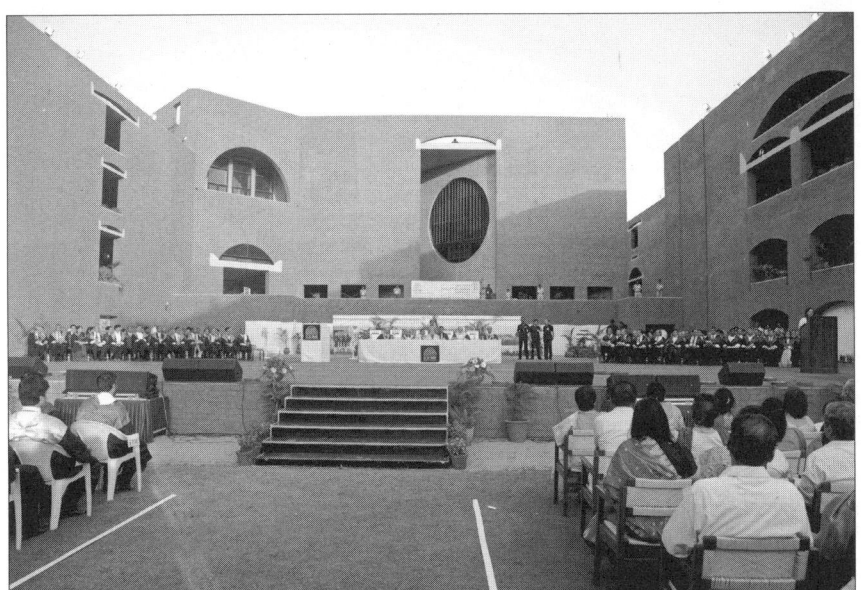

The 2011 convocation